Is Fiscal Policy the Answer?

Is Fiscal Policy the Answer?

A Developing Country Perspective

Blanca Moreno-Dodson, Editor

THE WORLD BANK
Washington, D.C.

ISBN (paper): 978-0-8213-9630-8
ISBN (electronic): 978-0-8213-9631-5
DOI: 10.1596/978-0-8213-9630-6

Cover art: Rapids in the Ebro River (Rapidos en el Ebro), Aurora Herrero, Zaragoza, Spain; photographed by Columna Villarroya, Zaragoza, Spain.
Cover design: Debra Naylor, Washington, D.C.

Library of Congress Cataloging-in-Publication Data
Is fiscal policy the answer? : a developing country perspective / edited by Blanca Moreno-Dodson.
  p. cm.
  Includes bibliographical references.
  ISBN 978-0-8213-9630-8 — ISBN 978-0-8213-9631-5 (electronic)
1. Fiscal policy—Developing countries. 2. Financial crises—Developing countries. 3. Economic development. I. Moreno-Dodson, Blanca.
  HJ1620.I8 2012
  339.5'2091724—dc23   2012030189

Contents

Boxes

Figures

Tables

Foreword

This book brings together the thoughts of several World Bank economists on a subject of considerable importance for developing countries: the potential contributions of fiscal policy to strengthening long-term growth in national income and wealth, and achieving greater equity in their distribution.

Admittedly, much of the renewed attention given to fiscal policy since 2008 and the start of the "Great Recession" has focused on its role as an instrument for countercyclical stabilization in the face of large macroeconomic shocks, and on the importance of ensuring long-run fiscal sustainability. And yet a growing interest in the longer-run development potential of fiscal policy is also apparent and is only likely to grow over time. For one thing, there is the troubling possibility that, far from being an ordinary cyclical downturn, the Great Recession may have opened a more extended period of sluggishness and volatility in the global economic environment. In this climate, both developing and developed countries have strong incentives to seek out new domestic engines for efficiency and productivity growth as well as for greater equity. As this book seeks to document, fiscal policy can be an important instrument for these purposes.

The first chapters in this volume sketch out a framework that policy makers can use in adopting a more cohesive or integrated approach to the short- and long-term dimensions of fiscal policy. Here the traditional threefold rationale for fiscal policy proposed by Musgrave—stabilization, resource allocation, and distribution—continues to be useful. Well-designed and well-implemented public spending can improve resource allocation by supplying critical public goods, for example, thereby boosting longer-run growth prospects. Even when the primary focus is on stabilization, *what* the government spends money on and *how* it finances that spending—through various kinds of taxation or borrowing—also have significant implications for resource allocation and distribution. A careful evaluation of the trade-offs and complementarities between the various rationales and final objectives of fiscal policy is therefore always important, as is a proper awareness of the fiscal sustainability, institutional, and political economy constraints within which fiscal policy operates.

Other chapters in this volume take up some of the critical institutional challenges in implementing fiscal policy for longer-term growth and development. These chapters also look at the tools and approaches being developed to address these challenges. Improving the quality of public investment management is a particular priority in view of the recent evidence that as little as half of all public investment expenditure translates into productive capital stock. As Harberger has observed, strengthening the quality of public investment management is one of the few reforms that can be expected to raise productivity growth and have a permanent, continuing impact on a country's rate of economic growth, in contrast to a one-off increase in the level of output. Improving the institutional and policy framework for managing revenues and public spending in natural resource–rich low-income countries is also a priority. The sustained high prices and revenues generated by many natural resources in recent years could—with adequate fiscal management— prove to be a great lever for rapid development in many low-income countries. But if those natural resources are mismanaged, it could blight prospects for development. Better tools are also needed to help policy makers analyze the distributive impacts of fiscal policy, particularly in low-income country contexts, where the institutional capacity for this kind of work is often limited.

The last chapter in this volume is a case study of fiscal responses to the Great Recession in low-income Sub-Saharan Africa, looking at both stabilization and the longer-run growth, as well as distributional aspects of such responses. Broadly speaking, the message from that experience is one of hope, and one that is consistent with many of the messages elsewhere in the book. African countries that had improved their fiscal position over the course of the 2000s had the fiscal space to undertake a greater degree of countercyclical stimulus than in previous crises, as well as to better protect critical productive spending important for long-term growth. The growing depth of domestic financial markets in many African countries rather unexpectedly is turning out to be a critical source of financing for fiscal policy responses. Improvements in the quality of the institutional capacity for prudent revenue management, budget execution, and public investment management appear to have been an important factor in the success of fiscal plans. All told, the African experience during the recent Great Recession may be viewed as a source of guarded optimism about the prospects for fiscal policy for longer-term growth and development going forward.

Otaviano Canuto
Vice President and Head of Network
Poverty Reduction and Economic Management—PREM
World Bank

About the Editor and Authors

Editor

Blanca Moreno-Dodson is a Lead Economist in the Poverty Reduction and Economic Management (PREM) Network, currently assigned to the Investment Climate Department of the World Bank Group (Joint IBRD-IFC-MIGA). She has 20 years of service, with extended experience in Africa and Latin America and the Caribbean, as well as other regions. Her background is in macroeconomics and public finance for developing countries, with a focus on growth and poverty reduction, as well as tax reform, public expenditure analysis, and fiscal policy. Previously, she was a junior economist at the European Union (European Commission and European Parliament). She is the editor of *Reducing Poverty on a Global Scale* (World Bank 2005) and co-editor of *Public Finance for Poverty Reduction* (World Bank 2007). She has published several articles on macroeconomics, public finance, growth, and poverty issues in the *National Tax Journal, Banca d'Italia Fiscal Policy Annual Volume, Hacienda Pública Española,* and the *Bulletin of Economic Research,* and several World Bank Working Papers and Notes. She holds a PhD and masters degrees in international economics and finance from the Aix-Marseille II University, France, as well as a masters in economics from the Madrid Autonomous University, Spain.

Authors

Milan Brahmbhatt is Senior Adviser to the Vice President of the World Bank's PREM Network. In this capacity, he advises and leads work on a range of macroeconomic and structural policy issues, including on fiscal policy and on the economics of climate change and sustainable growth. He has been adviser to the Chief Economist of the World Bank's East Asia and Pacific Region, and he was leader of the global economic prospects and forecasting team in the Development Economics Department. He was a research manager at Data Resources Inc. (DRI/Standard & Poor's), where he consulted on international economic, trade, and environmental issues with corporate and government clients and was the Director for DRI's Asian Economic Service, where he focused on macroeconomic prospects for Asian economies. He holds an M.Sc. from the London School of Economics and is a former member of the Institute of Chartered Accountants in England and Wales.

James Brumby is a Sector Manager and Lead Economist, Indonesia, for the World Bank. He has worked on public management reform at state, national, and international levels for 30 years. Prior to joining the World Bank in 2007, he was Division Chief in the Office of Budget and Planning, Deputy Division Chief in the Fiscal Affair Department at the International Monetary Fund, and Division Chief in the Public Management Group at the Organisation for Economic Co-operation and Development. He held various positions at the treasuries of New Zealand and the state of Victoria in Australia.

Otaviano Canuto is the Vice President and Head of the PREM Network, a division of more than 700 economists and other professionals working on economic policy, poverty reduction, and analytic work for the World Bank's client countries. He previously served as the Vice President for Countries at the Inter-American Development Bank. He was Executive Director of the Board of the World Bank in 2004–07 and also served in the Brazilian Ministry of Finance, where he was Secretary for International Affairs. He was a professor of economics at the University of São Paulo and University of Campinas in Brazil. He holds a PhD in economics from University of Campinas and a masters degree from Concordia University in Montreal. He has written extensively on development economics and growth.

José Cuesta is a Senior Economist at the World Bank and an Affiliated Professor at Georgetown University, Washington, D.C. Previously, he was a Senior Research Economist at the Inter-American Development Bank. He taught development economics at the Institute of Social Studies, The Hague, and worked as a research economist for the United Nations Development Programme in Honduras. He has advised multiple governments on social policies and has extensive operational experience in social development projects in Latin America. Currently, he leads the production of the *Food Price Watch*, a World Bank quarterly publication following global and national food price trends. He is a founding member of the World Bank's Food Security and Nutrition Knowledge Platform, *SecureNutrition*. His research interests include development economics, poverty and social protection, crime and conflict, and the analytics of public policy. He has published numerous articles in international academic journals and is co-editor of the *European Journal of Development Research*. He has a PhD in economics from Oxford University.

B. Essama-Nssah is an Evaluation Methods Specialist with DevTech Systems, Inc., working for the United States Agency for International Development (USAID) Program Cycle Service Center, where he leads efforts to help build the capacity of staff to plan, design, and manage credible and useful evaluations. He worked for 17 years for the World Bank in Washington, D.C.; for the past 11 years, he was Senior Economist with the Poverty Reduction and Equity Group. At the World Bank, he performed economic analyses to support operations in client countries, designed and conducted studies of the social impact of development strategies and economic policies in a variety of countries, and developed and conducted an annual training course on impact evaluation methodologies for headquarters- and field-based staff members and their in-country government counterparts. He also wrote several policy research and technical guidance papers on policy impact and growth incidence analysis. He was a Senior Research Associate with the Food and Nutrition Policy Program at Cornell University from 1990–92. He was the Vice Dean of the Faculty of Law and Economics and Head of the economics department at the University of Yaoundé, Cameroon. He holds a PhD in economics from the University of Michigan in Ann Arbor.

Norman Gemmell holds the Chair in Public Finance at Victoria University of Wellington, New Zealand. He was previously Chief Economist and Principal Adviser (Tax) at the New Zealand Treasury, an Assistant Director of the U.K. Inland Revenue's Analysis and Research Department, and Professor of Development Economics at the University of Nottingham, U.K. Norman's research experience spans more than 30 years, with interests across a range of topics in economics and political economy, public finance (taxation, public expenditure, and public debt), and economic growth. He has authored several books and numerous papers, including *Modelling Corporation Tax Revenue* (with John Creedy, 2010) and articles in academic and policy journals such as the *American Economic Review, Economic Journal, Fiscal Studies, International Tax and Public Finance, Journal of Public Economics, National Tax Journal,* and *Journal of Development Economics.*

Kirk Hamilton is a Lead Economist in the Development Economics Research Group of the World Bank and co-author of *World Development Report 2010: Development and Climate Change* (World Bank 2009). He is principal author of the World Bank's (2005) report, *Where Is the Wealth of Nations?* and leads research on the links between poverty and the environment, the greening of national accounts, and the economics of climate change. Prior to joining the Bank, he served as Assistant Director of National Accounts for the government of Canada, where his responsibilities included developing an environmental national accounting program.

Kai Kaiser is a Senior Economist with the World Bank East Asia PREM, based in Manila. He served in the Public Sector Group, specializing in issues on fiscal decentralization and intergovernmetal finance and on governance of service delivery and reform. He is co-author of *Rents to Riches? The Political Economy of Natural Resource-Led Development* (World Bank).

Kathie Krumm worked with the World Bank for over 25 years in leadership positions with PREM, including Sector Manager for East Africa and the Horn, Deputy Director for the East Asia and Pacific Region, and Lead Economist for China in Beijing. She holds a PhD in economics from Stanford University and a BA from Columbia University, with postgraduate studies at Harvard University and University of Chicago. She has published on development issues, including trade and exchange regimes, poverty and social protection, and debt and fiscal risk. Her recent publications include a contribution on Africa to this volume, the co-editing of *East Asia Integrates* (World Bank and University of Oxford 2004), and a contribution on China for *Government at Risk* (World Bank 2007).

Chandana Kularatne is an economist in the PREM Network. He has also worked in the East Africa Unit of PREM. Before joining the World Bank in 2009, he served as the Deputy Director in the Economic Policy Unit of the National Treasury of South Africa. He holds a PhD in economics from the University of Cape Town. His research focuses on economic growth, industrial policy, and political economy.

Eduardo Ley is a Lead Economist in the Economic Policy and Debt Department in PREM, where he works on fiscal issues. Before joining the Bank in 2006, he served at the International Monetary Fund (IMF) in the Fiscal Affairs Department, the Research Department, and the IMF Institute. Previously, he held research positions at the Fundación de Estudios de Economía Aplicada (FEDEA), Madrid, and Resources for the Future (Washington, D.C.), and academic positions at the University of Michigan and the Universidad Carlos III de Madrid. He has published about 30 papers in refereed academic journals and books on topics from environmental and fiscal issues to statistical methodology. During 2006–09, he was the managing editor of the *Spanish Economic Review*, and he has served on the editorial boards of several other journals, including the *IMF Staff Papers*, for six years.

Jorge Martinez-Vazquez is Regents Professor of Economics and Director of the International Center for Public Policy in the Andrew Young School of Policy Studies at Georgia State University in Atlanta. He has published over 20 books and numerous articles in academic journals, such as *Econometrica*, *Journal of Political Economy*, *Journal of Public Economics*, *Southern Economic Journal*, and *Review of Economics and Statistics*. He has directed multiple fiscal reform projects worldwide, including the USAID Fiscal Reform Project in the Russian Federation (1997–2000) and the World Bank Tax Policy Review Project in Pakistan (2008–09). His expertise in fiscal decentralization, taxation, and fiscal management has led to consulting assignments with federal agencies and state governments in the United States and over 60 countries including China, Indonesia, Mexico, the Russian Federation, and South Africa. He has consulted with the World Bank, the Asian Development Bank, the United Nations, and the Inter-American Development Bank, and he has been a member of the IMF Panel of Fiscal Experts since 1994.

Florian Misch is a Senior Researcher in the Corporate Taxation and Public Finance Department at the Centre for European Economic Research in Mannheim, Germany. His current research interests include the impact of fiscal policy on economic performance and fiscal policy making when governments are imperfectly informed. He obtained a PhD in economics from the University of Nottingham, and he holds a postgraduate certificate in International Economic Policy Research from the Kiel Institute for the World Economy. He worked as a consultant on public finance–related projects for organizations such as the World Bank, the German Development Institute (DIE), and the New Zealand Treasury, and he led country missions on taxation sponsored by the German Agency for International Cooperation (GIZ).

Acknowledgments

This volume was prepared by a team led by Blanca Moreno-Dodson at the Poverty Reduction and Economic Management (PREM) Network of the World Bank under the Vice Presidency of Otaviano Canuto. Peer reviewers were Milan Brahmbhatt and Jack Mintz.

The team contributing to the book consisted of Milan Brahmbhatt and Otaviano Canuto (Overview); B. Essama-Nssah and Blanca Moreno-Dodson (chapter 1); Norman Gemmell, Florian Misch, and Blanca Moreno-Dodson (chapter 2); James Brumby and Kai Kaiser (chapter 3); Kirk Hamilton and Eduardo Ley (chapter 4); José Cuesta and Jorge Martinez-Vazquez (chapter 5); and Kathie Krumm and Chandana Kularatne (chapter 6).

The team leader wishes to thank all the people who were instrumental in bringing this initiative to fruition. First and foremost, Otaviano Canuto for his inspiration and leadership to launch the Fiscal Policy for Growth and Development business line under which the team was created with members of the Economic Policy, Poverty, and Public Sector Governance PREM units; Milan Brahmbhatt for his guidance through the process; and Linda Van Gelder for her support in the finalization of the book in the Public Sector Governance unit. In addition, the team is very grateful to our external partners from the University of Notthingham (Florian

Misch), the New Zealand Treasury (Norman Gemmell), Georgia State University (Jorge Martinez-Vazquez), and the University of Calgary (Jack Mintz), as well as the government of the Republic of Korea for its external support.

Excellent research assistance for chapters 1 and 2 was provided by Nihal Bayraktar (University of Pennsylvania). Amelia Yuson provided efficient administrative support. Sabra Ledent served as copy editor with previous contributions from the late Christine Cotting. Finally, the production of this volume was made possible by the World Bank Office of the Publisher.

Abbreviations

ADB	Asian Development Bank
aNNI	adjusted net national income
ANS	adjusted net saving
ARRA	American Recovery and Reinvestment Act
CCAGG	Concerned Citizens of Abra for Good Government
CFA	central finance agency
CGE	computable general equilibrium
CMDT	Compagnie Malienne pour le Development des Textiles
CoST	Construction Sector Transparency Initiative
DfID	Department for International Development
FMIS	financial management information system
GDP	gross domestic product
GFS	government finance statistics
GNI	gross national income
GNU	Government of National Unity
ICGFM	International Consortium on Governmental Financial Management
ICT	information and communication technology
IFAC	International Federation of Accountants
ILO	International Labour Organization

IMF	International Monetary Fund
IPSASB	International Public Sector Accounting Standards Board
LIC	low-income country
LISGIS	Liberian Institute for Statistics and Geo-Information Services
MDG	Millennium Development Goal
MIC	middle-income country
MTEF	medium-term expenditure framework
NNI	net national income
NRF	natural resource fund
ODA	official development assistance
OECD	Organisation for Economic Co-operation and Development
PBB	program-based budgeting
PEFA	public expenditure and financial accountability
PFM	public financial management
PIM	public investment management
PIMI	Public Investment Management Index
PPP	public-private partnership
PSI	Policy Support Instrument
R&D	research and development
SOE	state-owned enterprise
SVAR	structural vector autoregression
TASAF	Tanzania Social Action Fund
TBM	tax-benefit microsimulation
TFP	total factor productivity
UNICEF	United Nations Children's Fund
UNRISD	United Nations Research Institute for Social Development
WEO	*World Economic Outlook*

OVERVIEW

Fiscal Policy for Growth and Development

Milan Brahmbhatt and Otaviano Canuto

The global financial and economic crisis that broke out in 2008 has reawakened interest in fiscal policy. In the early stages of the crisis, there was a widespread turn to fiscal instruments for countercyclical stimulus, as many developed countries experienced a massive negative shock to aggregate demand, which was then transmitted to developing countries through various channels.[1] More recently, the instability in the Euro Area has exposed how the need to restore long-term fiscal sustainability can itself contribute to harsh recessionary pressures and constraints on policy, especially when countries fall into a spiraling "bad equilibrium" of negative sovereign debt dynamics.[2]

More subtly, the global crisis has refocused interest in fiscal policy as an instrument for longer-term growth and development, particularly among developing countries. In the potential "new normal" of continued sluggishness in the advanced world, developing countries have strong incentives to seek out new domestic engines for efficiency and productivity growth, as well as for greater equity in development. The potential of fiscal policy to raise an economy's long-run growth rate and promote equitable development is therefore of great interest to developing country policy makers. And that is the main focus of this book.

This introduction begins with a brief overview of how developing countries have fared so far in this crisis, particularly in the evolution of

1

fiscal policy and fiscal positions. In doing so, it touches on some emerging policy lessons. It then sketches a useful conceptual framework for thinking about the connections between fiscal policy and longer-term growth and development, aspects of which are fleshed out in more detail in chapter 1. The remainder of the introduction highlights some of the main findings in the rest of the volume about the connections between fiscal policy and development: chapter 2 on public expenditure and long-run growth, chapter 3 on the critical role of good public investment management (PIM) in achieving development results, chapter 4 on the special issues of fiscal policy in natural resource–rich developing economies, chapter 5 on the impact of fiscal policy on distribution and equity, and chapter 6 on how fiscal policy played out during the crisis in one developing region, Sub-Saharan Africa.

Context, Recent Trends, and Lessons from the Crisis

There is a fairly common perception that economic performance in developing countries during and after the global crisis held up much better than in developed countries. But this perception can be questioned in some respects. For example, the drops in growth of gross domestic product (GDP) among developing economies were fully comparable in magnitude to those in the developed world (Didier, Helvia, and Schmukler 2011). However, the common perception is correct in that even after these declines, growth rates in developing countries during the crisis generally remained much higher than in developed countries.

Figure O.1 shows the emergence in the decade of the 2000s of a large *growth premium* in developing countries relative to developed countries, averaging about 4 percentage points a year (on a GDP-weighted basis). This premium persisted even in 2009—the trough of the recession—when developing countries grew by about 2 percent, compared with a steep 4 percent contraction in the advanced world, and it has continued during the recovery. This resilience was not just a matter of strong growth in big economies such as China and India. Figure O.2 indicates that 2009 growth in *most* developing countries, big and small, was somewhat higher than in the developed world.

Among the reasons for the emergence of a large developing-country growth premium in the 2000s and its persistence during and after the crisis, favorable external circumstances, such as low international interest rates and relatively high commodity prices, are likely to have played some

Figure O.1   World Output Growth, 1961–2012

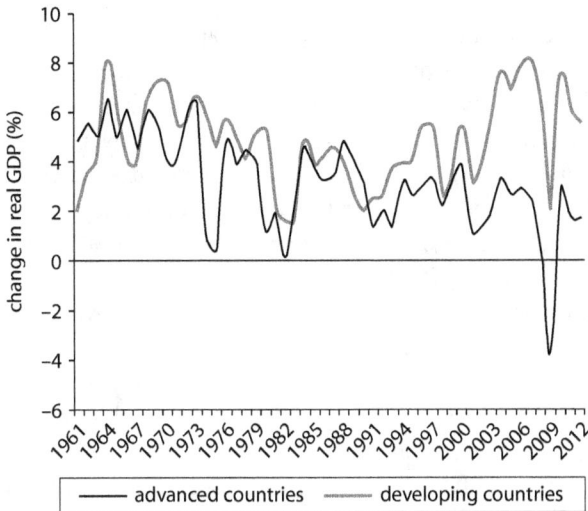

Sources: World Development Indicators and World Bank forecasts.
Note: GDP = gross domestic product.

Figure O.2   Frequency Distribution of GDP Growth, Developed and Developing Countries, 2009

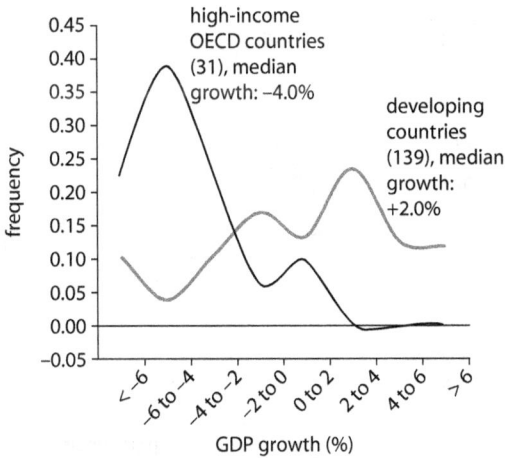

Source: World Development Indicators.
Note: GDP = gross domestic product; OECD = Organisation for Economic Co-operation and Development.

part. But there is also much evidence and a growing consensus that
another important reason was a substantial improvement in economic
policies in developing countries. They therefore entered the crisis in
much stronger macroeconomic and financial positions than in the past.
Compared with previous crises, this one found them with, in general,
much smaller fiscal and current account deficits, lower inflation, higher
international reserves, more flexible exchange rates, lower public and
external debt burdens, and less financial sector vulnerability associated
with excessive domestic credit expansion (Canuto and Giugale 2010;
Kose and Prasad 2010; Gourinchas and Obstfeldt 2012).[3]

The improvement in the fiscal position of many developing countries
during the 2000s was reflected in a substantial decline in their public
debt. Among middle-income countries (MICs), the median ratio of general government debt to GDP almost halved, from close to 60 percent in
2002 to just over 30 percent in 2008. Median debt in a sample of low-
income countries (LICs) fell even more precipitously over this period,
aided by substantial debt relief (figure O.3).

Figure O.3   General Government Debt, Medians, 2002–11

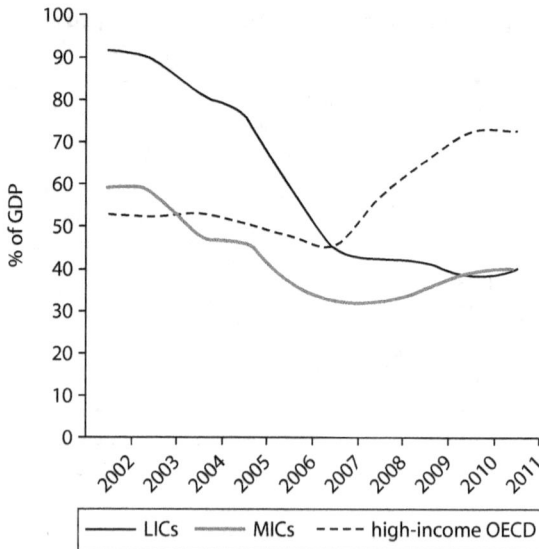

Source: World Economic Outlook database, International Monetary Fund.
Note: LIC = low-income country; MIC = middle-income country; OECD = Organisation for Economic
Co-operation and Developmentl; GDP = gross domestic product.

Linked to this improvement in fiscal positions was a swing to greater countercyclicality in the fiscal policy stance in many economies, in contrast to the norm in the past when policy in most countries was procyclical, expanding fiscal stimulus during booms and reducing it during downturns and recessions. Frankel, Vegh, and Vuletin (2011) present evidence that the proportion of developing countries effectively pursuing countercyclical fiscal policies increased from less than 10 percent in 1960–99 to over one-third in 2000–09.[4] As chapter 2 in this volume by Gemmell, Misch, and Moreno-Dodson notes, many developing countries were able to increase real government spending in 2009, at the depths of the recession, despite weaker fiscal revenues. This scenario was in sharp contrast to the common one in earlier crises, when countries were often obliged to cut spending, and not least on investment projects, social expenditures, or both. Generally, countries that had greater fiscal space before the crisis were able to undertake more significant increases in countercyclical fiscal stimulus, something also documented by Krumm and Kularatne in chapter 6 of this volume on Sub-Saharan Africa (Aizenmann and Jinerak 2010; IMF 2010a, 2010b).

How effective were countercyclical programs in developing countries in bolstering short-term growth during the recent crisis? The International Monetary Fund (IMF 2010b) presents some preliminary evidence that the strength of the postcrisis recovery was positively correlated with higher public spending as well as with flexible exchange rates and the extent of precrisis foreign exchange reserve coverage, among other factors. Several chapters in this volume also document, to the extent allowed by the currently available data, the preliminary impacts of the recent countercyclical fiscal policies in developing countries in bolstering near-term growth and in pursuing social objectives such as protecting the poor and vulnerable.

It is worth noting that the impact of countercyclical fiscal policies on near-term growth is likely to be very context dependent. It is likely to be affected, for example, by various structural characteristics of an economy and by a country's overall macroeconomic policy regime. This is one of the useful results emerging from recent debates in developed countries over the potential effectiveness of countercyclical fiscal policy. DeLong and Summers (2012) note that what they call the "policy-relevant fiscal multiplier" depends in particular on how monetary policy reacts to fiscal policy shocks. They presume that in normal times monetary policy will be the primary tool for macroeconomic stabilization and will tend to offset fiscal policy shocks, so that estimates of the fiscal multiplier will tend to be quite small. In a depressed economy, however, the situation may be different, particularly when nominal policy interest rates have reached a zero lower bound and political factors constrain the central bank from undertaking "nonstandard" monetary easing on a large scale. Then monetary policy may be much more accommodating of fiscal stimulus, and the policy-relevant fiscal multiplier would be much larger.[5]

Recent work by Ilzetzki, Mendoza, and Vegh (2010) indicates that fiscal multipliers in developing countries are generally estimated to be much smaller than in developed countries but also clearly documents the dependence of multipliers on the structural and macroeconomic context. This work finds a clear difference between countries with flexible exchange rates, where the multipliers are essentially zero, and countries with predetermined exchange rates, where they are significantly positive and over one. This gap essentially relates to the different features of monetary policy under the two exchange rate regimes. Under predetermined exchange rates, monetary policy is passive and obliged to accommodate fiscal policy. Under flexible exchange rates, it is autonomous and able to offset fiscal policy shocks. These results are very much in line with theoretical predictions from standard open economy macro models. Fiscal multipliers are also found to be smaller for more open, international trade–dependent economies (because of greater import leakage) and even to be negative in the long run for economies with high public debt (defined as central government debt of over 60 percent of GDP). The latter result likely arises because private agents anticipate that near-term fiscal stimulus will in fact endanger longer-term fiscal sustainability and will require sharp fiscal consolidation going forward.

These results suggest that developing countries need to evaluate the case for countercyclical fiscal stimulus on a careful case-by-case and context-specific basis. A growing number of developing countries are moving toward more flexible exchange rate regimes—something that in fact proved of great value in adjusting to shocks during the recent crisis—which suggests that monetary policy may become a more relevant and effective instrument for short-term macroeconomic stabilization over time. Many developing countries are also small, open economies, a fact that, according to the findings of Ilzetzki, Mendoza, and Vegh (2010), further limits the effectiveness of short-term fiscal stimulus.

Concerns about fiscal sustainability are perhaps less likely to pose a constraint on the use of short-term fiscal stimulus in view of the great decline in the public debt–to–GDP ratios in developing countries in the years leading up to the crisis. Nevertheless, although median debt ratios in LICs are still a moderate 40 percent of GDP, they have risen by almost 10 percentage points since the start of the crisis in MICs, and so this is a trend worthy of ongoing scrutiny (figure O.3). Furthermore, not all developing economies are in a relatively benign position: public debt–to–GDP ratios remain over 55 percent in about one-quarter of developing countries (figure O.4).

These observations do not mean that countercyclical fiscal policies cannot continue to be a useful instrument for short-term macroeconomic stabilization in developing countries if the appropriate macroeconomic and structural conditions are in place. What they do suggest is that short-term stabilization should not be the only or primary lens through which developing countries assess the usefulness of fiscal policy. Its role in addressing key market failures, improving resource allocation and efficiency, increasing the long-run growth properties of the economy, and addressing issues of distributional equity and social inclusion is likely to have at least as large, if not a greater, influence on social welfare over the long haul.

Fiscal Policy for Growth and Development—A Framework

It may be useful to start with a simple framework that helps to organize some of these issues. First, what are the *development objectives* to which

Figure O.4   General Government Debt, All Developing Countries, 2002–11

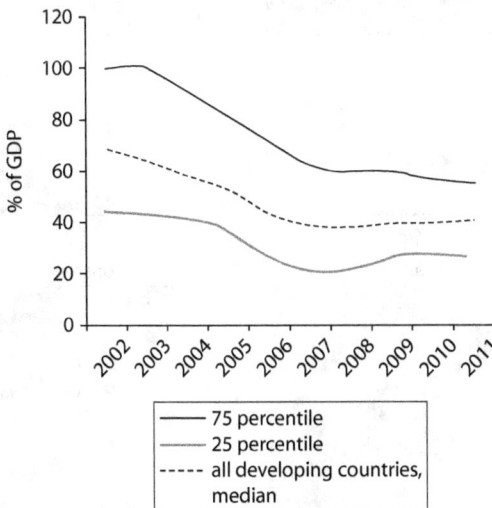

Source: World Economic Outlook database, International Monetary Fund.

fiscal policy should contribute (see figure O.5)? *Growth* is clearly one, though policy makers may sometimes want to go beyond the standard focus on growth of real GDP and consider broader measures of income or even to expand the focus to growth in a comprehensive measure of a country's *wealth* (a point explored further by Hamilton and Ley in chapter 4).[6] *Poverty reduction, social inclusion,* and *equity* have complex links to growth but also are rightly viewed as independent development objectives, because the distributional outcomes of market processes may not necessarily jibe with a society's normative views on equity. Finally, although sometimes overlooked, there is *protection against risk and vulnerability to shocks,* which, assuming that most people are risk averse, is also an element of social welfare. Social risk management has long been among the most powerful drivers of public spending and fiscal interventions in advanced economies, and it is of growing importance in developing countries as well.

However, one cannot simply assume that government has a clear role in advancing these development objectives. There must be a *clear rationale for public action* rather than relying on the private markets or on the kinds of self-organizing, voluntary meso-institutions for collective action

Figure O.5   Fiscal Policy for Growth and Development, A Framework

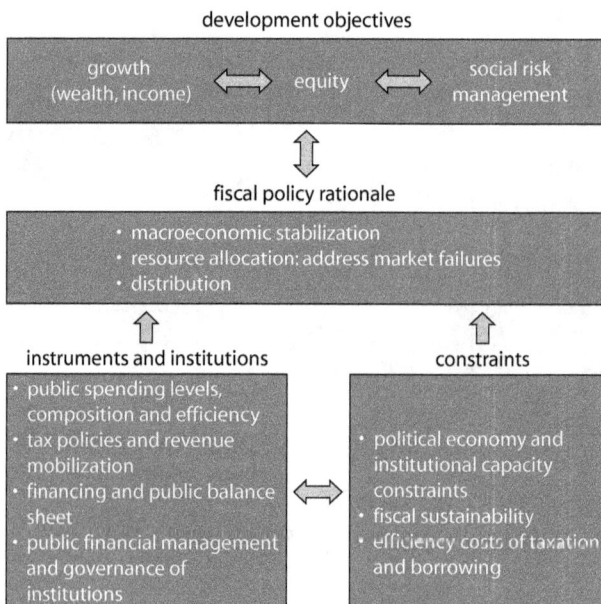

studied by Ostrom (1990). Chapter 1 of this volume by Essama-Nssah and Moreno-Dodson elaborates on aspects of this framework and notes that the traditional threefold rationale for fiscal policy proposed by Musgrave (1959) is still useful. Under that rationale, fiscal policy should aim to promote macroeconomic stabilization, improving resource allocation and addressing distributional disparities.

The *stabilization rationale* has both short- and long-run aspects. The short-run aspect focuses on the possibility of using countercyclical fiscal policy to offset the impact of macroeconomic shocks that create large or persistent gaps between aggregate demand and potential output, thereby helping to avert both excessive cyclical unemployment and inflationary pressure. (However, as the previous section indicated, there is considerable debate over whether fiscal policy is the best policy instrument for this purpose.) From a longer-run perspective, stabilization is also concerned with keeping fiscal deficits and public debt on a *sustainable* path, so that the public finances do not themselves become a source of macroeconomic stability.

As for the *resource allocation rationale* of fiscal policy, the focus is on the potential for the government to improve economic performance through expenditure and tax policies that boost efficiency (technical and allocative) and improve long-term development performance by dealing with critical market failures. For example, the government might spend on public goods such as law and order, justice, and basic infrastructure, the supply of which also raises productivity and growth in the private sector. Market failures in this context refer not only to the familiar issues of public goods, externalities, and increasing scale returns but also to a variety of information failures and problems of missing markets that can, for example, lead to failures in private insurance markets, creating an efficiency rationale for social insurance policies.

Finally, the *distribution rationale* underpins fiscal policies that aim to adjust the distribution of income, opportunities, assets, or risk that emerge from private market activity so that it better reflects the ethical views endorsed by society.

There is no simple mapping from rationales to objectives. Fiscal policy undertaken under one or more rationales will typically affect all three development objectives. Thus, for example, a reallocation of public spending toward roads with a net positive effect on growth will also have implications for income distribution and social risk management. If, for example, a new road links a poor remote area to the big city, it could improve the income possibilities for the poor (access to new markets, cheaper farm inputs), as well as their ability to cope with shocks (such as more diverse job opportunities, urban migration possibilities). A road between two wealthy cities might be even better for growth but worse on the other two counts.

Even when fiscal policy has a clear rationale, key decisions must be made about the appropriate fiscal policy instrument to use, the financing or balance sheet implications of public spending or tax policies, and the institutions that are available to implement such policies in practice, taking into account key constraints and linkages (see figure O.5). For example, how will changes in the composition of public expenditure or tax structure affect growth and income distribution? The taxes or borrowing needed to finance spending also have their own efficiency costs, and so the benefits of public spending always need to be evaluated net of those costs, as discussed in chapter 2.

In addition, as noted, fiscal policies need to remain *sustainable* if they are not themselves to become a source of macroeconomic instability. The government must therefore remain solvent (able to pay off its debts at some future time), liquid (able to meet its current outgoings), and credible (retaining the confidence of investors in its solvency and liquidity). The effectiveness of fiscal programs—for example, the efficiency with which revenues are raised, the cost-effectiveness of public service delivery, or how well public resources are protected from corruption and waste—all depend crucially on the quality of public financial management institutions in a country. Indeed, the costs of government failures may even exceed the costs of the market failures the government is trying to address. Political economy factors and institutional capacity intimately affect a country's ability to actually implement sound fiscal policies.

The sections that follow briefly survey other chapters in this volume and some of their findings about fiscal policies and institutions for growth and development.

Public Spending and Long-Run Growth

It is now well understood that specific kinds of public expenditure can make a significant contribution to the level and growth rate of economic output. The government may be able to supply key goods or services such as infrastructure, research and development, or education that raise the productivity of capital and labor in the private sector but that the private sector itself is unable to provide in optimal quantity or quality because of market failures. The reasons for such failures could be that those goods and services are public goods, or that credit market imperfections or human capital externalities are a factor.[7]

Yet relatively little is known about the likely size of the growth effects of various kinds of public spending, particularly in developing countries, or about the circumstances that may affect these growth outcomes. Chapter 2 in this volume explores the existing empirical research on the growth effects of public spending in developing countries using a consistent conceptual framework.

Estimating these effects is not easy, as the authors of chapter 2 note, because, for one thing, the growth benefits of a change in public expenditure need to be measured net of the effects of how the expenditure is financed. Most taxes generate distortions and efficiency costs that can affect growth. Public borrowing and growing debt (representing future taxes) can affect growth as well—for example, through financial crowding out, particularly in situations in which investors lose confidence in the sustainability of the government's fiscal position.

The authors therefore restrict their attention to the limited number of empirical studies on the growth effects of government spending in developing countries that take proper account of the government's budget constraint and meet some other quality standards. Some of these studies divide government spending along functional lines, using an a priori definition of productive spending common in this literature that includes education, health, housing, transportation and communication, general services, and defense. Broadly speaking, these studies find that more productive expenditures do have a positive impact on growth if they are financed through reductions in other less productive expenditures or through relatively small fiscal deficits, or both. Financing through large deficits appears to be associated with weaker or even negative impacts on growth (Adam and Bevan 2005). However, there is fairly high variation in the size and statistical significance of the estimates in these studies.

Other studies break down government spending along economic classification lines, in particular between capital and current spending. The effects of capital spending appear to also depend crucially on how it is financed. An important finding in a number of studies is that there is no great growth payoff from boosting capital spending by cutting current spending—indeed, there may be a negative impact. This finding supports the idea that properly selected capital and current spending are complements rather than substitutes—for example, spending on operations and maintenance. Results on the effects of more disaggregated spending by sector or function are less robust within and across studies, possibly because of differences in measurement across countries.

In chapter 2, Gemmell, Misch, and Moreno-Dodson also point out that changes in public spending can be triggered by a variety of motivations other than long-run growth. Fiscal stimulus to counter cyclical downturns and spending to address distributional and equity issues are two examples. They survey public spending trends in developing countries following the recent global crisis, noting the composition of spending packages and potential trade-offs between the different motivations for expenditure programs, in particular between near-term stimulus and long-term growth.

Finally, the chapter looks at directions for future research that could help improve the robustness and precision of estimates of the impact of government spending on long-run growth. Although government can help overcome market failures, it can also generate institutional failures that reduce incentives and productivity in the private sector. In other words, empirical work in this area will likely be affected by unobserved heterogeneity in governance, institutions, and the overall quality of public spending.[8] Greater use of subnational expenditure data and firm-level data are other promising areas for research.

Public Investment Management: Challenges and Tools

Chapter 3 by Brumby and Kaiser explores what is perhaps the most important variable conditioning the impact of public spending: the quality of public investment management (PIM). A newly developed index of PIM quality shows that only about half of public investment expenditure in developing countries translates into productive capital stocks (Dabla-Norris et al. 2011; Gupta et al. 2011). There is also evidence that public investment spending is higher in countries in which institutional quality is lower because of the opportunities for corruption and rent seeking it provides (Keefer and Knack 2007). Poor governance thus leads to more public resources being committed precisely in those circumstances in which the resources are most likely to be squandered on poorly chosen, implemented, and managed public investments.

Public investment takes place under a complex and diverse variety of institutional arrangements among central, state, and local governments, public corporations, state-owned enterprises, and the private sector. Careful attention must therefore be paid to the institutional arrangements, contexts, and, above all, incentives by which investment projects are created and maintained.

Brumby and Kaiser delve into several of the institutional challenges of PIM. One is the optimal assignment of roles and responsibilities for the creation and maintenance of public assets across various agencies and levels of government. A particularly important issue here is how to achieve sufficient coordination between capital and current spending on the operations and maintenance needed to keep assets working effectively. Other important institutional challenges are how to strike an optimal balance between different stages of project selection and management and how to balance fiscal resource allocation and execution of capital assets. In the latter area, budget planning and execution of public investment projects are ideally nested in the context of a medium-term expenditure framework (MTEF), which may help address problems arising from excessive political discretion over projects, myopia, and seesaw or ratchet effects.

The chapter also surveys some new tools that hold promise for helping improve PIM. Benchmarking tools such as the IMF's PIM Index (PIMI) and the World Bank's recently developed public expenditure and financial accountability (PEFA) diagnostic framework for public capital spending provide useful information on the general quality of appraisal, selection, implementation, and evaluation, as well as the broader public financial management practices surrounding public capital spending. Accounting innovations, such as the gradual adoption of accrual accounting for public investments, can help strengthen the quality of information available for evaluating fiscal policy, long-term fiscal sustainability, and public asset management in an intertemporal context.

Greater transparency is a powerful tool for improving public investment performance, particularly when coupled with mechanisms that allow stakeholders to provide decision makers with feedback. Stakeholders can include a wide range of actors—civil society organizations, concerned citizens, the users of public infrastructure, and contractors—each with distinct capabilities and perspectives. Feedback from these social monitoring initiatives complements formal reporting and monitoring mechanisms. When stakeholders have access to the relevant information, they can assess progress against plans, the quality of investments, and value for money. They also can identify risks arising from shortcomings in project design or corruption. The development of information and communication technology (ICT) can further enhance transparency and the impact of social monitoring, while facilitating the adoption of reliable modern financial management information systems (FMIS). Still, the political frictions that might hamper social monitoring initiatives should not be underestimated.

Fiscal Policy for Sustainable Development in Resource-Rich LICs

Why is a special perspective needed on fiscal policy in resource-rich developing countries? In chapter 4, Hamilton and Ley observe many distinctive features of these countries that make such a perspective worthwhile. For one thing, taxation and royalties from the natural resource sector often become a predominant source of government revenue. However, international resource prices are highly volatile, tending in turn to induce high volatility in government revenues and economic activity. "Point source" natural resources, such as minerals and oil, become a tempting target for corruption and rent seeking. The struggle to control such assets is sometimes a source of civil strife and war. Because natural resources themselves are depleting assets, a key question arises about how much to consume today and how much to save for future generations. The problems of natural resource–led development are exacerbated in LICs, where governance conditions are weak, where present consumption demands by the large numbers of poor are hard to resist, and where it is hard for governments to commit and stick to rational plans for natural resource depletion.[9]

This chapter sets fiscal policy in resource-rich countries within a broader setting of the theory of capital and long-run growth. The key to increasing future living standards lies in increasing overall national *wealth*, which includes not only traditional measures of capital such as produced and human capital but also natural capital. Hamilton and Ley argue that standard economic measures of GDP and savings can be inadequate for indicating whether national wealth is indeed rising. Measures of *adjusted* net national income and savings are needed, which, among other things, take into account the depletion of natural assets as a form of depreciation, complemented by comprehensive measures of the stock of wealth. This is a matter of much practical importance. For example, conventionally measured GDP growth has been strong in some countries in Sub-Saharan Africa in recent years, but it may be unsustainable because adjusted savings rates are estimated to be negative, which would suggest that the overall wealth of these countries is declining.

To ensure that their long-run growth is sustainable, resource-rich countries need to ensure that they capture an efficient and fair share of natural resource rents and then invest that share effectively in order to increase the country's wealth. This is where fiscal policy and good public sector governance become crucial.

As for upstream taxation of resources, the chapter notes that the optimal form of taxation will depend on the information available to the parties, their risk tolerance, their ability to make credible commitments, and the balance of strategic bargaining power between the government and international mineral companies. Multiple fiscal instruments may well be required to protect the interests of all parties.

Natural resource funds (NRFs) have long been advocated as an important tool for securing and rationally managing the use of government revenues from natural resources. Why? Hamilton and Ley argue that NRFs are a type of rules-based fiscal policy instrument intended to help overcome political economy problems that favor excessive consumption and plunder of natural resource revenues. Three traditional functions of NRFs are macroeconomic stabilization (to insulate the economy from large fluctuations in resource prices and revenues), stable budget financing (to smooth out the government budget fluctuations), and more optimal savings and investment (to preserve wealth for future generations). Such funds are also useful in maintaining the quality of public spending by providing a "speed limit" on excessively rapid and wasteful expenditures in boom times. However, experience shows that NRFs only work if they change the underlying incentives facing political actors. Chapter 4 reviews some of the approaches that have been considered. On the whole, it seems that, to change the incentives facing government decision makers, it is helpful to increase transparency in the operation of the NRF and to broaden accountability to include actors outside the executive— for example, the legislature, technical experts, and appropriately qualified civil society organizations.

Having securely placed revenues in an NRF, the government still faces difficult decisions on how much to pass on to citizens directly through tax cuts or transfers (for example, through a "national dividend") and how much to retain in public hands; on how much of the public share to consume and how much to save and invest; and on how to allocate public investment optimally (for example, between holding foreign assets and engaging in domestic public investments such as infrastructure). On the last decision, a good case could be made for using resource revenues to fund high-return public investments in what are, after all, capital-scarce LICs. However, this strategy requires that countries "invest in their capacity to invest"—that is, they appropriately appraise, select, and manage public investments so that potential high returns become a reality. Hamilton and Ley highlight a crucial point made by Harberger (2005): a strengthening of the PIM system increases productivity growth and thus should have a permanent, continuing impact on the country's rate of economic growth, in contrast to reforms that yield a one-off increase in the level of economic output.

Analyzing the Distributive Effects of Fiscal Policies: How to Prepare (Analytically) for the Next Crisis

In chapter 5 of this volume, Cuesta and Martinez-Vazquez review evidence on the distributive consequences of fiscal policy, focusing in particular on the recent global crisis. They look at the merits and limitations of the analytical tools currently available for distributional analysis, keeping in mind practical considerations such as the limited resources, urgency, and strategic questions facing hard-pressed policy makers in the midst of an economic crisis. Using Liberia as a case study, the chapter suggests some simple new analytical tools that would help policy makers conduct better social analysis in the next crisis.

Because of the relatively little time that has elapsed since the crisis and the paucity of good disaggregated data, there is as yet little detailed information on the poverty and income distribution impacts of the crisis and crisis-related policies. Aggregate cross-country studies have typically found that the net impact was to slow down rather than reverse the ongoing decline in the global poverty rate, which was estimated to fall from 42 percent in 2008 to 39 percent in 2009, compared with an estimated counterfactual 38 percent without the crisis (Chen and Ravallion 2009). Some in-depth country-level microsimulation studies that link macro-level crisis impacts with detailed household survey data have produced additional interesting findings. For example, households made newly poor by the crisis tended to have characteristics different from those of the structural poor; they were more urban, skilled, and less reliant on agricultural income. However, there is relatively little information on the poverty and distributional effects of specific fiscal policy decisions made during the crisis.

Cuesta and Martinez-Vazquez then turn to evaluating the three main types of analytical tools that could be used in efforts to understand the distributional implications of fiscal policies. The first tool, conventional incidence analysis, is a relatively well-developed set of techniques to estimate how much of a given category of expenditure is received by a particular group in society and how much taxation is borne by each group. Some advantages of this methodology are the simple but powerful set of results it produces and the relative ease with which policy messages can be developed from the results. These analyses produce the observed results on the basis of a particular set of assumptions, and although in some cases these are supported by well-established evidence, there is no guarantee that the assumptions actually hold in a given case. This approach also typically does not allow for secondary or general equilibrium effects.

The second tool is tax-benefit simulation models. These models offer the advantage of allowing analysis of the impact of economic shocks or policy changes all the way down to the level of a microdata sample of heterogeneous households. They also allow much greater precision in the specification of policies and potential behavioral responses by households, although the sensitivity of results to the behavioral assumptions made is also one of the caveats associated with this type of tool.

The third type of tool studied, computable general equilibrium models, allows in principle for a flexible combination of micro- and macro-level analysis. For example, the Maquette for MDG Simulations (MAMS) model developed at the World Bank draws on micro-level information about the determinants of outcomes in sectors such as health and education. It then uses this information as inputs for macro- and sectoral-level analysis of government policies. Finally, it points to implications for income distribution, drawing on microdata from household surveys. Here, too, various shortcomings and caveats should be kept in mind—for example, the high sensitivity of results to modeling assumptions.

In practice, how should one go about choosing among the available techniques? Cuesta and Martinez-Vazquez observe that in terms of desirable features, there is no single superior technique but rather trade-offs among the simplicity of data needs, analytical assumptions, readiness to implement, and comprehensiveness and richness of results to guide policy making. Cuesta and Martinez-Vazquez propose two additional tools that may help policy makers better prepare to address the distributional impacts of the next crisis. The first is a simple qualitative questionnaire on fiscal decisions implemented at the sectoral level in a given period. This information is intended to complement, not replace, aggregate spending trends and more sophisticated ex post microanalyses. The second tool is an approach to conducting ex ante microsimulations that focus on *opportunities* rather than on outcomes in the hope that the traditional short-term analysis of welfare outputs may be complemented with a discussion of the longer-term effects on equality of opportunity. A case study of

Liberia provides an example of this method in action. It traces the likely impacts of a theoretical cut in educational spending on the probability of access to education for different individuals. This information should be useful in designing more effective policy responses to a crisis.

Fiscal Policy Lessons from the Global Crisis in Sub-Saharan Africa

Chapter 6 by Krumm and Kularatne assesses the fiscal response to the 2009 global crisis in 15 LICs in Sub-Saharan Africa. The crisis required short-term responses, but these responses have implications for the medium- and long-term challenges related to growth and poverty reduction—issues that are particularly pressing in Sub-Saharan Africa.

In evaluating what happened, it is important to note that many African economies came into the crisis on the heels of significant improvements in economic and fiscal performance over the preceding decade. Over 70 percent of them ran primary fiscal surpluses (compared with less than 30 percent in the early 1990s); public debt–to–GDP ratios had declined sharply, in part because of debt relief but also because of domestic fiscal adjustment; and many countries were experiencing higher growth and expanding productive public and private investment.

In most African LICs, where automatic fiscal stabilizers are limited, the principal fiscal impact of the crisis was a drop in government revenue. Revenue declines were particularly large in highly commodity-dependent economies. The main fiscal policy instrument available to governments in Sub-Saharan Africa was a discretionary change in expenditure. In principle, these governments had a number of fiscal policy options available: *adjustment*, defined as a cut in spending in response to the revenue drop; *accommodation*, defined as maintaining spending unchanged; and *stimulus*, defined as increasing spending notwithstanding the revenue decline. Krumm and Kularatne find that the bulk of the countries in the sample undertook full or partial accommodation of revenue declines, and some even undertook countercyclical stimulus.

Only a relatively small number of countries undertook full adjustment in the face of revenue declines. Also important, the authors find a close link between the availability of fiscal space and low risk of debt distress and the type of fiscal policy response to the crisis: the more fiscal space a country had built up before the crisis, the less it was obliged to undertake full adjustment and the more options it had in accommodating the revenue shock or even undertaking stimulus.

Krumm and Kularatne ask how countries in Sub-Saharan Africa that undertook countercyclical fiscal stimulus were able to finance such programs. By and large, official grants and concessional lending remained stable, although there was some front-loading by multilaterals. As for external private capital markets, African LICs traditionally have had limited access to such markets, and, in any case, these markets became largely inaccessible during the depths of the crisis. However, these governments were able to draw on domestic financial markets for the bulk of fiscal stimulus financing. Such markets have been growing in depth and scope over the last decade, and it appears they were able to partly meet the financing challenge raised by the crisis. Because of the reduction in private sector credit demand stemming from the crisis, governments were able to borrow without much evidence of crowding out. Going forward, countries in Sub-Saharan Africa will need to ensure that the countercyclical increases in government spending undertaken during the crisis do not contribute to a longer-term deterioration in fiscal sustainability.

Chapter 6 also looks at how the crisis affected the planned composition of government budgets. An important consideration in many countries was to protect public infrastructure programs that had been launched before the crisis with a view to promoting long-term growth. The ability to do this depended crucially, however, on whether countries had built up adequate fiscal reserves during the precrisis boom. In natural resource–dependent countries, this ability was linked to the presence of fiscal rules (such as the type of NRFs described in chapter 4) that encourage saving resource-linked revenues during boom times. Where governments had little fiscal space, spending cuts affected more public investment. As for protection of the vulnerable, although well-targeted cash transfers and public works are generally thought to be the most efficient tools in an LIC context, their use in Sub-Saharan Africa has been limited and poorly coordinated. A few governments scaled up spending on such programs where they were already in place. Other governments, however, were tempted to adopt less efficient measures, such as fuel subsidies or producer price supports, for specific export commodities.

Krumm and Kularatne also point to the critical importance of institutional capacity to actually execute budgets and manage public investments well, underlining the points made in chapter 3. Although many countries made excellent fiscal plans on paper, the actual execution of plans often lagged. In most cases, actual expenditures were lower than those budgeted, so that the actual fiscal stance was less of a stimulant than intended. The need to steadily improve institutional capacity for budget and PIM is indeed one of the important lessons from the crisis in Sub-Saharan Africa. In addition, the importance of maintaining a prudent, sustainable fiscal stance over the medium term was well demonstrated, in particular the importance of building up fiscal space during good times in order to have resources during a crisis for countercyclical spending, including social spending to protect the vulnerable and spending on infrastructure and other productive sectors that will yield benefits for long-term growth. Experience from other regions has demonstrated that it is often difficult to reverse the discretionary fiscal programs undertaken during a crisis, and so it is important for countries in Sub-Saharan Africa to build safety nets that are effective and affordable in the long run and to ensure that exit strategies from temporary crisis programs are in place, especially where this is important for rebuilding fiscal space, ensuring fiscal sustainability, and maintaining policy credibility.

The Way Forward

The afterword at the end of this volume draws on the discussions in the various chapters to present suggestions for continued research and learning on the contributions of fiscal policy to growth and development.

Notes

1. In this volume, *developing countries* are defined as the group of low-income and middle-income countries (LICs and MICs) using the standard World Bank per capita income criteria for these groups; *developed countries* are defined as high-income countries.

2. Blanchard (2011) briefly discusses the potential for multiple equilibria in sovereign debt dynamics in the aftermath of the 2008 global crisis.

3. Such a broad assessment is inevitably subject to individual exceptions. For example, several countries in Central and Eastern Europe experienced major private sector credit bubbles financed by foreign borrowing.

4. Frankel, Vegh, and Vuletin (2011) define countercyclicality as a negative correlation between the cyclical components of government expenditure and gross domestic product (GDP).

5. For a more skeptical view of the efficacy of fiscal policy at even the zero lower interest rate bound, see Mankiw and Weinzierl (2011).

6. On such broader measures of income and wealth, see Arrow et al. (2010); Stiglitz, Sen, and Fitoussi (2010); and World Bank (2010).

7. Agénor and Moreno-Dodson (2006) identify a variety of other indirect channels through which public spending can affect growth—for example, by

reducing the adjustment costs of private investment or by facilitating the re-allocation of factors of production between sectors.

8. World Bank expenditure tracking surveys, for example, find large variations across countries in the extent to which public spending translates into actual public services or infrastructure.

9. Also see Brahmbhatt and Canuto (2010) for a brief survey of these issues.

References

Adam, Christopher S., and David L. Bevan. 2005. "Fiscal Deficits and Growth in Developing Countries." *Journal of Public Economics* 89: 571–97.

Agénor, Pierre-Richard, and Blanca Moreno-Dodson. 2006. "Public Infrastructure and Growth: New Channels and Policy Implications." Policy Research Working Paper 4064, World Bank, Washington, DC.

Aizenmann, Joshua, and Yothin Jinerak. 2010. "De Facto Fiscal Space and Fiscal Stimulus: Definition and Assessment." Working Paper 16539, National Bureau of Economic Research, Cambridge, MA.

Arrow, Kenneth J., Partha Dasgupta, Lawrence H. Goulder, Kevin J. Mumford, and Kirsten Oleson. 2010. "Sustainability and the Measurement of Wealth." Working Paper 16599, National Bureau of Economic Research, Cambridge, MA.

Blanchard, Olivier. 2011. "2011 in Review: Four Hard Truths." IMF Direct: The International Monetary Fund's Global Economy Forum, posted December 21.

Brahmbhatt, Milan, and Otaviano Canuto. 2010. "Natural Resources and Development Strategy after the Crisis." *World Bank Economic Premise*, no. 1 (February).

Canuto, Otaviano, and Marcelo Giugale, eds. 2010. *The Day after Tomorrow: A Handbook on the Future of Economic Policy in the Developing World.* Washington, DC: World Bank.

Chen, S., and M. Ravallion. 2009. "The Impact of the Global Financial Crisis on the World's Poorest." http://www.voxeu.org/index.php?q=node/3520.

Dabla-Norris, Era, Jim Brumby, Annette Kyobe, Zac Mills, and Chris Papageorgiou. 2011. "Investing in Public Investment: An Index of Public Investment Efficiency." Working Paper WP/11/37, International Monetary Fund, Washington, DC.

DeLong, J. Bradford, and Lawrence H. Summers. 2012. "Fiscal Policy in a Depressed Economy." Paper presented to the Spring 2012 Brookings Panel on Economic Activity, Washington, DC, March 20.

Didier, T., C. Helvia, and S. Schmukler. 2011. "How Resilient Were Developing Economies to the Global Economic Crisis?" Policy Research Working Paper 5637, World Bank, Washington, DC.

Frankel, Jeffrey, Carlos Vegh, and Guillermo Vuletin. 2011. "On Graduation from Procyclicality." Working Paper 17619, National Bureau of Economic Research, Cambridge, MA, November.

Gourinchas, P. O., and M. Obstfeldt. 2012. "Stories of the Twentieth Century for the Twenty-First." *American Economic Journal: Macroeconomics, American Economic Association* 4 (1): 226–65.

Gupta, Sanjeev, Alvar Kangur, Chris Papageorgiou, and Abdoul Wane. 2011. "Efficiency-Adjusted Public Capital and Growth." WP/11/217, International Monetary Fund, Washington, DC.

Harberger, A. C. 2005. "On the Process of Growth and Economic Policy in Developing Countries." Issue paper 13, Bureau for Policy and Program Coordination, U.S. Agency for International Development, Washington, DC.

Ilzetzki, Ethan, Enrique G. Mendoza, and Carlos A. Vegh. 2010. "How Big (Small) Are Fiscal Multipliers?" Working Paper 16479, National Bureau of Economic Research, Cambridge, MA.

IMF (International Monetary Fund). 2010a. "Emerging from the Global Crisis: Macroeconomic Challenges Facing Low-Income Countries." IMF Policy Paper, IMF, Washington, DC, October 5.

———. 2010b. "How Did Emerging Markets Cope in the Crisis?" IMF Policy Paper, IMF, Washington, DC, June 15.

Keefer, Philip, and Stephen Knack. 2007. "Boondoggles, Rent-Seeking and Political Checks and Balances: Public Investment under Unaccountable Governments." *Review of Economics and Statistics* 89 (3): 566–72.

Kose, M. Ayhan, and Eswar Prasad. 2010. *Emerging Markets: Resilience and Growth amid Global Turmoil.* Washington, DC: Brookings Institution Press.

Mankiw, Gregory N., and Matthew Weinzierl. 2011. "An Exploration of Optimal Stabilization Policy." Papers on Economic Activity, Brookings Institution, Washington, DC.

Musgrave, Richard. 1959. *The Theory of Public Finance: A Study in Public Economy.* New York: McGraw-Hill.

Ostrom, Elinor. 1990. *Governing the Commons: The Evolution of Institutions for Collective Action.* Cambridge, U.K.: Cambridge University Press.

Stiglitz, Joseph, Amartya Sen, and Jean-Paul Fitoussi. 2010. *Mismeasuring Our Lives: Why GDP Doesn't Add Up. Report of the Commission on the Measurement of Economic Performance and Social Progress.* New York and London: New Press.

World Bank. 2010. *The Changing Wealth of Nations: Measuring Sustainable Development in the New Millennium.* Washington, DC: World Bank.

CHAPTER 1

Fiscal Policy for Growth and Social Welfare

B. Essama-Nssah and Blanca Moreno-Dodson

Fiscal policy is an important instrument for maintaining and improving living standards. Such living standards can be viewed as an outcome of the interaction between the opportunities offered by society and the readiness and ability of each person to exploit them. Under certain circumstances, public finance can make an important contribution to the creation of opportunities within a given society by raising resources from the private sector through taxation or borrowing (domestic and external)[1] and allocating those resources effectively and equitably in the form of public spending, including through public goods and transfers. These considerations put fiscal policy at the front and center of development policy making and raise a central question: how should fiscal resources be mobilized and deployed in order to improve social welfare? The answer to this question is complex. In part, it is positive and depends on the expected outcomes of fiscal policy. However, in part, it is also normative, because it depends on the desirability of those outcomes.

The appropriate role of government must also be assessed in terms of its comparative advantage relative to the market or nongovernmental institutions. In particular, Musgrave (1959) notes three fundamental public finance functions of government: *allocation*, *distribution*, and *stabilization*.

The *allocation* function is related to the mix of private and public goods in the economy, as well as the composition of public goods. A potential role for public finance policies arises when market failures of various kinds lead to Pareto inefficient outcomes.[2]

The *distribution* function is related to the pursuit of equity with respect to the income and nonincome dimensions of the living standards. Consistent with the distributive role of government, the "United Nations Millennium Declaration" (UN 2000) and the *World Development Report 2006* (World Bank 2005) promote poverty reduction and equity as fundamental objectives of socioeconomic development worldwide. Thus, in a market economy,[3] public finance could help all members of society achieve a standard of living that is acceptable on the basis of the prevailing norms on human needs and rights.

Finally, the *stabilization* function is related to the achievement of economic growth in a stable macroeconomic environment characterized by full employment of labor and other resources, low inflation, low fiscal deficits, and a sustainable external account.

The purpose of this chapter is to present a methodical way of thinking about public finance policy design in developing countries, taking into account the implementation challenges that emerge in times of economic crisis when a government needs to carefully balance the three Musgravian functions. The government must adjust its role to meet emerging needs in an imperfect market environment and to stabilize the economy, all while protecting the poor and most vulnerable.

Public finance policy options are usually assessed on the basis of a three-dimensional criterion that involves a rationale for state intervention, a determination of the appropriate type of intervention, and the social desirability of induced outcomes.

The design of public finance policy can therefore be informed by ex ante analysis of the likely growth and equity consequences of alternative options. Economic growth creates opportunities, and social inclusion can preserve and promote the ability of individuals to take advantage of those opportunities. The effects of fiscal policy on economic growth are mediated through its impact on input accumulation and productivity, which we refer to as the "engine of growth." This effect ultimately hinges on the nature of the linkages between growth and the economic environment characterized by individual endowments and behavior as well as on the sociopolitical arrangements that govern interaction between economic agents.

Social inclusion can be viewed as encompassing, first, policies to pro-mote equity, because the distribution of income and wealth yielded by market outcomes may not necessarily agree with a society's ethical per-spectives. In addition, because of market failures that lead to imperfec-tions in and the incompleteness of insurance markets, there has been a growing role for governments in social risk management and protection against vulnerability to shocks. Grosh et al. (2008) argue that fiscal policy can promote social inclusion by means of (1) *prevention* through social insurance to manage the risk from economic shocks; (2) *protection* through resource transfers against significant losses in human capital; and (3) *promotion* through the provision of services that foster an individual's ability to participate in economic growth.

Although economic growth generates the resources needed for social protection, growth in turn benefits from appropriate risk management, which is conducive to private investment (prevention), safeguarding of human capital from temporary shocks (protection), and development of the human resource potential of the economy (promotion). As we note later in this chapter, the impact of fiscal policy on the pattern of distribu-tion also has implications for growth dynamics. Ultimately, growth and social inclusion determine social welfare.

This chapter is organized as follows. The first section presents an evaluative framework that establishes a link between fiscal policy and the ultimate objective of improving social welfare by promoting inclu-sive growth. In the medium to long run, the impact of fiscal policy works through the induced *pattern of growth* (see chapter 2) and through the nature of *social inclusion*, which includes distributional impacts and implications for social risk management. The next section discusses the potential impact of fiscal policy on long-run growth using endogenous growth theory as a conceptual framework. It also reviews tools to assess the growth impact of fiscal changes. The sections that follow review the basic methods for assessing the redistributive effects of fiscal policy, in particular the burden of taxation, the incidence of public expenditure, and the net incidence of the fiscal system; the need to implement countercyclical fiscal policy in times of crises; the provi-sion of social safety nets; and the trade-offs between the different objectives of public finance and how they can be bridged, relying on actual fiscal policy design evidence during crises, in particular the 2008–09 global crisis and its subsequent impact. The final section pres-ents concluding remarks.

This review reveals that allocation, distribution, and stabilization issues are all intertwined in analysis of the impact of fiscal policy on growth and social welfare. Because of the social objective and the heterogeneity of the interests involved, the best fiscal policy must be incentive compatible and time consistent.

Evaluative Framework for Fiscal Policy Making

Policy recommendations should be grounded in a framework that allows an evaluation of policy alternatives. Assessing the effects of fiscal policy requires (1) a metric for identifying desirable outcomes; (2) a way of attributing outcomes to explanatory factors, including policy; and (3) a criterion for ranking social outcomes. Based on the selected metric, the framework therefore comprises a positive component that explains outcomes (based on individual behavior and social interaction) and a normative one that ranks them socially (for example, pro-poorness).

As for identifying desirable outcomes, the policy objective provides the yardstick by which to assess its impact. The ultimate objective of public finance policy is to maintain and improve the living standards of the population. Income and consumption expenditure are commonly used as living standard indicators. In addition, indicators measuring access to social services and inequality coefficients capture human development dimensions and distributional issues, which affect inequality (income and nonincome) patterns.

The attribution of outcomes to policy in order to learn about the implications of fiscal policy for growth and social welfare requires a social policy model that clearly links fiscal policy instruments—mainly *public spending, taxation,* and *borrowing*—to outcomes that in turn include the pattern of *growth* and how it shapes *social welfare.*

Figure 1.1 suggests that the implementation of fiscal policy may affect growth, social inclusion, and income distribution, which ultimately shape the social welfare on which social impact analysis is based.

In turn, understanding the impact of fiscal policy on growth and social welfare requires a theory of individual behavior and social interaction. Such a theory must be consistent with the constraints imposed on agents' behavior by preferences, endowments, and social relations through the relevant institutional arrangements.[4]

Endogenous growth models assume that the impact of fiscal policy on growth is mediated by *factor accumulation* and *productivity* (quantity and quality of inputs), which are the fundamental drivers of growth. The

Figure 1.1   Framing the Impact of Fiscal Policy on Growth and Social Welfare

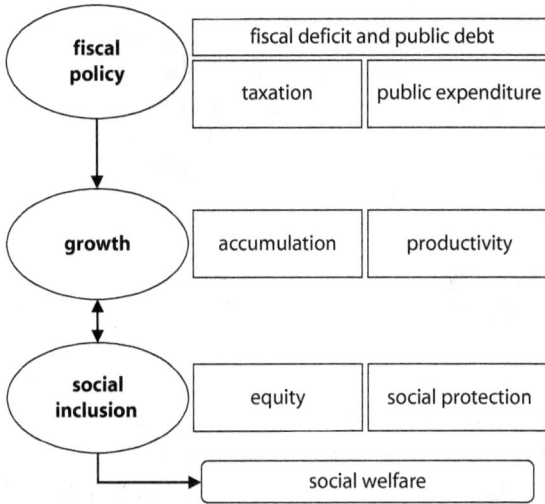

growth of output can therefore be broken down into two components: one attributable to the growth of inputs and a residual not related to change in input levels.[5] This residual is interpreted as the rate of growth of *total factor productivity* (TFP). This indicator reflects the way in which all inputs interact within the production process. It is important to keep in mind that the contributions of these two components to output growth depend on how inputs are measured. Thus, any unmeasured improvements in the quality of inputs will be attributed to TFP (Helpman 2004). Yet such improvements may be due to new technology, better organization of production, or changes in fiscal policy such as a reduction in distortions associated with taxes or bad regulations, more productive public spending, or better public institutions.[6]

In turn, fiscal policy promotes social welfare by protecting and enhancing the ability of individuals to take advantage of the opportunities created by the growth dynamics. In the broader context of socioeconomic development, growth has an instrumental rather than an intrinsic value, to the extent that it focuses only on income per capita[7]—a measure of the amount of means of well-being available to people, which says nothing about the way those means are distributed or about what the people involved can achieve with those means in view of their life plans (Sen 1988).[8]

Social progress accordingly must be defined and assessed in terms of what society cares about. This conclusion prompts us to consider a criterion for ranking social outcomes, which requires an evaluation function summarizing the value judgments once the observed outcomes have been causally linked to policy. Because the implementation of fiscal policy implies a distribution of burdens and advantages (income and nonincome), which modifies the initial distribution of economic welfare within society, social evaluation entails a comparison of the postpolicy distribution with the relevant counterfactual.

Growth creates opportunities, but what individuals are able to make of them depends critically on individual behavior and endowments, as well as the sociopolitical arrangements that govern social interaction. From this perspective, Ravallion (2001) argues that disparities in access to human and physical capital, and differences in returns to such assets, are the main determinants of income inequality. Furthermore, these disparities are most likely to inhibit overall growth prospects. This is a good reason for fiscal policy to be directed at helping those with low levels of endowments—that is, the poor.

The view that some elements of redistribution can be growth enhancing is consistent with the argument in the *World Development Report 2006* that missing or failing markets prevent resources from flowing where returns would be highest (World Bank 2005). This is a consequence of the three key assumptions underlying a similar conclusion reached by Aghion and Williamson (1998): (1) unequal distribution of capital endowments across individuals; (2) production technology characterized by decreasing returns to individual investments; and (3) credit market failures. The assumption about technology implies that the poorly endowed would experience higher marginal returns to investment than the nonpoor. Therefore, an incentive-compatible redistribution to the less endowed would be growth enhancing. Thus, if correcting these failures is not feasible, then improved efficiency can be achieved through some form of incentive-compatible redistribution of access to services, assets, or political influence.

Using a simple endogenous growth model that includes wealth heterogeneity or differences in human capital endowments across individuals and capital market imperfections, Aghion and Williamson (1998) develop the idea that redistribution can be good for growth, asserting that there is no fundamental trade-off between efficiency and equity. These authors explain that such a trade-off does not hold in the case of heterogeneous human capital endowments and credit market imperfections. If the poor are excluded from the credit market, it is harder for them to invest in education or in other forms of assets. Such a situation would perpetuate the wage differentials associated with skill distribution. In those circumstances, redistribution policies would be growth enhancing.[9]

Ravallion (2001) cites evidence from cross-country comparisons of growth rates showing that countries with higher initial income inequality tend to experience lower rates of growth, controlling for other factors such as openness to trade and inflation. This empirical evidence is consistent with the theoretical and political economy arguments and has led to the view that countries with a more equitable distribution are more likely to escape bouts of populist policies in which the government feels compelled to distort incentives or divert scarce public resources under the pretext of helping the poor and the disadvantaged.[10]

When one analyzes the ultimate impact of fiscal policy on social welfare, it becomes essential to find out how the poorest segments of society are being affected—in other words, whether any distributional change is "pro-poor."[11]

One must address two important issues in the formulation of a poverty-focused evaluation criterion (Duclos 2009). The first relates to whether the standard of evaluation should be relative or absolute. According to the relative approach, a policy that benefits the poor more than the nonpoor must be considered pro-poor. As for the absolute approach, a pro-poor policy increases the poor's absolute standard of living. Thus, a distributional change that causes poverty to fall is considered pro-poor in the absolute sense.[12]

The second issue that one must confront is whether more weight should be given to outcomes for the poorer of the poor.[13] Evaluation functions that give more weight to the poorer of the poor are consistent with the Pigou–Dalton transfer principle, which requires that a progressive transfer of resources leads to an improvement in social welfare, other things being equal. Progressivity is based on vertical equity, which demands that differences in people's circumstances be appropriately taken into consideration in both the formulation and the implementation of public policy.[14]

Finally, because any fiscal policy choice entails a distribution of burdens and advantages that creates winners and losers, two basic approaches to policy making can inform the specification of the social welfare evaluation functions used for fiscal policy making. On the one hand, the *normative* approach seeks to maximize social welfare subject to the economy's resource, technology, and institutional constraints.[15] Considerations of growth and equity are combined in an abbreviated social welfare function defined by the mean multiplied by a distribution adjustment factor.[16] The resulting social evaluation function is known as the equally distributed equivalent outcome.[17]

On the other hand, the *positive* approach views policy making as a political process driven by conflicts of interest, which involves strategic interactions among various socioeconomic agents, subject to potential conflict and cooperation. As Kanbur (1995) explains it, the outcome depends crucially on the threshold at which a gain or a loss becomes so significant that an individual or a group feels compelled to organize and fight. The *political feasibility*[18] of a policy recommendation therefore depends on the way gainers and losers form coalitions and use the political system to their advantage. These considerations also argue for a participatory approach to policy evaluation to ensure that the views of all stakeholders are accounted for by the social evaluation criterion.

Potential Impact of Fiscal Policy on Growth

The impact of public finance policy on long-term economic growth depends on the way its implementation affects growth dynamics. Endogenous growth theory provides an appealing framework for linking fiscal policy with growth outcomes. This appeal stems mainly from the assumption that technological progress is driven by profit-seeking individuals who can earn rent on the fruits of their labor in chasing newer and better ideas (Jones 1998).

As for public expenditure, endogenous growth theory suggests that certain categories of public expenditure, referred to in the literature as "productive" or "core," are expected to be more growth enhancing than others.[19] Consistent with the Musgrave framework, allocating public resources to those types of expenditures is conducive to growth because they contribute to increasing the accumulation of production factors, mainly capital and labor, or to increasing productivity—in other words, the way in which those inputs interact in the production process.

Although the composition of productive public spending must be determined at the individual country level, it usually includes education expenditure, which increases the level of human capital. Public expenditure on health, safety nets, infrastructure, and research and development (R&D) is also expected to have a positive impact on growth, especially when planned and implemented in an integrated manner because of the synergies between them.[20] In the particular case of health expenditure, it is widely believed that productive spending on health reduces sickness, morbidity, and mortality, thereby increasing the labor supply with beneficial effects for growth. Good health also improves the ability of workers to acquire new skills and better education, with an additional potential beneficial effect on growth. Finally, infrastructure public spending is expected to affect growth positively through traditional and nontraditional channels by means of its positive impact on both health and education (Agénor and Moreno-Dodson 2006).

On the revenue side of the general government constraint, taxation produces the resources needed to finance public spending, and it is generally considered to be a less distortionary alternative to other forms of financing such as inflation or debt (González-Páramo and Moreno-Dodson 2003), although its effect on growth depends on the composition of the tax system.[21] To the extent that taxation interferes with private decisions to save and invest, it is expected to have an impact on the input accumulation process, which is one important determinant of economic growth. A high effective tax rate on corporate and individual income or on capital gains along with low depreciation allowances could dampen the rate of private investment. Furthermore, taxation can affect the marginal productivity of capital by distorting the allocation of investment between the sectors of the economy that are heavily taxed and those that are lightly taxed or not taxed at all. Moreover, it can distort asset diversification and the choice of organizational form. One would also expect special tax preferences to be detrimental to efficiency because capital may be allocated to low-return projects.

The impact of a tax on labor depends on the effect of such a tax on labor force participation, occupational choice, labor supply, and the acquisition of education and training. Zagler and Dürnecker (2003) explain that taxation on earnings can have a negative impact on the quality of labor input. This impact stems from the fact that the acquisition of new knowledge and skills is driven by the expectation of higher future earnings. Optimality of schooling decisions implies that marginal benefits (in terms of higher future earnings) are equal to marginal costs. If tuition costs are kept constant, then a tax on labor income will induce individuals to cut back on their efforts to obtain schooling, thereby reducing the average quality of the workforce, with a detrimental effect on growth.

The net effect of public spending and taxation on growth ultimately depends on their levels and composition. Although a combination of productive spending and less distortionary taxes is expected to affect growth positively, this positive effect seems to predominate only up to a certain point—that is, up to a certain percentage of the gross domestic product (GDP)—at which the distortions associated with taxation overcome the positive effects associated with additional public spending.[22]

The joint impact of fiscal policy (spending and taxes) on growth is also determined by whether the path of fiscal policy is expected to be sustainable—that is, on whether the government remains solvent. Fiscal deficits are commonly expected to have a negative impact on growth because they can lead to higher interest rates and crowding out of private sector investments. In addition, they may lead to rising public debt, the accumulation of which is expected to affect growth in different ways, depending on how the private sector reacts to the reduction in public saving, as well as the possibility that the country receives external financing, which in turn reflects risk levels as perceived by foreign creditors.

It has been argued that if households consider an increase in deficit spending as postponed taxation, they will decide to save an amount equivalent to their future tax liability under *Ricardian equivalence* (Elmendorf and Mankiw 1999).[23] Under these circumstances, there will be no change in national saving and thus no change in national investment. If the rather stringent conditions for Ricardian equivalence do not hold, however, then one would expect an increase in budget deficits driven by rising public consumption to reduce national saving and investment. Over time, this situation will lead to a smaller capital stock and thus a reduction in national income. Gale and Orszag (2003) argue that bigger deficits imply lower future national income regardless of the interest rates, other things being equal.

A crude or naive focus on maintaining fiscal sustainability by reducing cash budget deficits in the short term can, however, sometimes have perverse effects on long-term fiscal sustainability if it fails to properly account for and protect productive public spending.[24]

Perry et al. (2008) discuss two basic approaches to dealing with anti-investment bias. One is to exclude selected investment spending from fiscal targets.[25] There is a risk, however, of having the investment program artificially biased toward the favored categories of investment.

The second approach is to use fiscal targets and rules designed to reduce the bias against investment spending. The *golden rule*, for example, forbids deficits on the current account but allows borrowing for the creation of capital assets. However, its limitation is the lack of certainty that the assets involved will yield a return commensurate with the interest on the debt incurred for their acquisition. Furthermore, even when the returns are high enough, the state may not be able to capture them. The golden rule also creates incentives for expenditure misclassification and creative accounting. Unproductive expenditures could be labeled "investment" to facilitate debt financing[26] (see chapter 2 for a more detailed discussion).

Referring to Brazil's Fiscal Crimes Law, Perry et al. (2008) argue that authorities are more likely to comply with fiscal responsibility rules when there are enforceable penalties and little room for cheating. Based on a review of the experience with such arrangements in Latin America, these authors suggest that simple rules, which adjust cyclically and cover the whole budget, work better than unadjusted ones or those that restrict only part of the budget, such as commodity stabilization funds. They also warn that an excessively rigid rule may limit the flexibility needed to adapt to changing circumstances and may not enhance credibility.[27] Ultimately, the effectiveness of these rules, like any other institutions, depends on the extent of the underlying political consensus. Grosh et al. (2008) note that the overall performance of fiscal rules has been mixed, indicating that they are neither necessary nor sufficient for overall fiscal discipline. Furthermore, they are unable to ensure that a single rubric of spending, such as safety nets, behave countercyclically.

The use of automatic and enforceable stabilizers can also help deal with the problems associated with procyclicality. Automatic stabilizers are essentially income taxes and transfer payments embedded in the fiscal system. The effectiveness of these automatic stabilizers depends on the size of government, the structure of taxation, and, of course, the underlying political system. These factors determine the responsiveness of the stabilizers to cyclical conditions.[28] To speed recovery from an economic crisis and improve the prospect for long-term economic growth, Arnold et al. (2011) argue that it is desirable to reduce the income tax (including social security contributions) for low-income families. Furthermore, increasing recurrent taxes on immovable property and consumption can help to increase revenues after recovery from a shock in a manner that is the least harmful to growth.

The arguments just presented help to assess the growth effects of fiscal policy qualitatively, but they provide little indication about the magnitude of the effects. In turn, the government budget constraint always implies that any fiscal change needs to be offset by another fiscal change. Frequently, the direct growth effects and the indirect growth effects induced by the offsetting change have opposing signs. The magnitude of the net effect of fiscal policy on growth must be measured using quantitative techniques.[29]

Assessing the Redistributive Effects of Fiscal Policy

As indicated earlier, the social dimension of fiscal policy includes the distribution function of government, the third function in the Musgravian framework, and concerns both policy making and the ultimate beneficiaries of fiscal policy.

Fiscal policy has both a direct and an indirect impact on the distribution of welfare. The indirect impact comes from the pattern of growth and human development induced by it. For example, even if health and education expenditures finance public health and education institutions, access to them may not be equal and the poor may be disadvantaged for different reasons.

The direct impact relates to the immediate distribution of burdens and advantages associated with fiscal policy implementation. Several tools and instruments can be used to assess the direct distributive effects of fiscal policy in practice.[30] These tools can help in a search for answers to the following key questions: Who really bears the burden of taxation? Who benefits from public expenditure and by how much? How desirable is the induced distribution of economic welfare? At this stage, we provide only a quick overview of the basic ideas used in searching for answers to these questions.[31]

Fiscal incidence analysis entails comparing the *original income* (without government activity) with the *final income* (including taxes, transfers, and benefits from spending). Final income is obtained from the original income by first allocating taxable cash transfers to obtain the distribution of *total income*. Then direct taxes are subtracted to obtain the distribution of *posttax income*. Based on this distribution, indirect taxes, nontaxable cash, and in-kind transfers are assigned to obtain the distribution of *net income*. The distribution of *final income* is obtained by allocating benefits from public spending by net income classes (Hemming and Hewitt 1991).

Incidence of Taxation

The effective distribution of the tax burden can be determined by identifying as accurately as possible the people who end up bearing the burden of the tax in question and the extent of their share of that burden.[32] *Tax shifting* reflects the fact that the imposition of a tax at a particular point in the chain of production and distribution may end up affecting the economic welfare of people at different points. The possibility of shifting the tax burden stems from the fact that socioeconomic agents can change their *behavior* in response to a tax, subject to the prevailing *institutional arrangements*.

As a rule of thumb, the extent to which a tax can be shifted and thus who ends up bearing the burden depends on the alternatives available to the parties in the taxed transaction. Thus, one is less likely to bear the tax burden when one has better alternatives to what is taxed (Slemrod and Bakija 1996). For taxes on labor income, leisure or unpaid work at home are the alternatives open to workers. For employers, the alternative to hiring workers is determined by an employer's ability to switch to more capital-intensive modes of production. Thus, a tax on labor income can be shifted to employers if workers have better alternatives than employers.

Because economic agents can change their behavior in response to taxation and thereby shift the tax burden to other actors, it is evident that the allocation of the tax burden to policy-relevant socioeconomic groups[33] depends critically on the assumptions made about this behavior and the interaction among economic agents. It is difficult in practice to obtain an accurate estimate of tax shifting. Most empirical studies rely on data on the sources and uses of income in each socioeconomic group to construct the distribution of the tax burden on the basis of some assumptions about incidence. The quality of the results thus depends on the extent to which such assumptions are reasonable and defensible (Slemrod and Bakija 1996).

Martinez-Vazquez (2008) describes a set of assumptions used in conventional tax incidence analysis. Because the role of incidence assumptions is to facilitate the allocation of the tax burden to different income groups, they rely heavily on the fact that income sources and expenditure patterns vary significantly among such groups. For example, one can expect income from capital to be concentrated in the highest tail of the income distribution. In certain countries, this component of income can also be found in a lower-income population segment because retired workers may be living off their past savings.

Shah and Whalley (1991) caution that a mechanical application of conventional tax incidence analysis to developing countries can lead to significantly erroneous results and thus to the wrong policy recommendations. Indeed, this standard analysis assumes an institutional setting that may not prevail in developing countries—a competitive market economy.

For a proper tax incidence analysis in developing countries, these authors urge that account be taken of the following special features, such as the informal sector, rural-urban migration, credit rationing, extent of unionization, tax evasion, and foreign and public ownership of firms. The presence of these factors requires special shifting assumptions, which may reverse the incidence pattern implied by conventional assumptions. For example, effective price controls may prevent producers from shifting sales and excise taxes to consumers, thereby rendering invalid the conventional assumption that such taxes are fully shifted forward to consumers. Rural-urban migration may lead to a partial shift of the income tax burden from urban to rural workers. This cautionary note from Shah and Whalley underscores the importance of modeling explicitly and accurately individual behavior and social interaction in improving estimation of the distribution of the tax burden.

Incidence of Public Expenditure

Estimation of the benefits derived from public expenditure is fraught with serious *valuation issues*. Public expenditure can take the form of cash transfers, subsidies, or the government's direct provision of goods and services. Measuring cash transfers to households or individuals is far easier than measuring the benefits accruing to individuals or households from publicly provided goods and services. The market system provides a convenient way of valuing private goods sold on the market. This convenience stems from the fact that the price of a good or service reflects the marginal benefit to the consumer. In general, this approach does not work in the case of public goods because their supply is either rationed or does not adjust to demand. Under these circumstances, whatever price is charged (for example, a user fee) cannot signal marginal benefit or the willingness to pay (Martinez-Vazquez 2008). The solution adopted in the context of benefit incidence analysis is to value benefits from an expenditure program on the basis of the *unit cost* of provision.

To obtain a distribution of the benefit from public spending, one combines information on the *cost* of provision with data on the *use* of the relevant public goods and services. Thus, the analysis can be applied only to assignable public expenditure—that is, expenditure for which beneficiaries can be identified. However, this approach poses a serious problem because most public goods are nonrival to the extent that every unit can be enjoyed by all people. In view of this fact, benefit incidence analysis is usually applied to a limited subset of public expenditure programs, mainly in education, health, and infrastructure.

Construction of the distribution of benefits associated with a particular public expenditure program involves three basic steps:

- Using data from public expenditure accounts and the operation of the program under study, estimate the unit cost or subsidy associated with the public service in question.
- From household survey data, estimate the rate of use[34] of the service by each household and impute the benefits on the basis of these estimates.
- Report the results by policy-relevant socioeconomic groups (for example, by quantiles of the distribution of some welfare indicator, or by region, gender, or ethnic group).

The interaction of demand and supply factors suggests that the way individuals react to an expenditure program is crucial in determining both the *welfare* and the *distributional outcome* of such a program. Ignoring behavioral responses to a spending program is bound to introduce some bias in the estimates of the distributional impact of the program in question. One can use simple tools to account for behavioral responses in the context of benefit incidence analysis. These tools rely on reduced-form relationships between interventions and outcomes. They do not attempt to bring out all behavioral interlinkages that may explain the outcome (van de Walle 2003).

Incidence of the Net Tax System

The ultimate question of interest in fiscal policy is the net incidence of fiscal policy or the combined incidence of taxes and public spending. After all, taxes are mostly justified on the basis of expenditures that must be paid for, if the role of government is accepted. Furthermore, Lambert (2001) notes that a welfare rationale for taxation can be found only by considering the way public spending affects people's economic well-being. Because of the importance of behavior in determining the welfare impact of policy, incidence analysis must account, to the extent feasible, for the interaction between tax and spending policies. Indeed, a progressive public spending program can dominate regressive taxation to make the overall net impact progressive. This dominance relation can also run the other way around. Martinez-Vazquez (2008) notes, for example, that a cost recovery scheme may be deemed regressive, and yet if the proceeds are used to finance better health services for the poor, the whole operation will be progressive. However, he adds that the fragmentation of the decision-making process for budgetary policy making implies that fiscal incidence analysis is relevant only for the entire government budget.

The Political Economy of Fiscal Volatility

The question of when it is appropriate to use countercyclical fiscal policies has, in the wake of the recent global crisis, become the subject of intense debate. Until recently, however, this debate would have been of limited relevance in developing countries, where, before the decade of the 2000s, most countries had tended to follow *procyclical* fiscal policies— that is, they applied fiscal stimulus during economic booms and fiscal contraction during downturns and recessions. Procyclical fiscal policy tends to reduce social welfare by exacerbating economic fluctuations, and it may have adverse effects on both growth and equity objectives—for example, by breeding fiscal instability and anti-investment bias, both of which have a negative impact on growth. There is now evidence that during the decade of the 2000s, a growing number of developing countries succeeded in shifting toward a more acyclical or countercyclical stance in fiscal policy, in the latter case building up fiscal reserves during the boom and undertaking fiscal stimulus during the 2008–09 crisis. Yet fiscal policy in many developing countries remains subject to procyclicality, and thus it continues to be important to understand the political economy and other potential factors that may be driving this phenomenon.[35]

How is procyclicality generated? Some possible explanations have been put forward. One is that macroeconomic crises tend to have a negative impact on government revenues, which, in the presence of the severe credit constraints that developing countries have traditionally faced in bad times, forces them to slash spending and severely constrains their ability to increase social outlays to meet the increased demands for assistance. This situation has led to procyclical financing of social protection, for example. However, Alesina and Tabellini (2005) doubt this view in light of the fact that these countries have an option to self-insure by accumulating reserves in good times in order to alleviate the credit constraint they will face in bad times.[36]

Tornell and Lane (1998) offer an alternative political economy explanation of procyclicality based on the notion of the *voracity effect* associated with the interaction of powerful interest groups in the absence of strong legal and political institutions. In this context, fiscal redistribution is the mechanism through which these interest groups struggle to capture national resources for themselves. The voracity effect is thus a loss of growth potential resulting from an uncooperative behavioral response to windfall gains in productivity (Strulik 2011).

The voracity effect is analogous to the *polarization* effect found by Woo (2005) in his study of fiscal policy making within societies characterized by ethnic fractionalization and a high degree of income inequality. Woo shows that the size of the fiscal deficit, the magnitude of the fiscal volatility, and the size of the reduction in output and growth rate increase with the degree of social polarization. This outcome stems from the fact that the heterogeneity of preferences—that is, whether there is sharp disagreement among socioeconomic groups about ideal government policies—may cause a failure of coordination in collective action that ultimately leads to fiscal instability and growth collapse. Furthermore, the sociopolitical instability associated with polarization may create political uncertainty and significantly shorten the horizon of politicians. The expectation of a shortened tenure in office creates incentives for policy makers to adopt policies that are rational from an individual perspective but inferior from a social point of view.[37]

In essence, both the voracity and polarization effects are a manifestation of the *common pool problem* (or tragedy of the commons) in which an overexploitation of a common resource stems from the fact that each claimant fails to internalize the full cost of his or her own appropriation (Woo 2005).

The Median Voter Theorem has also been invoked to explain distortionary policy outcomes on the basis of social polarization. In a highly unequal society, the median income is below average. Thus, the median voter would have a preference for redistribution. However, if such a policy is implemented, the economy would suffer a loss of efficiency through distortionary taxes and transfers. Such distortions may negatively affect individuals' investment decisions, stifle growth, and produce political instability.

Perry et al. (2008) attribute procyclicality to the *anti-investment bias* of fiscal policy. When faced with the necessity to cut public spending, many developing countries have found it easier to cut *investment expenditure* than *current expenditure*. Perry et al. note that in the 1980s and 1990s Latin America carried out fiscal adjustment at the expense of investment in infrastructure, despite the fact that such an approach tends to undermine the sustainability of economic growth and the productivity of tax collection efforts. These authors explain that the *anti-investment bias* of fiscal policy is intimately linked to its procyclical nature.[38]

In many countries with procyclical fiscal policies, fiscal expansion in booms is driven mainly by current expenditure, whereas the contraction in downturns is delivered mostly in the form of investment cuts. One of the political factors explaining this asymmetric response of public investment to booms and busts is the myopia of policy makers that leads them to favor policies with immediate benefits for their constituents.[39] For example, in good times policy makers would rather increase public sector employment than invest in long-lasting infrastructure whose impact on growth might occur under a future government. Similarly, in bad times the same policy makers would find cutting public sector employment or the wage bill costlier politically than cutting public investment.

Because of the political nature of fiscal volatility, one wonders whether fiscal discipline is attainable. The anti-investment bias and procyclicality of fiscal policy share the same root. We would therefore expect the same principles that underpin the solution to procyclicality to be of help in dealing with anti-investment bias. In particular, institutional reforms designed to correct the perverse political economy incentives facing policy makers can help protect productive investment in bad times and achieve some degree of countercyclicality. Frankel, Vegh, and Vuletin (2011) provide empirical evidence on the link between low institutional quality and procyclicality.

Social Safety Nets

As part of the protective and preventive roles of public finance in promoting social inclusion, specific interventions may be required to prevent and protect the most vulnerable[40] individuals or households from suffering irreversible losses from adverse shocks. The vulnerability of an individual or a household to livelihood stress depends crucially on both *exposure* and the *ability to cope* with and recover from the shock. Fiscal policy therefore should aim at enhancing the capacity of individuals to mitigate the effects of shocks and help the most vulnerable cope with them.

There are two main sources of vulnerability. An aggregate or *covariate shock* is one that emanates from the environment in which a household is situated. Such a shock could be a natural disaster, a climate-related shock, or a macroeconomic crisis affecting the entire economy (for example, a financial crisis, a debt crisis, a terms-of-trade shock, or a food or fuel crisis). A covariate shock affects all members of a community, as opposed to an *idiosyncratic shock*, which is household specific. Family death and illness are typical examples of idiosyncratic shocks.[41]

Broadly speaking, *safety nets* or *social assistance* programs are non-contributory transfer programs that target the poor and vulnerable (Grosh et al. 2008). They include cash and in-kind transfers (unconditional or not), price subsidies, public works schemes, and fee waivers for essential services, not all of which are equally effective in accomplishing their goals.[42]

Public works, programs can act as safety nets by helping poor communities maintain and construct infrastructure that supports livelihoods in the community. A cost-effective program of public works, should be able to provide employment for the poor and vulnerable who are looking for a job and are able to work, without interfering with the other fiscal policy instruments already in place.[43]

Safety nets are usually a component of a broader social protection policy that includes contributory social insurance programs (for example, pensions and unemployment insurance) and other labor market intervention.[44] In addition, a carefully targeted program of microcredit can assist recovery from a crisis by helping the poor and vulnerable avoid selling their productive assets under duress. The fungibility of credit implies that microfinance can also facilitate consumption smoothing over seasonal cycles (Pitt and Khandker 2002).

Both idiosyncratic and covariate shocks can irreversibly reduce the assets of the population, especially the more vulnerable. For example, health shocks and decline in local economic prosperity are two of the main reasons why people fall into poverty across the developing world (Dudwick, Hull, and Tas 2009). A household is bound to suffer a loss of income when the main breadwinner becomes sick or dies, or when income earners in the family stop working to become caregivers. Families may even have to sell off their assets in order to cover medical expenses.[45]

Most covariate shocks—macroeconomic crises, for example—affect more than one individual and family, challenging any existing social risk management mechanisms such as self-insurance, informal insurance, and market-based consumption smoothing mechanisms (for example, credit). This implies that the most vulnerable are unable to protect themselves from those shocks, which can irreversibly damage their assets, including human capital. Safety nets are specifically designed to help smooth consumption and stabilize asset bases.

Furthermore, safety nets have a social insurance function. They help households manage risk by preventing irreversible losses in assets that support their livelihoods and therefore contribute to social inclusion. In addition, they help remedy credit market failures (Grosh et al. 2008).

Resource transfers through a safety net program can improve nutritional and educational outcomes for households by making more and better food available and helping them afford schooling. There is also evidence that safety nets have helped households invest in physical capital.

An effective social protection strategy involves actions to lessen a household's vulnerability to falling into poverty and policies to support the movement out of poverty (Dudwick, Hull, and Tas 2009). The formulation of interventions to lessen vulnerability requires identifying the vulnerable, the sources of vulnerability, and feasible coping mechanisms.[46]

The success of fiscal policy in preventing the potential impact of a shock or crisis on the living standard of the population generally depends on the nature of the shock and household characteristics. Ultimately, the efficacy of a social safety net depends on the degree of asset protection it provides and the speed at which those who are affected by shocks return to the preshock standard of living (Alderman and Haque 2006). What are the desirable properties of social safety nets in view of the important role they can play in policy making?

Grosh et al. (2008) propose the following properties: relevance, adequacy, equity, cost-effectiveness, incentive compatibility, sustainability, and adaptability. *Relevance* requires that the safety net program respond to the particular needs of the population and be consistent with country circumstances. *Adequacy* refers to the ability of the program to provide full coverage and meaningful benefits to various socioeconomic groups in need, including the chronic poor, the transient poor, and those who are adversely affected by policy reforms.[47] *Equity* requires that the program provide equal benefits to people who face the same set of circumstances (horizontal equity) and more support to the poorest among the beneficiaries (vertical equity). To achieve *cost-effectiveness*, the program administration uses the minimum level of resources required to effectively deliver the desired outcomes. *Incentive compatibility* entails the use of mechanisms that prevent individuals from engaging in counterproductive behavior. This outcome is usually accomplished by conditioning resource transfers on some desirable behavior. *Sustainability* relates to the survival of the program over time, including both a financial and a political economy dimension. Finally, the system must be flexible enough to *adapt* to changing conditions in a growing economy.

Social safety nets must be able to expand as needs increase and contract in good times when the demand for social assistance goes down.

Such flexibility would contribute to making fiscal policy countercyclical. That idea does not apply to the planning and financing of preventive social safety nets, which should be articulated on the basis of anticipated potential needs. To adequately protect the poor and the vulnerable when their number is increasing and their needs are rising because of a macro-economic crisis, the social safety net must be prefunded. Thus, adequate budget allocations need to be made in times of strong economic growth.[48] In fact, a consensus has emerged about the need to build social protection mechanisms permanently into long-term development strategies, because it is very difficult to weave an effective safety net during a crisis, and a preexisting good safety net could even prevent a crisis (Ferreira, Prennushi, and Ravallion 1999).

The design and implementation of social safety nets in a decentralized system of government raise the issue of the distribution of responsibility between the central and local governments. The conventional wisdom is that the central government should finance[49] safety nets and define eligibility criteria because it is better placed to handle risk pooling and interregional inequality. It is indeed desirable to base social protection programs on the largest possible risk pool. Yet local governments have a comparative advantage over the central government in administering such programs because they are more knowledgeable about the client base. This knowledge can be used to improve the targeting of safety net programs. The division of responsibilities between central and local governments creates a *principal-agent* relationship between the central government and subnational jurisdictions.

Effective delivery of social protection and promotion thus requires a combination of incentive and oversight mechanisms capable of aligning the agents' actions and the principal's goals at a reasonable cost (Grosh et al. 2008). At the same time, economies of scale and the possibility of limited implementation capacity at local levels argue against administrative decentralization. In any case, these factors must be taken into consideration when deciding on a case-by-case basis the distribution of responsibilities among various levels of government.

Evidence from Fiscal Policy Responses to the Crisis

Since the 2008–09 global crisis, a number of developed and developing countries alike have implemented fiscal stimulus packages. Especially in developing countries, such discretionary fiscal stimulus policies were facilitated by the availability of fiscal space generated by a combination of a long period of strong growth before the crisis and relatively prudent fiscal policies during the boom (see chapter 2). This section reviews country experiences in accommodating growth and social inclusion goals in the design of their fiscal responses to the crisis. It also reflects on other measures taken in response to previous crises. The composition of those fiscal response packages, by type of fiscal measure, indicates to what extent governments have been trying to achieve simultaneously different fiscal policy objectives and how the trade-offs between them have been reconciled.

A few studies have focused on cross-country comparisons of fiscal policy responses following the 2008–09 global crisis. For example, Khatiwada (2009) examines the composition of postcrisis stimulus packages in 12 developing countries. He finds that tax cuts amounted only to 3 percent on average of the total fiscal packages, perhaps the result of concerns that tax cuts would undermine efforts to strengthen domestic revenue mobilization, which is central for fiscal stability, long-run growth, and state building. Because a large share of the poor either work in the informal economy or earn incomes that are below income tax thresholds, they do not benefit from such tax cuts.

Khatiwada (2009) also finds that for the same sample of countries the share of infrastructure spending in the total fiscal stimulus packages was 46.6 percent. In principle, this category is well suited to contribute to long-run growth and can also have significant poverty reduction effects if projects have a strong employment effect or are planned and executed in connection with education and health objectives in an integrated manner. However, as chapter 2 argues, in practice this balance between growth and social objectives has not been easy to achieve in many countries. On the one hand, because of implementation lags, employment opportunities do not always materialize on time. On the other hand, where infrastructure spending as part of stimulus packages is guided primarily by a desire to create employment, unproductive investments may be selected, with only weak benefits for growth.

Another finding by Khatiwada (2009) is that transfers to low-income households represented only 6.8 percent of fiscal stimulus programs, despite the fact that protecting the poor during crises is desirable in the short term and should not jeopardize long-run growth if that protection is adequately designed and targeted. For example, increased transfers may prevent social unrest, which hampers private investment and may help prevent reversing of previous gains in social inclusion. However, the nature of the link (if any) between transfers during an economic crisis and long-run growth and whether such programs are administered effectively to target the poor depend on country-specific circumstances and cannot be generalized.[50]

In another cross-country study, Zhang, Thelen, and Rao (2010), using data on planned stimulus measures from 35 developed and developing countries, shed more light on the extent to which stimulus packages have included social protection measures. They broadly define social protection as "policy interventions that are intended to reduce poverty and vulnerability (including transitory poverty and vulnerability due to economic or other shocks) and to improve human welfare." Their examples of "social protection measures" are diverse and include interventions in the fields of public education and health, housing, labor market policies, social services, and both contributory social insurance programs and noncontributory safety net (social assistance) programs. Based on this definition, they find that social protection measures represented on average 25 percent of the (planned) fiscal stimulus packages, and that 29 out of 35 countries spent more than 10 percent of their fiscal stimulus on social protection.

According to the findings of Zhang, Thelen, and Rao (2010), the amount of spending on social protection appears to be sizable, and the countries reviewed have made efforts to simultaneously protect vulnerable groups while stimulating the economy. However, from a growth perspective, these findings are difficult to interpret. The type of measures labeled as "social protection" suggests that the long-run growth impact is uncertain. However, to the extent that such measures help prevent greater inequality and marginalization, they also likely help make growth more socially sustainable (Stiglitz 2011).

The correlation between the growth performance in 2010 and the share of social protection expenditures in total spending as planned in 2009 is presented in figure 1.2, based on the data set of Zhang, Thelen, and Rao (2010). There appears to be no correlation, which suggests that, taken in isolation, a large share of social protection spending does not necessarily have to be detrimental to stabilize output over the short run. However, this type of evidence is obviously limited because it refers only to selected countries where data are available and omits a range of other potentially relevant factors.[51]

Although our review is not meant to be used as a substitute for a rigorous incidence analysis (see chapter 5) and although targeting the poor is certainly difficult in practice, judged solely by the composition of public spending across countries, some governments in developing countries

Figure 1.2   Correlation between the Growth Performance and Social Protection Expenditures, Selected Countries

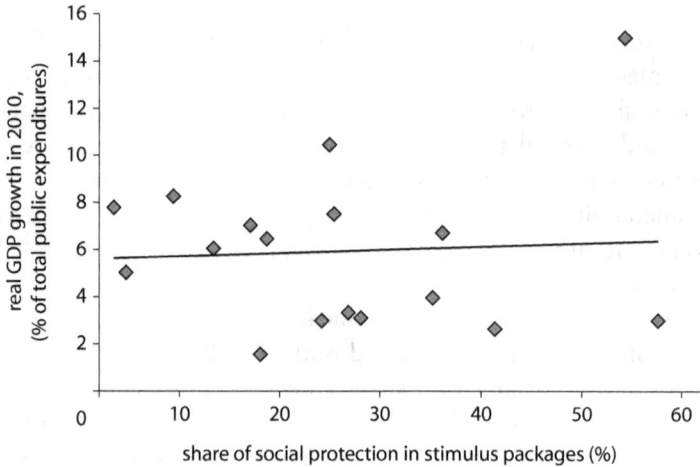

Source: Data from Zhang, Thelen, and Rao 2010.
Note: GDP = gross domestic product.

may have succeeded in accommodating social protection and output stabilization, at least to some extent. The long-run growth impact is much harder to assess. However, these governments have largely refrained from measures that may be detrimental for long-run growth such as dramatic tax cuts that erode previous efforts to mobilize domestic revenue and are hard to reverse. Nevertheless, the long-run growth impact of the stimulus measures is more uncertain than the impact on social protection and the poor and is harder to assess.

Clear-cut conclusions about how well governments appear to have accommodated output stabilization, social objectives, and long-run growth are often difficult. Nevertheless, the reviews of these country experiences still suggest that several governments made at least some efforts to achieve all three objectives simultaneously, even if some of the measures may not have been the most appropriate. For example, when one investigates the composition of stimulus packages and the patterns of fiscal policy in Brazil, China, and India, it can be seen that their policy responses have tried to balance the specific measures taken to help the most affected groups of people, basically the poor, with other policy actions taken to stabilize their economies and promote long-run growth.[52]

Many governments chose to take specific actions to help the groups most affected in times of crisis, mainly lower-income groups, as a countercyclical policy response. For example, Argentina engaged in higher social spending to allocate more resources to lower-income groups (see box 1.1).

Box 1.1

Social Spending in Argentina in Times of Crisis

One problem detected in policy responses during previous crisis periods in Argentina was the procyclicality of social spending items, especially ones targeting the poor. Evidence from the 1980s and 1990s suggests that the elasticity of social spending with respect to total government spending was 2.14, which implies that a 1 percent *decrease* in total government spending *lowers* social spending by 2.14 percent (World Bank 2009a). Thus, social spending in Argentina in 2009 was declining when it was most needed to support the poor.

By contrast, during the 2002 economic crisis Argentina was able to change the nature of procyclical social spending. According to the World Bank (2009a), although the total government budget contracted by 25 percent, spending on public health expanded by 70 percent in real terms. This policy change could also explain the improvements in child and maternal health outcomes after 2002, suggesting that there were positive longer-lasting effects as well. After the 2002 crisis, GDP grew 8.8 percent on average from 2003 to 2007, and unemployment dropped to 8.5 percent in 2007, from almost 20 percent in 2002. GDP growth for 2008 was 6.8 percent, but it declined to 0.5 percent in 2009 as the global crisis hit Argentina. Unemployment dropped from 8.5 percent in 2007 to 7.9 percent in 2008, increasing to 8.7 percent in 2009. With the strong economic rebound, unemployment fell to 7.7 percent in 2010. The size of the stimulus package was about 5 percent of GDP, and it covered both major structural policies (renationalization of the pension system and a large public works program), and temporary measures to provide relief to specific industries, to maintain higher employment, and to protect lower-income people (ILO 2010a).

With the help of employment retention and social protection policies, the government has tried to prevent layoffs, expand cash transfer programs aimed at improving people's skills and employability, and extend child benefits to vulnerable families.

Sources: World Bank 2009a; ILO 2010a.

Because many developing or emerging economies lack adequate social safety nets, their governments usually need to allocate more funds to social spending items in times of economic crises. For example, the Republic of Korea made serious efforts to increase social spending during the East Asian economic crisis of 1997 and after the 2008–09 global crisis to protect lower-income groups. On the revenue side, the Korean government has also been successful in helping low-income groups. Several studies indicate that the tax system has contributed to reducing income inequality. Box 1.2 summarizes the Korean case, focusing on social spending and tax policy both before and during the crisis.

Box 1.2

Social Spending and Tax Policy in the Republic of Korea

Prior to the recent global crisis, public expenditures on social safety nets—especially housing benefits, unemployment and active labor market programs, family services and benefits for the elderly and disabled people, and disability and sickness benefits—had been much lower than the Organisation for Economic Co-operation and Development (OECD) average (Feyzioglu 2006). But in recent years, the Korean government has tried to increase spending in those categories. The Expansion of the Basic Livelihood Guarantee System is increasing the number of people that receive such support, increasing the medical support to low-income children under 18, providing housing support for low-income families, and introducing an Emergency Welfare Support System (Ministry of Planning and Budget, Republic of Korea 2006).

Even though the share of social spending is still relatively low in Korea, it has increased during crisis periods to protect vulnerable groups. During the East Asian economic crisis of 1997, the unemployment rate in Korea jumped from 2.6 percent to 6.8 percent between 1997 and 1998. In response, the government introduced both employment generation and income maintenance programs that involved 2.6 percent of the Korean labor force (World Bank 2009a). Meanwhile, additional programs for job preservation and hiring subsidies were initiated, self-employment was promoted, more changes were made in job security legislation to help displaced workers, and public unemployment insurance coverage was extended to smaller firms.

However, when one looks at the total stimulus packages introduced between 2008 and 2010, the share of spending on social protection in the Korean stimulus

(continued next page)

Box 1.2 *(continued)*

package was less than in many developing countries. Zhang, Thelen, and Rao (2010) calculate that the share of expenditure on social protection in the stimulus package was 11.5 percent in Korea, with the stimulus package introduced between 2008 and 2010 itself representing 6.5 percent of GDP. The average share of expenditure on social protection in the stimulus packages of the countries included in the study by Zhang, Thelen, and Rao was 24 percent, for an average stimulus package size of 6 percent of GDP.

When one focuses on 2009 alone instead of the total package introduced between 2008 and 2010, the share of social spending appears much larger. During 2009, almost 25 percent of the stimulus package in Korea was allocated to support low-income households, which is high by both G-20 and Asian standards (Eskesen 2009; Khatiwada 2009). One expenditure item in the package expected to most affect the poor was the amount directed at farmers and fishermen, corresponding to almost 10 percent of the package (World Bank 2009b).

An ILO report (2010b) gives more detailed information on the social protection crisis response measures in the G-20 countries. Similar to other G-20 countries, Korea spent public funds on old age and disability, cash transfers for family and children, unemployment and employment policies, and health and education.

Fiscal policies have contributed to reducing income inequality in Korea. For example, Kang (2001) explains that the government's education policy in particular has played a key role in this area. The share of education expenditure in the budget has been increasing continually in Korea since the 1960s (Kang 2001).

Not only education policies but also income tax policy has contributed to improving income inequality in Korea. The Gini index after taxes was almost 6 percent lower than before taxes in 2000 (Hyun and Lim 2005). In an article that investigates the redistributive effects of Korea's fiscal policies, especially in the 2000s, Sung and Park (2011) conclude that taxes and transfers reduced income inequality in Korea by 14 percent. They show that in-kind benefits, direct taxes, and social security contributions all contributed to decreasing the Gini coefficient.

Sources: Kang 2001; Hyun and Lim 2005; Feyzioglu 2006; Ministry of Planning and Budget, Republic of Korea 2006; Eskesen 2009; Khatiwada 2009; World Bank 2009a, 2009b; ILO 2010b; Zhang, Thelen, and Rao 2010; Sung and Park 2011.

Other recent country examples imply that the size and adequacy of fiscal policy responses, including social spending, have been critically determined by the availability of fiscal space (lower budget deficit and lower public debt) and preexisting fiscal rules before the crisis hit. When such fiscal space is available, governments can engage in the required

amount of stimulus, and, if needed, they can expand fiscal policy packages more easily. Their exit strategies can be shaped less painfully as well.
Two country examples, Peru and Indonesia, are presented in box 1.3.
Thanks to fiscal rules introduced before the recent crisis, both countries
had a relatively low fiscal deficit, even surplus in some years, and their

---

Box 1.3

Policy Responses in Peru and Indonesia

Peru

One advantage of Peru in Peru's and Indonesia's responses to the global economic crisis was that the fiscal position of the country was relatively flexible,
thanks to a set of fiscal rules introduced since 1999 (Perny 2003; World Bank 2003).
Prudent fiscal policies before the crisis allowed the country to build fiscal buffers
and apply a timely countercyclical policy response. The share of central government debt in GDP dropped from 31.2 percent to 24.3 percent between 2006 and
2010. The central government budget deficit as a percentage of GDP declined to
3.5 percent in 2000 and then turned into a 3.5 percent surplus in 2007 (Carranza,
Daude, and Melguizo 2011). The immediate impact of the stimulus packages on
fiscal balance was a 2 percent budget deficit in 2009, from an almost 2 percent
surplus in 2008. But the government cut the deficit quickly to 0.3 percent in 2010
and is expected to achieve fiscal surpluses of 1.5 percent of GDP in 2011 and
1.0 percent of GDP in 2012.

The size of the stimulus package intended to mitigate the adverse impact on
the global economic crisis was 3.5 percent of GDP (Perez-Novoa 2011). The main
goals of that package were (1) accelerating expenditures on social programs,
including maintenance of educational and health facilities, as well as subsidies
for government housing programs; (2) supporting construction levels through a
higher public investment in infrastructure; and (3) helping individuals seeking
mortgages through expanded credit lines. The economic stimulus plan mainly
involved expenditure on infrastructure; tax cuts were very limited. The social protection components made up about 14 percent of the fiscal stimulus package in
Peru and included funding for health and education and social programs and
support for workers in affected sectors (Zhang, Thelen, and Rao 2010). In March
2011, it was announced that Peru's social spending had reached 41 billion soles
in 2010 and was distributed primarily in the education, culture, health, sanitation, social protection, and welfare sectors. The 2010 numbers correspond to a

(continued next page)

Box 1.3 *(continued)*

63 percent increase over those from five years ago (Living in Peru 2011). The share of targeted programs for extreme poverty in GDP increased significantly, from 1.4 percent in 2008 to 1.5 percent, 1.7 percent (expected), and 1.8 percent (expected) in 2009, 2010, and 2011, successively (IMF 2010a). At the same time, the share of gross fixed public investment jumped to 4.3 percent of GDP in 2008 from 3.3 percent in 2007, and increased further to 5.1 percent in 2009 and 5.85 percent in 2010, thanks to the stimulus package introduced in 2009 (Calderón and Servén 2010).

The growth rate was very strong in Peru before the 2008–09 crisis hit: 7.7 percent in 2006, 8.9 percent in 2007, and 9.8 percent in 2008. It dropped sharply to 0.9 percent in 2009 as the negative effects of the crisis were felt strongly. But Peru's real GDP grew by 8.8 percent in 2010. The unemployment rate was already high even before the global crisis (8.4 percent between 2006 and 2009) but dropped to 7.9 percent in 2010. Poverty rates in Peru have dropped to 36 percent, and they were expected to reach 33 percent during 2010, mostly because of ongoing fiscal efforts to reduce poverty (Guerra 2010).

In response to continuing instability in the global economy and as an effort to stop any slowdown in domestic activity, in 2011 the government introduced a second set of stimulus packages constituting about 1 percent of GDP to finance public sector investment in domestic infrastructure (Perez-Novoa 2011). In September 2011, Peru's government approved a stimulus plan of US$325 million, and in October 2011, the second part of a fiscal stimulus program totaling US$587 million.

Indonesia

In Indonesia, similar to other developing countries, the government's decision to undertake a discretionary fiscal stimulus was justified in part by the relative weakness of automatic stabilizers (Basri and Siregar 2009; Doraisami 2011). Thanks to a fiscal law introduced in Indonesia in 2003 that capped the budget deficit at 3 percent of GDP and public debt at 60 percent of GDP, the government was in a good position to expand spending within the available fiscal space (OECD 2008). The impact of the stimulus packages introduced in response to the global economic crisis was an increase in the fiscal deficit from 0.1 percent of GDP in 2008 to 2 percent in 2009, keeping the debt level at 30 percent of GDP (Abidin 2010). The growth rate in Indonesia was maintained at a sturdy 4.5 percent in 2009, unlike the negative growth experienced in numerous other economies.

(continued next page)

Box 1.3 *(continued)*

The stimulus package included both higher government spending and tax cuts. The main goals were to sustain purchasing power to continue household consumption, maintain business resilience, and create jobs (Ministry of Finance, Indonesia 2009). The combined stimulus package (about 2 percent of GDP) was 33 percent social assistance, 38 percent tax cuts, 22 percent capital mainte-nance and materials, and 7 percent infrastructure (ADB 2011). Social spending has been relatively low in Indonesia, but in the stimulus package there were several items targeting middle-income groups—for example, a 15 percent basic salary increase for civil servants, military personnel, police, and pension-ers, as well as a direct cash transfer payment to 18 million poor households for two months at the rate of Rp 100,000 per household per month (Budina and Tuladhar 2010).

Preliminary estimates indicate that, overall, the fiscal stimulus package con-tributed 1.6–1.8 percentage points to GDP growth in 2009 (ADB 2011). The unemployment rate declined slightly, from 8.1 percent in 2008 to 7.9 percent in 2009 and then to 7.4 percent in 2010. It is estimated that the government's infrastructure stimulus program created about 1.1 million wage jobs in 2009. Declining unemployment, stable prices (lower rice and fuel prices), and direct cash transfers helped to lower the poverty rate in 2009 to 14.15 percent from 15.42 percent in 2008 (Ministry of Finance, Indonesia 2009; Simorangkir and Adamanti 2010). It fell to 13.3 percent in 2010, 2 percentage points lower than in early 2008. Compared with other groups, the rural poor benefited from fiscal stimulus actions the most. Their consumption increased by 2.63 percent in 2009, whereas the consumption levels of the nonpoor increased by only 1 percent.

The fiscal stimulus measures had been designed to be temporary, and the government did prepare an exit strategy. A fiscal contraction of 0.95 percent of GDP was achieved in 2010; subsequent expansions were introduced in 2011 and 2012 in response to concerns about renewed weakening of the global economic environment with the aim of reaching the targeted growth rate of 6.7 percent in 2012 (Samboh 2011).

Sources: Perny 2003; World Bank 2003; OECD 2008; Ministry of Finance, Indonesia 2009; Basri and Siregar 2009; Abidin 2010; Budina and Tuladhar 2010; Calderón and Servén 2010; Guerra 2010; IMF 2010a; Simorangkir and Adamanti 2010; Zhang, Thelen, and Rao 2010; ADB 2011; Carranza, Daude, and Melguizo 2011; Doraisami 2011; Living in Peru 2011; Perez-Novoa 2011; Samboh 2011.

level of foreign debt was low. They were able to introduce timely stimulus packages and so improve the growth performance of their economies relatively quickly and reduce unemployment and poverty. In 2012, both governments are planning to introduce new stimulus measures as the global economic problems continue.

When countries have limited fiscal space, their room for policy response is more restricted. The Philippines has historically grappled with a problem of high public debt, although the general government debt-to-GDP ratio in 2007 on the eve of the crisis, at 46 percent (according to International Monetary Fund estimates), was well below levels earlier in the decade. However, it was still relatively high compared with the median of 33 percent for all middle-income countries. The country, nevertheless, introduced a stimulus package, which has been judged to have had a positive impact on growth, although not very successful in lowering either unemployment or poverty, both of which were already high before the crisis (see box 1.4 for details).

Box 1.4

Limited Fiscal Space and Stimulus Policies in the Philippines

Faced with a history of concerns about its high public debt, the Philippines had to balance the need for higher expenditure in the short term against the need to maintain fiscal sustainability in the longer run. A stronger revenue effort is required to finance the country's growing expenditure on social services while protecting fiscal sustainability. Recognizing the limited fiscal space available, government plans call for protecting the poorest and improving the medium-term prospects of the economy (World Bank 2009c, 2009d).

The Philippines has one of the highest poverty rates in the region, but its social safety nets are limited, as they were during the 1997 Asian crisis. Habib et al. (2010) and the World Bank (2010) find that the 2008–09 global crisis increased both the level and the depth of aggregate poverty. As a result, the poverty rate is calculated to be 1.45 points higher in 2009 than in 2008 and 2.07 points higher in 2010 than in 2009. In addition to high poverty, another major problem, despite some minor improvements, is high and persistent unemployment. The

(continued next page)

Box 1.4 *(continued)*

unemployment rate increased slightly to 7.5 percent in 2009 and then dropped modestly to 7.3 percent in 2010.

In light of concerns about rising poverty and unemployment, the government in the Philippines reacted to the global crisis of 2008–09 by introducing a stimulus package corresponding to 4 percent of GDP. Infrastructure items (48 percent of the package) included maintenance of government buildings and the hiring of teachers, police, soldiers, and doctors (Abidin 2010). Another important item was the program designed to provide some 800,000 temporary jobs in government departments (30 percent of the package). Twelve percent of the package represented a reduction in the corporate income tax and a waiver of the personal income tax for minimum wage earners, and 9 percent was used for expanding access to public health services and waiver of penalties on loans from social security. Before the crisis, the country had one of the lowest shares of public investment in percentage of GDP, 2 percent in 2008 (Paderanga 2001; IMF 2010b). In part thanks to the stimulus package, starting in 2008 this share increased to 3 percent of GDP and was expected to stay at this level until the end of 2011.

Despite the remaining concerns, the outcome of the stimulus package can be considered positive. Real GDP growth, which was 3.5 percent in 2008 and 7.8 percent in 2007, dropped sharply to 1.1 percent in 2009, but then jumped to 6.2 percent in 2010. It was expected to be 4.6 percent in 2011. It is estimated that the fiscal expansion added between 1.7 and 1.9 percentage points to GDP in 2009.

The fiscal deficit rose from 0.9 percent in 2008 to 2.3 percent in 2009. As a part of an exit strategy, in 2009 the government announced a medium-term fiscal consolidation plan, with a budget deficit at or below 2.0 percent of GDP by 2013.

Sources: Paderanga 2001; World Bank 2009c, 2009d; Abidin 2010; Habib et al. 2010; IMF 2010b; World Bank 2010.

Many countries are facing large budget deficits because of the stimulus packages introduced during the global economic crisis and the declining revenues stemming from slower growth and the remaining uncertainty about the global economy. The presence of automatic stabilizers is among the factors affecting how quickly governments are able to unwind deficits and restore fiscal balance. Box 1.5 considers the case of Thailand, which has one of the largest automatic stabilizers among emerging

Box 1.5

Fiscal Policies and the Help of Automatic Stabilizers in Thailand

When the global crisis hit, Thailand had a fiscal surplus (averaging 1.3 percent of GDP between 2005 and 2007) and a relatively low public debt-to–GDP ratio (42 percent in 2008). The availability of fiscal space allowed the government to introduce a large and timely stimulus package. The other advantage of Thailand was that the value of its automatic spending stabilizers was larger than in other countries in the region (Budina and Tuladhar 2010). The first stimulus package (1.2 percent of GDP) basically included measures with a direct impact on low-income groups, whereas the second package mainly targeted infrastructure spending (Abidin 2010). With additional spending on infrastructure, the share of public investment increased to 8 percent of GDP from 7 percent starting in 2009.

According to the World Bank data, the poverty rate in Thailand declined to 8.1 percent in 2010 from 9 percent in 2009. Despite a low growth rate in 2009, the drop in poverty can be explained by the success of the stimulus package, which introduced new social safety nets. The outcome of the stimulus package can also be considered successful in terms of much higher growth in 2010. The growth rate declined sharply in 2009 to −2.2 percent and then recovered to 7 percent in 2010. It was projected to be 4.5 percent in 2011. As a result of higher expenditure and lower taxes, the fiscal deficit jumped from 0.1 percent in 2008 to 3.2 percent in 2009, higher than its historical trend (Budina and Tuladhar 2010). Thanks to automatic spending stabilizers, the deficit is expected to decline gradually to 1.4 percent by 2014. In 2011, the government had already begun a gradual exit from fiscal policy support.

Sources: Abidin 2010; Budina and Tuladhar 2010.

market economies in the East Asia region. As in other countries, the government introduced a stimulus package, including social and invest-ment spending. It was able to lower poverty, but it faces a large fiscal deficit as a result of the fiscal expansion. However, this deficit is expected to abate with the help of relatively large automatic stabilizers.

Concluding Remarks

The ultimate role of public finance is to maintain and improve the living standard of the population. This entails raising resources from the private sector through taxation or borrowing and allocating them effectively and equitably in the form of public spending in a way that improves social welfare. This chapter presents a general framework that can guide fiscal policy making toward achieving those objectives.

The framework described here can be translated into a two-part policy model. The first part is positive in nature to the extent that it explains outcomes on the basis of individual behavior and social interaction. The second part is normative and is designed to assess social states in terms of what individuals and society care about. An important consideration is the ability of such a model to control for confounding factors, such as initial endowments, so that policy effects can be clearly identified.

The impact of fiscal policy on individual and social welfare works through the induced pattern of fiscal stability and growth, and the levels of social inclusion, including both equity and social protection. Growth creates opportunities, whereas social inclusion enhances the ability of individuals to take advantage of those opportunities.

Growth and social inclusion are intermediate objectives of fiscal policy. Both are affected by fiscal stability. Thus, in light of the Tinbergen principle, which says that a policy instrument must be assigned to each policy objective, it is clear that the simultaneous pursuit of growth and social progress requires that an effective social inclusion program be an integral part of fiscal policy because growth-enhancing fiscal instruments alone may not fully accomplish these two intertwined objectives.

The impact of fiscal policy on economic growth also depends on how the distribution of burdens and advantages (income and nonincome) associated with the implementation of fiscal policy affects the accumulation and productivity of factors of production. Although both neoclassical and endogenous growth models identify technological progress affecting productivity as the "engine of growth," the ability of the neoclassical model to predict the impact of fiscal policy on long-term growth is limited by the assumption that technological progress is exogenous.

Endogenous growth theory links the engine of growth to the socioeconomic environment characterized by the behavior of and interaction among agents. Because these agents are bound to react to the incentives and opportunities created by the redistributive effects of fiscal policy, the endogenous growth paradigm establishes clear channels of transmission on the impact of fiscal policy on social welfare.

An important message that emerges from this review is the fact that, beyond the impact of individual policy instruments, the overall quality of fiscal policy making matters greatly for policy outcomes, especially when exogenous shocks challenge its implementation. Procyclical fiscal policy may have adverse effects on both growth and equity objectives, and it tends to reduce social welfare by exacerbating economic fluctuations. Ill-judged efforts at fiscal adjustment may squeeze out productive public spending that is supportive of both growth and fiscal sustainability in the long term.

As part of the protective and preventive roles of public finance in promoting social inclusion, specific interventions such as safety nets are required to prevent and protect the most vulnerable individuals or house-holds from suffering irreversible losses from adverse shocks. For them to be fully effective, such interventions must be created in good times, must be consistent with fiscal stabilization goals, and must be flexible enough to adapt to evolving circumstances and external shocks.

Finally, fiscal policy implementation requires institutions capable of correcting the perverse political economy incentives facing policy makers. The basic idea is to reward compliance while making the cost of noncompliance unbearable. This is what fiscal targets and similar mechanisms attempt to do. In the end, whether fiscal policy leads to growth and improves social welfare depends crucially on its incentive properties and the supporting governance apparatus.

Notes

1. Official aid grants are an additional source of financing in low-income countries.

2. Stiglitz (1997), for example, argues that whenever there are imperfections of information or competition or when markets are incomplete, there is a potential for government actions to improve living standards, provided that government intervention does not lead to worse outcomes. Essentially, he views the role of government as establishing six types of *infrastructure* for the economy: educational, technological, financial, physical, environmental, and social.

3. In a market economy, each person's claim to available goods and services is limited to the amount of income obtainable from that person's successful sale of something of value on the market. Thus, distribution by the market system is based on quid pro quo (Lindblom 2001).

4. Given a causal model, identification strategy seeks fundamentally to isolate an independent variation in causal exposure (participation in a policy intervention) and link it to the outcome for the estimation of a causal effect (policy impact). This is exactly what is done in the case of endogenous growth models. Although the validity of any causal effects of fiscal policy on

growth hinges on the reliability of the theory used to justify the maintained assumptions, such effects are well established and in line with stylized facts.

5. Helpman (2004) explains that the contribution of an input to the growth of output is equal to the elasticity of the output level in relation to the input in question times the rate of growth of the input. Assuming perfect competition and constant returns to scale implies that the output elasticity with respect to an input is equal to that input share in total output.

6. Helpman (2004) cites evidence that total factor productivity is a major determinant of the observed variation in per capita income and patterns of economic growth across countries.

7. Economic growth is commonly measured by the rate of change of per capita real income.

8. This view was recently upheld by the Commission on Growth and Development in its 2008 report, which notes that growth is not an end in itself but creates opportunities for the achievement of other important objectives about which individuals and society care (Commission on Growth and Development 2008).

9. This conclusion hinges critically on the assumption of capital market imperfections. Without this assumption, the optimal level of individual investments is determined by the equality between the marginal product of capital and the opportunity cost of investing—that is, the interest rate (the same for lenders and borrowers). Those with wealth above the optimal level will lend and those with wealth below will borrow. Wealth distribution policies cannot have a positive impact on aggregate output and growth. Aghion and Williamson (1998) also show that redistribution enhances growth in the context of an imperfect credit market with moral hazard.

10. However, some other evidence casts doubt on the significance of the median voter hypothesis in this context (Helpman 2004).

11. The distribution of economic welfare is improved when the poorest become better off, thereby diminishing their differences in relation to the average and richer segments of society.

12. This is the definition of pro-poorness proposed by Ravallion and Chen (2003) and Kraay (2006).

13. Duclos (2009) explores ways of rendering pro-poor judgments robust in the choice of evaluation functions and the choice of poverty lines.

14. Thus, for example, the tax burden must be distributed according to an indicator of the ability to pay (usually some indicator of living standard). When income tax is progressive, taxpayers in the higher income brackets pay a higher proportion of their income in taxes. The principle of horizontal equity requires an equal treatment of equals. It can be shown that the violation of

horizontal equity dampens the redistributive effect of a progressive income tax (Lambert 2001).

15. In the classical version, the resulting optimal program is supposed to be implemented by a set of competitive and complete markets in view of the prevailing ownership of resources (Dixit 1996).

16. The latter is usually defined as 1 minus a measure of relative inequality (such as the Gini coefficient or the Atkinson index).

17. This is the bedrock concept in Atkinson's 1970 framework for social evaluation of inequality (Atkinson 1970). When income is used as an indicator of well-being, the equally distributed equivalent income is the level of per capita income that, if enjoyed by every individual, would yield the same level of social welfare as the current distribution for some choice of utility of income.

18. Thus Kanbur (1995) explains that desirability is determined by welfare economics, whereas feasibility stems from political economy.

19. The transmission channels of public spending on growth are reviewed in detail in chapter 2.

20. The composition of productive public spending that is conducive to growth, taking into account both level and intrasectoral composition, must be determined at the individual country level.

21. Zagler and Dürnecker (2003) explain that a debt-financed tax cut could enhance economic growth due to reduced distortions relative to taxes.

22. This well-known "Barro hypothesis" is also supported by economists such as Vito Tanzi, who affirms that beyond 30 percent of the GDP, additional public spending usually leads to inefficiencies (Tanzi 2011).

23. Bernheim (1987) provides the following list of assumptions on which Ricardian equivalence rests, either explicitly or implicitly: (1) each generation is concerned with the well-being of its heirs and therefore leaves bequests; (2) capital markets function perfectly; (3) the timing of taxes has no redistributive effects within generations; (4) taxes are nondistortionary; (5) deficits cannot create value; (6) consumers are rational and forward looking; and (7) the political process is not affected by the availability of deficit financing as a fiscal instrument.

24. In the past, fiscal policy in developing countries has often been highly procyclical, with fiscal adjustment efforts occurring during economic downturns, often led by sharp cuts in public infrastructure spending. As Easterly, Irwin, and Servén (2007) argue, fiscal adjustment through infrastructure cuts can be like walking up the down escalator: the short-run effect is to raise cash flows, but the indirect effect is to reduce the supply of productive services, growth, and thus future tax bases. Over time, this effect may undo much of the short-term fiscal adjustment, requiring yet more spending cuts.

These considerations are especially important in countries in which poor infrastructure is a major obstacle to growth.

25. This approach can be achieved through devices such as public-private partnerships based on service purchase agreements or revenue guarantees. Essentially, such arrangements let the government assume the investment risk of private sector projects. They are hidden liabilities to the extent that they are kept off budget.

26. Other rules have been suggested to deal with the limitation of the golden rule. They include the permanent balance rule, the net worth fiscal rule, and a modified golden rule. The permanent balance rule attempts to impose an intertemporal budget on the government by setting a constant tax to GDP ratio at a level that enables the government in the long run to link present and future expenditures. The net worth fiscal rule ties spending and financing decisions to a desired net worth trajectory. The design of both the permanent balance and the net worth rules entails demanding informational requirements that limit their applicability. This limitation has led to a modification of the golden rule that allows debt financing of assets that can "pay for themselves" either through user fees or through tax revenues (see Perry et al. 2008 for a more detailed discussion of these issues).

27. The design of rules incorporates a trade-off between flexibility and credibility. A rule may be so rigid that it becomes untenable. Such a rule will lose credibility once agents perceive it as unsustainable (Perry et al. 2008).

28. Perry et al. (2008), in discussing the case of Latin America, note that the size of government in the region is relatively small compared with that in the more industrialized countries. Furthermore, income taxes represent a larger share of tax revenues in higher-income countries than in Latin America. These authors also cite empirical evidence showing that automatic stabilizers built into tax codes in the region have failed to deliver a significant smoothing effect. These countries could therefore consider improving the size and effectiveness of automatic stabilizers by increasing the share of income taxes and adopting countercyclical transfer schemes.

29. Chapter 2 describes several tools for policy makers who wish to estimate the growth effects ex ante. The most obvious option is to base policy decisions on ex post estimates of the growth effects of fiscal policy. Chapter 2 also develops criteria to assess the usefulness of existing estimates and summarizes them in detailed tables as a tool for policy makers. It also suggests other sources of information that policy makers may use.

30. These tools are presented in more detail in chapter 5.

31. We focus mainly on the issues related to the estimation of distributional change. Our summary account relies heavily on Essama-Nssah (2008)

32. See chapter 4 for a more complete analysis.

33. One conventional type of socioeconomic group used in incidence analysis is that obtained by arranging the population in increasing order according to some welfare indicator (for example, income or consumption expenditure) and allocating individuals to income deciles or quintiles.

34. In the case of education and health, this information relates to enrollment rates or clinic visits reported by members of a household.

35. See the introduction to this volume for further comments on the recent debate on fiscal policy and the evidence on more developing countries recently moving toward a countercyclical fiscal policy stance. Manasse (2006) argues that procyclical fiscal policy increases macroeconomic volatility, depresses investment in both real and human capital, and thus limits the prospects for long-term growth. See also Alesina and Tabellini (2005) and Ilzetzki and Vegh (2008).

36. These authors suggest a deeper explanation of procyclicality based on a *political agency model* of a democracy in which the government is able to appropriate part of the budget surplus in the form of unproductive public consumption.

37. Ayuso-i-Casals et al. (2009) explain that the uncertainty of reelection pushes a government to neglect the long-term implications of budgetary imbalances and to use fiscal policy to enhance the likelihood of its reelection. This is made possible because voters suffer from "fiscal illusion" in the sense that they seem to care more about the short-term benefits of lower taxes and increased spending than the long-term cost induced by such policies. This fiscal illusion makes it possible for governments to get away with policies that lead to high, unsustainable deficits.

38. In this context, an anti-investment bias should be broadly interpreted to include the tendency to cut resources for the maintenance of productive public capital. Maintenance spending is critical to extending the useful life of capital (Perry et al. 2008).

39. See chapter 2 for more details.

40. The term *vulnerable* comes from the Latin word *vulnerabilis* used by the Romans to designate the state of a wounded soldier on the battlefield and to convey the sense that the current injury puts him at risk of further attack. In the context of natural hazards, Kelly and Adger (2000) explain, by analogy, that the vulnerability of an individual or group to a given hazard is essentially determined by their current capacity to deal with that hazard rather than by some future conditions. This analogy extends to other socioeconomic shocks.

41. Considering the experience of Latin America and the Caribbean in the 1980s and the 1990s, Lustig (2000) identifies macroeconomic crises as the single most important cause of large increases in poverty besides wars. Indeed, crises in that region also tend to be associated with increases in inequality.

42. When such programs focus on public infrastructure based on projects proposed by local communities and selected by a central agency, their results are expected to be better (Ferreira, Prennushi, and Ravallion 1999). Argentina's Trabajar Program and India's Employment Guarantee Scheme in the state of Maharashtra are commonly cited as examples of well-designed public works programs.

43. Countercyclical programming is easily achieved when communities have on standby a set of feasible public works investments so that feasibility studies do not have to be undertaken in a crisis mode (Alderman and Haque 2006).

44. The overall social policy includes programs in social protection, health, and education, and sometimes elements of housing and utility policy (Grosh et al. 2008).

45. Lustig (2000) cites evidence that macroeconomic downturns in the Latin America region had an adverse impact on human capital accumulation because of their effects on investment in education, health, and nutrition. Such effects could lock poor people into poverty traps for generations.

46. In this context, vulnerability may be considered as the likelihood that, at a given point in time, individual welfare will fall short of some socially acceptable benchmark (Hoddinott and Quisumbing 2008).

47. In this context, Alderman and Haque (2006) note the informational challenges implied by the distinction between permanent and transient poverty. Transfer programs to deal with the former must target individuals or households on the basis of wealth or earning potential. Transient poverty requires programs that serve an insurance purpose. Targeting in this case is based on income loss. These considerations lead to a distinction between static and dynamic targeting.

48. Gurenko and Lester (2004) point to countries such as India, Mexico, and the Philippines that hold reserve funds for relief programs.

49. The following mechanisms may be used to transfer resources to local governments: capitation grants, block grants, matching grants, or specific grants. Obviously, any of these has both advantages and disadvantages. See Grosh et al. (2008) for details.

50. The remaining share of the stimulus packages in the data by Khatiwada (2009) is difficult to evaluate because it includes mostly "other spending."

51. In addition, budgetary plans may have been revised and not fully executed as indicated in the data.

52. In Brazil, the total size of the stimulus package represented 0.3 percent of GDP in 2009 and 0.2 percent in 2010. The measures targeting low-income groups were extension of Bolsa família (a conditional cash transfer program) to include 5 million more citizens, an increase in the minimum wage by 12 percent, and tax cuts on consumer loans and personal income (Khatiwada

2009; World Bank 2009b). China introduced one of the largest fiscal packages in the world (almost 13 percent of GDP), and almost 25 percent of the package was spent on social protection (Zhang, Thelen, and Rao 2010). Over 2009 and 2010, India planned to spend 1.4 percent of GDP. In this package, 0.4 percent of GDP was allocated to low-income housing, irrigation, rural employment, and social assistance, corresponding to 0.4 percent of GDP (World Bank 2009b).

References

Abidin, Mahani Zainal. 2010. "Fiscal Policy Coordination in Asia: East Asian Infrastructure Investment Fund." Working Paper Series No. 232, Asian Development Bank Institute, Tokyo.

ADB (Asian Development Bank). 2011. "Completion Report—Indonesia: Countercyclical Support." Program number 43317, loan number 2563, ADB, Manila, August.

Agénor, Pierre-Richard, and Blanca Moreno-Dodson. 2006. "Public Infrastructure and Growth: New Channels and Policy Implications." Policy Research Working Paper 4064, World Bank, Washington, DC.

Aghion, Phillippe, and Jeffrey G. Williamson. 1998. *Growth, Inequality and Globalization: Theory, History and Policy.* Cambridge, U.K.: Cambridge University Press.

Alderman, Harold, and Trina Haque. 2006. "Countercyclical Safety Nets for the Poor and Vulnerable." *Food Policy* 31: 372–83.

Alesina, Alberto, and Guido Tabellini. 2005. "Why Is Fiscal Policy Often Procyclical?" Working Paper 11600, National Bureau of Economic Research, Cambridge, MA.

Arnold, Jens Matthias, Bert Brys, Christopher Heady, Asa Johansson, Cyrille Schwellnus, and Laura Vartia. 2011. "Tax Policy for Economic Recovery and Growth." *Economic Journal* 121: F59–80.

Atkinson, Anthony B. 1970. "On the Measurement of Inequality." *Journal of Economic Theory* 2: 244–63.

Ayuso-i-Casals, Joaquim, Servaas Deroose, Elena Flores, and Laurent Moulin. 2009. "Introduction: The Role of Fiscal Rules and Institutions in Shaping Budgetary Outcomes." In *Policy Instruments for Sound Fiscal Policies: Fiscal Rules and Institutions,* ed. Joaquim Ayuso-i-Casals, Srevaas Deroose, Elena Flores, and Laurent Moulin. New York: Palgrave Macmillan.

Basri, Muhammad Chatib, and Reza Yamora Siregar. 2009. "Navigating Policy Responses at the National Level in the Midst of the Global Financial Crisis: The Experience of Indonesia." *Asian Economic Papers* 8 (3): 1–35.

Bernheim, B. Douglas. 1987. "Ricardian Equivalence: An Evaluation of Theory and Evidence." *NBER Macroeconomics Annual* 2: 263–316.

Budina, Nina, and Anita Tuladhar. 2010. "Post-Crisis Fiscal Policy Priorities for the ASEAN-5." Working Paper WP/10/252, International Monetary Fund, Washington, DC.

Calderón, C., and L. Servén. 2010. "Infrastructure in Latin America." Policy Research Working Paper 5317, World Bank, Washington, DC.

Carranza, Luis, Christian Daude, and Angel Melguizo. 2011. "Public Infrastructure Investment and Fiscal Sustainability in Latin America: Incompatible Goals?" Working Paper 301, OECD Development Centre, Paris.

Commission on Growth and Development. 2008. *The Growth Report: Strategies for Sustained Growth and Inclusive Development.* Washington, DC: World Bank.

Dixit, Avinash K. 1996. *The Making of Economic Policy: A Transaction-Cost Politics Perspective.* Cambridge, MA: MIT Press.

Doraisami, Anita. 2011. "The Global Financial Crisis: Countercyclical Fiscal Policy Issues and Challenges in Malaysia, Indonesia, the Philippines, and Singapore." Working Paper Series 288, Asian Development Bank Institute, Tokyo.

Duclos, Jean-Yves. 2009. "What Is "Pro-Poor?" *Social Choice and Welfare* 32: 37–58.

Dudwick, Nora, Katy Hull, and Emcet Tas. 2009. "A Note on Vulnerability: Findings from Moving Out of Poverty." PREM Notes 132, World Bank, Washington, DC.

Easterly, William, Timothy Irwin, and Luis Servén. 2007. "Walking Up the Down Escalator: Public Investment and Fiscal Stability." Policy Research Working Paper 4158, World Bank, Washington, DC.

Elmendorf, Douglas W., and N. Gregory Mankiw. 1999. "Government Debt." In *Handbook of Macroeconomics*, vol. 1, ed. J. B. Taylor and M. Woodford, 1615–69. Amsterdam: Elsevier Science and North-Holland.

Eskesen, Leif Lybecker. 2009. "Countering the Cycle—The Effectiveness of Fiscal Policy in Korea." Working Paper WP/09/249, International Monetary Fund, Washington, DC.

Essama-Nssah, B. 2008. "Assessing the Redistributive Effect of Fiscal Policy." Policy Research Working Paper 4592, World Bank, Washington, DC.

Ferreira, Francisco H. G., Giovanna Prennushi, and Martin Ravallion. 1999. "Protecting the Poor from Macroeconomic Shocks." Policy Research Working Paper 2160, World Bank, Washington, DC.

Feyzioglu, Tarhan. 2006. "Long-term Fiscal Challenges." In *Republic of Korea: Selected Issues.* IMF Staff Country Report No. 06/381. Washington, DC: International Monetary Fund.

Frankel, Jeffrey A., Carlos A. Vegh, and Guillermo Vuletin. 2011. "On Graduation from Procyclicality." Working Paper 17619, National Bureau of Economic Research, Cambridge, MA.

Gale, William G., and Peter R. Orszag. 2003. "Fiscal Policy and Economic Growth: A Simple Framework." *Tax Notes*, February 3, 759–63.

González-Páramo, and Blanca Moreno-Dodson. 2003. "The Role of the State and Consequences of Alternative Forms of Public Expenditure Financing." WBI Working Paper 37225, World Bank, Washington, DC.

Grosh, Margaret, Carlo del Ninno, Emil Tesliuc, and Ouerghi Azedine, with the assistance of Annamaria Milazzo and Christine Weigand. 2008. *For Protection and Promotion: The Design and Implementation of Effective Safety Nets.* Washington, DC: World Bank.

Guerra, Isabel. 2010. "Poverty Rates in Peru Drop to 33 Percent, Finance Minister Says." LivinginPeru.com, February 23.

Gurenko, Eugene, and Rodney Lester. 2004. "Rapid Onset Natural Disasters: The Role of Financing in Effective Risk Management." Policy Research Working Paper 3278, World Bank, Washington, DC.

Habib, Bilal, Ambar Narayan, Sergio Olivieri, and Carolina Sánchez-Páramo. 2010. "Assessing Poverty and Distributional Impacts of the Global Crisis in the Philippines: A Microsimulation Approach." Policy Research Working Paper 5286, World Bank, Washington, DC.

Helpman, Elhanan. 2004. *The Mystery of Economic Growth.* Cambridge, MA: Harvard University Press.

Hemming, Richard, and Daniel P. Hewitt. 1991. "The Distributional Impact of Public Expenditure." In *Public Expenditure Handbook: A Guide to Public Policy Issues in Developing Countries*, ed. Ke-Young Cho and Richard Hemming. Washington, DC: International Monetary Fund.

Hoddinott, John, and Agnes R. Quisumbing. 2008. *Methods for Micro-econometric Risk and Vulnerability Assessments.* Washington, DC: International Food Policy Research Institute.

Hyun, Jin Kwon, and Byung-In Lim. 2005. "The Financial Crisis and Income Distribution in Korea: The Role of Income Tax Policy." *Journal of the Korean Economy* 6 (1): 51–65.

ILO (International Labour Organization). 2010a. "Argentina's Response to the Crisis." G20 Country Briefs, G20 Meeting of Labor and Employment Ministers, Washington, DC, April 20–21.

———. 2010b. "Employment and Social Protection Policies from Crisis to Recovery and Beyond: A Review of Experience." Geneva, ILO April.

Ilzetzki, Ethan, and Carlos A. Vegh. 2008. "Procyclical Fiscal Policy in Developing Countries: Truth or Fiction?" Working Paper 14191, National Bureau of Economic Research, Cambridge, MA.

IMF (International Monetary Fund). 2010a. "Peru: Staff Report for the 2010 Article IV Consultation." IMF Country Report No. 10/98 IMF, Washington, DC.

———. 2010b. *World Economic Outlook*. Washington, DC: IMF. (April).

Jones, Charles I. 1998. *Introduction to Economic Growth*. New York: Norton.

Kanbur, Ravi. 1995. "Welfare Economics, Political Economy and Policy Reform in Ghana." *African Development Review* 7 (1): 35–49.

Kang, Seoghoon. 2001. "Globalization and Income Inequality in Korea: An Overview." Paper prepared for FDI, Human Capital and Education in Developing Countries Technical Meeting, Paris, December 13–14.

Kelly, P. Mick, and W. Neil Adger. 2000. "Theory and Practice in Assessing Vulnerability to Climate Change and Facilitating Adaptation." *Climatic Change* 47: 325–52.

Khatiwada, Sameer. 2009. "Stimulus Packages to Counter Global Economic Crisis: A Review." Discussion Paper DP/196/2009, International Institute for Labour Studies, Geneva.

Kraay, Aart. 2006. "When Is Growth Pro-Poor? Evidence from a Panel of Countries." *Journal of Development Economics* 80: 198–227.

Lambert, Peter J. 2001. *The Distribution and Redistribution of Income*. Manchester, U.K.: Manchester University Press.

Lindblom, C. E. 2001. *The Market System: What Is It, How It Works and What to Make of It*. New Haven, CT: Yale University Press.

Living in Peru. 2011. "Peru's Social Spending, Average Incomes on the Rise." LivinginPeru.com, March 7.

Lustig, Nora. 2000. "Crisis and the Poor: Socially Responsible Macroeconomics." *Economia* 1 (1): 1–19.

Manasse, Paolo. 2006. "Procyclical Fiscal Policy: Shocks, Rules, and Institutions—A View from MARS." Working Paper 06/27, International Monetary Fund, Washington, DC.

Martinez-Vazquez, Jorge. 2008. "The Impact of Budgets on the Poor: Tax and Expenditure Benefit Incidence Analysis." In *Public Finance for Poverty Reduction: Concepts and Case Studies from Africa and Latin America*, ed. Blanca Moreno-Dodson and Quentin Wodon. Washington, DC: World Bank.

Ministry of Finance, Indonesia. 2009. *The 2009 Revised Budget Fiscal Stimulus Programme: Mitigating the Impact from the Global Crisis*. Jakarta, Indonesia: Ministry of Finance. http://www.bi.go.id/NR/rdonlyres/AE350D5E-BCB8-4AA4-BE29-9FB44C66B04B/15743/APBNPenyesuaian_2009_ENGLISH1.pdf.

Ministry of Planning and Budget, Republic of Korea. 2006. *Budget Overview, Fiscal Year 2006*. Seoul, Republic of Korea: Ministry of Planning and Budget.

Musgrave, Richard Abel. 1959. *The Theory of Public Finance.* New York: McGraw-Hill.

OECD (Organisation for Economic Co-operation and Development). 2008. *Economic Surveys: Indonesia Economic Assessment,* vol. 2008, July 17. Paris: OECD.

Paderanga, C. 2001. "Recent Fiscal Developments in the Philippines." Discussion Paper 2001-10, University of the Philippines School of Economics, Quezon City.

Perez-Novoa, Cesar. 2011. "Peru Begins to Shield from Global Crisis." *Investment Strategy,* October 21.

Perny, Guillermo. 2003. "Can Fiscal Rules Help Reduce Macroeconomic Volatility in the Latin America and Caribbean Region?" Policy Research Working Paper 3080, World Bank, Washington, DC.

Perry, Guillermo E., Luis Servén, Rodrigo Suescún, and Timothy Irwin. 2008. "Overview: Fiscal Policy, Economic Fluctuations, and Growth." In *Fiscal Policy, Stabilization and Growth: Prudence or Abstinence?* ed. Guillermo E. Perry, Luis Servén, and Rodrigo Suescún. Washington, DC: World Bank.

Pitt, Mark, and Shahidur Khandker. 2002. "Credit Programmes for the Poor and Seasonality in Bangladesh." *Journal of Development Studies* 39 (2): 1–24.

Ravallion, Martin. 2001. "Growth, Inequality and Poverty: Looking Beyond Averages." *World Development* 29 (11): 1803–15.

Ravallion, Martin, and Shaohua Chen. 2003. "Measuring Pro-Poor Growth." *Economics Letters* 78: 93–99.

Samboh, Esther. 2011. "Government Plans Fiscal Stimulus amid Uncertainties in Global Economy." *Jakarta Post,* September 16.

Sen, Amartya. 1988. "The Concept of Development." In *Handbook of Development Economics,* ed. Hollis Chenery and T. N. Srinivasan, vol. 1, 10–26. Amsterdam: North-Holland.

Shah, Anwar, and John Whalley. 1991. "Tax Incidence Analysis of Developing Countries: An Alternative View." *World Bank Economic Review* 5 (3): 535–52.

Simorangkir, Iskandar, and Justina Adamanti. 2010. "The Role of Fiscal Stimuli and Monetary Easing in Indonesian Economy during Global Financial Crisis: Financial Computable General Equilibrium Approach." *EcoMod2010* (Istanbul), July 7–10.

Slemrod, Joel, and Jon Bakija. 1996. *Taxing Ourselves: A Citizen's Guide to the Great Debate over Tax Reform.* Cambridge, MA: MIT Press.

Stiglitz, Joseph E. 1997. "The Role of Government in Economic Development." In *Annual World Bank Conference on Development 1996,* ed. Michael Bruno and Boris Pleskovic. Washington, DC: World Bank.

———. 2011. "Of the 1% by the 1%, for the 1%." *Vanity Fair,* May.

Strulik, Holger. 2011. "Poverty, Voracity and Growth." Discussion Paper 473, Leibniz University, Hannover, Germany.

Sung, Myung Jae, and Ki-Baeg Park. 2011. "Effects of Taxes and Benefits on Income Distribution in Korea." *Review of Income and Wealth* 57 (2): 345–63.

Tanzi, Vito. 2011. *Governments versus Markets: The Changing Economic Role of the State.* Cambridge, U.K.: Cambridge University Press.

Tornell, Aaron, and Philip R. Lane. 1998. "Voracity and Growth." Working Paper 6498, National Bureau of Economic Research, Cambridge, MA.

UN (United Nations). 2000. "United Nations Millennium Declaration." General Assembly Resolution 2, Session 55, New York, September.

van de Walle, Dominique. 2003. "Behavioral Incidence Analysis of Public Spending and Social Programs." In *The Impact of Economic Policies on Poverty and Income Distribution: Evaluation Techniques and Tools,* ed. François Bourguignon and Luiz A. Pereira da Silva. New York: World Bank and Oxford University Press.

Woo, Jaejoon. 2005. "Social Polarization, Fiscal Instability and Growth." *European Economic Review* 49: 1451–77.

World Bank. 2003. *Restoring Fiscal Discipline for Poverty Reduction in Peru: A Public Expenditure Review.* Washington, DC: World Bank.

———. 2005. *World Development Report 2006: Equity and Development.* Oxford, U.K.: Oxford University Press.

———. 2009a. *Averting a Human Crisis during the Global Downturn.* Conference edition (April). Washington, DC: World Bank.

———. 2009b. "Developing Countries and the Financial Crisis: Vulnerabilities and Fiscal Policy Options." Background paper prepared by World Bank staff for the IMF/OECD/World Bank Seminar on the Response to the Crisis and Exit Strategies, Washington, DC, February.

———. 2009c. *Philippines Development Report, 2009, Battling the Global Recession.* Washington, DC: World Bank.

———. 2009d. *Philippines Quarterly Update.* April. Manila, Philippines: World Bank.

———. 2010. *Philippines Quarterly Update: Stepping Up Reforms to Sustain Growth,* September. Manila, Philippines: World Bank

Zagler, Martin, and Georg Dürnecker. 2003. "Fiscal Policy and Economic Growth." *Journal of Economic Surveys* 17 (3): 397–418.

Zhang, Yanchun, Nina Thelen, and Aparna Rao. 2010. "Social Protection in Fiscal Stimulus Packages: Some Evidence." United Nations Development Programme, NY, March.

CHAPTER 2

Public Spending and Long-Run Growth in Practice: Concepts, Tools, and Evidence

Norman Gemmell, Florian Misch, and Blanca Moreno-Dodson

Among academics and policy makers alike, it is widely recognized (implicitly or explicitly) that public expenditure is central to growth, notably through the delivery of critical public services. The empirical growth literature that emerged over the last two decades or so and that shaped policy debates and research agendas identified a range of growth determinants—see, for example, Temple (1999) and Rodrik (2003).[1] In turn, anecdotal evidence suggests that many of these factors depend on public expenditure, at least to some extent. Outside academia, it is also widely assumed that public expenditure is of central importance to growth: to a large degree, international assistance to developing countries comes in the form of loans and grants to ultimately create fiscal space in the recipient countries (at least temporarily). Indeed, even policy reforms in areas other than fiscal policy that affect growth typically involve changes in public expenditure. However, despite the importance of public expenditure, it is still often difficult to make concrete and well-founded policy recommendations with respect to its level and composition because of the complex trade-offs involved. For example, policy makers faced with the choice of raising education expenditure at the expense of infrastructure expenditure or through higher taxes are likely to have difficulties making informed decisions. The objectives of this chapter are to conceptualize the evidence concerning the effects of public expenditure changes on growth and to present it with a view to predicting the growth effects of public spending reforms ex ante from the perspective of a policy maker in a developing country. We take into account the implications of the 2008–09 global crisis and the fiscal policy reactions it has triggered.

In principle, there is a range of transmission channels through which public expenditure affects long-run growth. In standard growth models that explain the level of total output as a function of factor inputs (such as capital and labor), as well as the productivity through which these inputs are combined, public expenditure could play a role by affecting both the level and the productivity of inputs. Several public spending categories potentially raise the marginal product of factor inputs in the production process of output—what we refer to as productive effects. For example, private capital such as machinery or vehicles can be used more productively when public infrastructure is in place. In addition, notably public investment may entail various indirect productive effects.[2] For example, public infrastructure may lower adjustment costs, slow private capital depreciation, or facilitate the provision of other productive public services such as education. In turn, higher productivity raises the returns on private investment, thereby resulting in a higher stock of private capital.

Recent growth models with public finance—that is, growth models in which various fiscal policy parameters are included that affect the behavior of private agents—attempt to capture these sorts of transmission mechanisms. While fiscal policy has been included in exogenous growth models since the work of Arrow and Kurz (1970), following the seminal contribution by Barro (1990), a number of endogenous growth models have been developed in which fiscal policy also affects the long-run growth rate of the economy. In the most basic version of these models, the government levies a flat tax on income to finance public services or to accumulate public capital. Both public services and public capital then enter the production function of private sector firms. These models assume constant returns to scale in private capital (which is typically considered to include both physical and human capital) and public inputs to private production that expand in parallel to each other, implying that long-run growth arises and that the level of public spending affects the growth rate of the gross domestic product (GDP).[3]

The theoretical effects of public spending composition on growth were explored subsequently by Devarajan, Swaroop, and Zou (1996). They consider several productive public inputs and show that the composition of public spending also affects the growth rate of the economy. Other papers extend the Barro (1990) framework in other ways, generally showing that the prediction that fiscal policy affects growth holds under a variety of different assumptions with respect to the characteristics of the economy and to the indirect effects of fiscal policy.

Increasing empirical evidence suggests that in both developed and developing countries fiscal policy affects long-run growth, which broadly confirms the predictions of endogenous growth models with public finance. This literature provides some information for policy makers. Although most of this existing evidence is confined to cross-country growth studies that have been somewhat challenged by various papers,[4] more recent studies that have resolved a number of econometric issues appear to be more robust, and few papers use subnational fiscal policy data from one country. Studies of this kind consider fiscal policy parameters as explanatory variables, in contrast to the large body of literature on the impact of the stock of public infrastructure on economic performance, which has been reviewed in detail by Romp and de Haan (2007) and Straub (2008) and which considers the stock of public capital as the central explanatory variable.

From a policy perspective, it is essential to understand the level and composition of public expenditure that are conducive to growth or, alternatively, the type of public expenditure reforms that enhance growth. Despite the wealth of empirical evidence, however, it is often difficult to derive well-founded policy implications for policy makers. Fiscal policy is subject to inherent trade-offs as a result of the government budget constraint, which are difficult to evaluate in practice (as discussed further in the section later in this chapter on conceptual issues in estimating the growth effects of public expenditure reform). Finally, fiscal policy may be used to pursue several policy objectives simultaneously. In addition to long-run growth, these objectives include equity by redistributing income and stabilization (to smooth output along the business cycle) and inevitably lead to trade-offs.

Following the discussion of conceptual issues, we review evidence from mostly aggregate-level cross-country and panel growth regressions. Whether a given parameter estimate is useful for predicting the effects of expenditure reforms from the point of view of a policy maker depends on several factors. First, it must be clear which fiscal change—including which *offsetting* change—is being considered. Otherwise, the estimated expenditure reform cannot be unambiguously identified and then replicated in practice. Second, it must be clear how far the evidence obtained from a particular sample of countries is relevant for the country or countries of interest. For example, evidence from the Organisation for Economic Co-operation and Development (OECD) countries need not be a good guide for the conditions observed in some developing countries. Finally, the parameter estimates must be robust in the sense that they address standard econometric concerns such as the endogeneity of the right-hand-side variables. Based on the discussion of these factors, the section on the existing evidence presents tables summarizing the particular growth estimates of public expenditure reforms as a type of tool for policy makers to predict ex ante the growth effects of public expenditure reforms. The focus of our study—to provide information that may be useful to policy makers based on results from the empirical literature—distinguishes this chapter from a more traditional literature review.

We then discuss whether and to what extent the growth objective conflicts with the short-run considerations that often induce public expenditure policy changes. In practice, public spending decisions are often triggered by cyclical fluctuations. Downturns, for example, may make fiscal adjustments seem inevitable or make governments implement fiscal stimulus packages to smooth output. In both cases, the level and composition of public spending change. We review these issues in greater detail, and, based on country-level examples, we analyze trade-offs with respect to the growth objective that may arise in practice—especially in the current context of global uncertainty and volatility.

Finally, we discuss the limitations of the existing empirical evidence reviewed and show how this evidence can be complemented in practice with country-specific information. We argue that poor efficiency of public spending that is primarily induced by bad governance—that is, active waste that entails utility for the public decision maker (Bandiera, Prat, and Valletti 2009)—may be the main concern of policy makers. That means that the econometric evidence on the growth effects of the composition of public spending may be less relevant. We then review new types of evidence on the growth effects of public expenditure that also could be used as tools in practice to inform public spending decisions. We point to directions for future policy-relevant research, including greater use of subnational public spending data, the use of firm-level data to estimate the effects of public spending at the microeconomic level, and the identification of beneficial public expenditure reforms through the use of internationally comparable indicators.

The chapter is organized as follows. The first section introduces the conceptual framework for estimating the growth effects of public spending, taking into account the government budget constraint. The second section is a review of the existing empirical evidence from a policy-making perspective. The third section is an analysis of existing evidence and country examples illustrating the trade-offs that arose in the context of public expenditure policy making during the recent global crisis. The fourth section then discusses the limitations of the existing empirical evidence for policy making and points to additional sources of information that are useful in evaluating the growth effects of expenditure reforms in practice. The final section presents our conclusions.

Conceptual Issues in Estimating the Growth Effects of Public Expenditure Reforms

In this section, we review the conceptual issues that must be addressed when estimating the growth effects of changes to public expenditure. Most important, we show that it is crucial to take into account the government budget constraint in the estimation. In addition, we reflect on various aspects of the existing theoretical and empirical literature as they relate to the expected growth effects of different types of public spending.

Theoretical Models of Fiscal Policy and Growth

It is well known that in exogenous (neoclassical) growth models, if the incentives to save or to invest in new capital are affected by fiscal policy, the equilibrium capital-to-output ratio and therefore the level of output but not its growth rate are altered. There are effects on growth only for a transitional period as the economy moves onto its new output path, although the length of this transition remains subject to debate.[5] The 1990s, however, saw the development of growth models with a more persistent role for fiscal policy such as those of Barro (1990); Futagami, Morita, and Shibata (1993); Devarajan, Swaroop, and Zou (1996); and Ghosh and Mourmouras (2002).

A novel feature of these models was that fiscal policy can determine both the level of the output path and the steady-state (long-run) growth rate.[6] Key aspects include some "productive" public expenditures that affect the productivity of the private sector, although other "unproductive" expenditures may affect citizens' welfare (including the possibility of zero welfare effects). In addition, some taxes levied to fund public spending may distort investment decisions. In a model with multiple productive expenditures, Devarajan, Swaroop, and Zou (1996) show that the growth effects depend on a combination of the *relative* productivities of these expenditures and their *relative* budget shares.

Categorizing public expenditures a priori as "productive" or "unproductive" and taxes as "distortionary" or "nondistortionary" (with respect to investment decisions) yields long-run growth impacts from fiscal policy that depend on both the level and the composition of public expenditures (those that affect social welfare or private sector investment and productivity), as well as the forms of taxation used to finance them (whether taxes discourage investment, including human capital accumulation). Positive, negative, or zero effects are each possible, depending on the tax/expenditure combinations used. When the models are extended to allow for the growth effects of deficits/surpluses, outcomes are again positive, negative, or ambiguous, depending on the other fiscal variables. In the context of this literature, corporate and personal income taxes are considered as more distortionary, while consumption taxes are usually seen as nondistortionary with respect to economic activity and growth.

Some empirical studies—such as Devarajan, Swaroop, and Zou (1996) and Ghosh and Gregoriou (2008)—have distinguished between "capital" and "current" government spending in their empirical tests, although most theoretical models do not yield direct predictions of the growth effects for this decomposition. In the context of endogenous growth models, capital spending results in the accumulation of the public capital stock, whereas current public spending flows finance public services. Although it could be hoped that, in practice, capital spending would be dominated by productive elements at the country level, both the distinction between capital and current and the composition of capital spending itself do not correspond to clear or common classification criteria and are often not reliable. It is also not clear that current spending (especially wages and salaries) would be unproductive, because it likely depends on how that spending complements capital spending and on the extent to which it generates government services that affect private sector production functions. For example, the salaries of doctors, nurses, and teachers would have private sector growth effects that are quite different from those associated with various forms of government subsidies, especially when politically driven. Conversely, "wasteful" expansions of public sector employment may lead to unnecessary increases in government wage bills, whereas well-targeted food subsidies may enhance the health and performance of private sector workers.

To the extent that both capital and current public spending entail productive effects, they may raise the returns of private investment (for example, by allowing more efficient operations and maintenance of investments), thereby resulting in increased private capital accumulation and promoting growth. In practice, both types of public spending categories are sometimes referred to as public investment, and there is no overall agreement among economists about this differentiation.[7]

An important aspect of the theoretical literature is that almost all growth models with public finance predict *short-term* growth effects as a result of public expenditure increases, with the signs and the magnitudes depending on the type of spending and how it is financed. The models disagree generally on "steady-state" effects. In empirical tests, this last property is examined by looking for *longer-term* effects—over 10 years or more. It is important to remember, however, that this evidence may not allow one to distinguish between the neoclassical and endogenous growth models without a clearer view of the expected length of transitional dynamics. Nevertheless, various models now generate hypotheses in which, at least for some types of public spending, impacts on growth are expected to persist for a number of years and possibly for decades.

These relatively simple growth models with public finance differ from the recent microfounded new Keynesian models that consider a wider range of issues critical to the short-run output effects of public expenditure (Beetsma and Jensen 2004; Galí, Vallés, and López-Salido 2007). In particular, the Keynesian models often analyze demand-side effects resulting from price rigidities and credit-constrained consumers, and they examine consumption and investment responses explicitly. However, they tend not to distinguish between productive and unproductive public spending: public spending frequently does not enter into the production of private output through the provision of public inputs, and therefore it does not have an impact on the productivity of private inputs.

As a result, the output effects of public expenditure predicted by the new Keynesian models arise mainly from other transmission channels, making it difficult to compare these models with growth models. Including productive expenditure in new Keynesian models, together with features such as implementation lags or time-to-build requirements, would allow one to make better-founded predictions of the short-run effects of public spending.

Several recent papers have modeled the relationship of particular public spending categories to growth. In a series of papers, Agénor (2005), and Agénor and Neanidis (2006) have examined various extensions of the Barro/Devarajan framework. These extensions explicitly model (1) infrastructure, education, or health spending as inputs to private production; and (2) interactions between these spending types (for example, by allowing the supply of health services or infrastructure spending to enter the production function for education).

In a similar vein, Semmler et al. (2007) developed an endogenous growth model to consider the growth effects of three types of spending—infrastructure, education, and health—in which the tax rate is assumed to be chosen optimally. They solve the model numerically and calibrate it to explore the impact of shifts between public investment in infrastructure assets that directly influence market production and public investment devoted to the production of human capital accumulation (education and health). Blankenau and Simpson (2004) also propose a model that focuses specifically on the relationship between public education expenditures and growth. They show that the relationship need not be monotonic when account is taken of tax financing methods (analogously to Barro) and specification of the "technology" of human capital production—for example, how public and private inputs to education and the input of human capital from preceding generations are combined.

Each of these models therefore provides plausible mechanisms by which long-run impacts on growth rates might be expected in association with changes in particular public expenditure categories, especially those related to infrastructure and human capital production (education, health, and so forth).

Guidance for Empirical Testing

An important contribution of the growth models just described is that they provide a framework for thinking about empirical testing for public expenditure growth effects. They identify a set of potential control variables (factor inputs, technology, and the like), provide guidance on how to categorize public expenditure in terms of growth-affecting properties, and highlight the importance of short- versus long-run effects (sometimes labeled "level" and "growth" effects, respectively). The models also demonstrate that the simultaneous impact of other fiscal variables must be taken into account in testing and interpreting evidence—that is, the government budget constraint is crucial.

Government budget constraint. The fundamental property of the government budget constraint (GBC) is that, like any other identity, it requires every fiscal change to be offset by a compensating change. Increases in a certain category of public spending must be financed by increases in tax revenue, in the deficit or in the level of grants. Otherwise, other types of spending would have to be lowered, or the offsetting mechanism could be a combination of some or all of those elements. The net effect of any fiscal change therefore depends on the way it is offset. The direct and indirect growth effects of the offsetting element may have similar or opposite signs. In addition, the growth effects of the alternative offsetting changes are likely to differ in magnitude and time horizon. For example, the direct effects of increasing public spending on education are certainly expected to be beneficial, but these positive effects may be reversed by the negative growth effects of distortionary taxation, especially in the short run. Thus the net effects of the policy change are likely to be different from, say, an increase in public education expenditure financed by a decrease in public infrastructure investment.

The intertemporal budget constraint requires that all debt is repaid in the long run, so that deficits are essentially either deferred spending cuts or tax increases. The effects of deficit-financed increases of productive public spending on long-run growth are therefore ambiguous. They depend on the way that debt is repaid in the future: the short-run supply-side effects may be positive, depending on expectations about future repayment of debt, and the long-run supply-side effects may be negative if taxes need to be increased. However, both effects are empirically difficult to disentangle, which explains why most empirical studies make no specific assumptions about how the intertemporal budget constraint is satisfied. Furthermore, most empirical papers exclude the fiscal deficit simultaneously with other fiscal categories, so there is no clear empirical evidence on this.

Short-run versus long-run testing. The strands of the literature examining aggregate short-run or long-run growth effects of fiscal policy generally use quite different methodologies. On the one hand, following Blanchard and Perotti (2002) and Perotti (2002), tests for the short-run effects of taxes or government expenditure typically apply the structural vector autoregression (SVAR) approach to quarterly or annual data, although relatively few studies are directed at developing countries.[8] On the other hand, empirical studies of long-run growth effects increasingly use multi-country panel regression methods, which typically include no short-run dynamics, and assumed homogeneity of short- or long-run responses across countries is required for tractability.

The SVAR method essentially treats all variables—GDP, fiscal variables, technology, factor inputs, and so forth—as endogenous. However, by making assumptions about the lags with which different elements of the government budget will affect output, it can test for the temporal precedence of these different fiscal elements and allow for feedback effects among them. A common assumption in SVAR approaches is that an exogenous public expenditure change affects output only with a lag, not contemporaneously. The approach is especially suited to examining the immediate effects of a spending stimulus or withdrawal, such as that occurring during and after the 2008–09 global crisis.[9] This allows the initial "shock" effect to be identified and the responses (including any tendency for changes in spending) to feed through to subsequent changes in budget deficits or tax revenues. However, SVAR methods have weaknesses.

First, their specification often dictates that there are no long-run fiscal impacts on output, and, second, it can be difficult to disentangle the spending from tax effects that, in combination, feed through to output. A third consequence of the SVAR approach is that even though SVARs typically include both tax and spending variables, the government budget constraint is not explicitly taken into account. As a result, for example, the sustainability of implied changes in long-run public debt levels and the resulting growth impacts are rarely considered. This implies that even if the effects of taxes and spending were all exhausted within a few periods, public spending—through its impact on public debt in the short run—could have longer-run growth consequences. For these and other reasons, SVAR approaches to testing may be best thought of as measuring mainly the demand-side stimuli associated with new Keynesian models.

Long-run regression models. As noted, most empirical tests of the long-run effects of fiscal policy on growth have used cross-section or panel regression methods applied to annual or period-averaged data. Unlike vector autoregression models, these regressions often are limited in their recognition of the joint determination of or interactions among taxes, public spending, and budget deficits, or between different spending compositions—see the review and meta-analysis of Nijkamp and Poot (2004).

To see how the government budget constraint affects these regression models, consider a simplified government budget decomposition in which expenditures (E) must be financed by revenues (R) and a budget surplus/deficit (D), each of which has potential growth effects. Following the Devarajan, Swaroop, and Zou (1996) model, growth may be affected by both the level of total expenditures (E) and the share of each

j (= 1, ..., n) spending category in that total, e_j/E. For a panel data set involving a set of countries and years (for example, GDP growth in country i at time t), g_{it} can be written as a function of a set of control and fiscal variables (as ratios of GDP) where the latter take the form of

$$g_{it} = \dots \gamma_1 \left(\frac{E}{GDP} \right)_{it} + \sum_{j=1}^{n-1} \gamma_{2j} \left(\frac{e_j}{E} \right)_{it} + \gamma_3 \left(\frac{R}{GDP} \right)_{it} + \gamma_4 \left(\frac{D}{GDP} \right)_{it} + \dots \quad (2.1)$$

However, because the government budget constraint specifies that $D_{it} \equiv R_{it} - E_{it}$, the three variables would be perfectly collinear in a regression. Arbitrarily choosing one variable (for example, D_{it}) to omit, equation (2.1) can be rewritten, and estimated, as

$$g_{it} = \dots (\gamma_1 - \gamma_4) \left(\frac{E}{GDP} \right)_{it} + \sum_{j=1}^{n-1} \gamma_{2j} \left(\frac{e_j}{E} \right)_{it} + (\gamma_3 + \gamma_4) \left(\frac{R}{GDP} \right)_{it} + \dots \quad (2.2)$$

This clarifies the correct interpretation of the growth effects of expenditure and revenue variables. The parameters in equation (2.2) capture the effect of increases in total expenditure or of decreases in revenues financed by changes in the budget deficit (the omitted category in this example). These effects can be seen to depend on the signs and relative sizes of γ_1, γ_3, and γ_4. By comparison, the interpretation of the coefficients on the individual expenditure share components of interest, γ_{2j}, remains unaffected. It is some version of equation (2.2) that empirical studies ideally estimate.

The γ_{2j} parameters measure the effect on growth of a change in the share of spending on each category, holding constant the other variables in equation (2.2), including total expenditure. Equation (2.2) can be derived from equation (2.1) by omitting any of the three budget constraint elements, E_{it}, R_{it}, or D_{it}. In each case, the interpretation of the parameters on the remaining GBC variables changes, depending on what is included or excluded. Finally, note that the approach in equation (2.2) can be used to examine the short-run or long-run growth effects of fiscal variables, depending on the form of the regression equation (principally its lag structure).

In regression specifications used in practice, up to $n - 1$ of the expenditure categories, ej, in equation (2.2) may be included, with the interpretation of the included parameters differing (depending on which and how many individual categories are included). For example, where the regression includes only one element of total expenditure, e_1/E, the parameter estimate represents the effect on growth of changing this spending category while reducing the remaining expenditure shares on a pro rata basis. Of course, the included expenditure category can be rotated across the set of expenditure categories to identify each separate growth impact.[10] In line with the predictions of growth models with public finance, and following Kneller, Bleaney, and Gemmell (1999), it is likewise possible to select those expenditure categories that are expected to be productive based on a priori reasoning and to exclude all remaining categories that are supposedly "unproductive."

The next section discusses empirical studies of the impact of different types of government expenditure on growth and the extent to which they consider the conceptual issues discussed in this section.

Existing Evidence on the Effects of Public Expenditure Reforms in Developing Countries

This section summarizes the existing estimates of the growth effects of public spending in developing countries from a policy perspective. In principle, ex post estimates may be used to predict the effects of expenditure reforms ex ante. However, we do not regard all studies and estimates as equally useful for policy makers, and therefore we develop a set of criteria to select the studies listed in the summary tables that follow.

Criteria for the Selection of Studies

We applied three criteria to the selection of studies: they must consider the government budget constraint; they must use data almost exclusively from developing countries; and their results must be robust and free from obvious econometric problems.

From a policy point of view, it is essential that the studies consider the government budget constraint to ensure that the fiscal change being estimated can be identified, at least broadly speaking, and actually replicated in practice. For example, we exclude all studies that include total public expenditure as the only fiscal variable in the analysis because interpretation of the parameters is difficult, and these studies only allow for limited (if any) policy conclusions.

We discuss only studies that use data almost exclusively from developing countries. The growth effects of public expenditure are likely to differ between developed and developing countries—for example, because private production in developed countries requires combinations of public inputs that differ from those required in developing countries. We also generally exclude those studies that are based on mixed data from developed *and* developing countries because they are likely to suffer from unobserved heterogeneity for precisely this reason. These exclusions increase the relevance of the estimates we examine.

Finally, the results of the studies we use must be robust and free from obvious econometric problems such as collinearity. In particular, we verify that the number of observations seems to be sufficient and that panel studies somehow address the problem of endogeneity of the fiscal variables.

Applying those three criteria to the literature enables us to identify papers containing estimates that we regard, in principle, as useful for practice. Unfortunately, much of the literature has not formally recognized the implications of the government budget constraint for testing or interpretation, especially studies of developing countries where data availability and quality are more limited. Nevertheless, following studies such as that by Kneller, Bleaney, and Gemmell (1999), some papers on developing countries have now incorporated the government budget constraint either explicitly or implicitly.

Table 2.1 summarizes the papers that meet our criteria and that we review in detail later in this section. They are all based on data from developing countries, but the type of data they use differs. Cross-country data are the most widely used data source in studies that estimate the long-run effects of public expenditure, despite the well-known disadvantages of those data. The reasons are that cross-country data are easily accessible, they have a panel structure that facilitates the estimation of structural relationships between fiscal variables and output, and they provide a much larger number of observations than do time series from one country.

Using subnational expenditure data from one country is an alternative to cross-country data. The growing trend toward fiscal decentralization in many developing countries is increasingly providing suitable fiscal policy data at the subnational level. Although only a few studies are based on such data, this source may have the largest potential for future research, as discussed shortly.

Because time series are typically short, often resulting in few observations, time series evidence produces perhaps the least reliable evidence on the effects of public spending in developing countries. In addition, most time series studies do not consider the government budget constraint.[11] We therefore do not include time series studies in our review.

The existing papers can be distinguished further by the time span the data cover and how they consider lags in the effects of public spending.

Table 2.1   Summary of Relevant Papers

Paper	Economies	Years	Type of expenditure changes	Expenditure decomposition
Adam and Bevan (2005)	45 developing countries	1970–99, 5-year averages	Level effects	By growth impact
Bayraktar and Moreno-Dodson (2010)	14 developing countries	1970–2005, annual/3-year moving averages	Composition effects	By growth impact
Bose, Haque, and Osborn (2007)	30 developing countries	1970–89, 10-year averages	Level effects	Economic and functional
Devarajan, Swaroop, and Zou (1996)	43 developing countries	1970–90, 5-year forward-moving averages of LHS variable	Composition effects	Economic and functional
Ghosh and Gregoriou (2008)	15 developing countries	1970–99, 5-year forward-moving averages of LHS variable	Composition effects	Economic and functional
Gupta et al. (2005)	39 developing countries	1990–2000, annual	Level effects	Economic
Haque (2004)	33 developing countries	1980–97, 5-year forward-moving averages of LHS variable	Composition effects	Economic
Hong and Ahmed (2009)	14 Indian states	1990–2002, 5-year moving averages	Composition effects	By growth impact
López and Miller (2007)	29 developing countries	1980–2004, 5-year averages	Mixed	By growth impact
Rocha and Giuberti (2007)	27 Brazilian states	1986–2002, 5-year forward-moving averages of LHS variable	Composition effects	Functional
Yan and Gong (2009)	31 Chinese provinces	1997–2007, 3-year forward-moving averages of LHS variable	Composition effects	Functional

Note: LHS = left-hand side (referring to regressions).

Most papers use three- to five-year static or moving averages. Both the number of years included and the type of averages used affect the number of observations. The use of multiyear averages of public spending data is the standard but ad hoc means of ensuring that coefficients are capturing longer-run growth effects, not short-run demand-side effects.

The advantage of this approach is that no specific assumptions about the exact lag structure are necessary. However, this could also be seen as a disadvantage because this specification does not allow drawing better-founded conclusions about the lag structure of public spending—that is, how long it takes for potential growth effects of productive public spending to unfold.

Based on the discussion in the section on conceptual issues, we distinguish composition and level effects. The former capture the changes in the growth rate that arise purely because of changes in the composition of public expenditure with the level of total public spending held constant. Level effects also capture changes in the composition, but with the level of total expenditure *not* held constant. For example, an increase in capital expenditure financed by a pro rata decrease in current expenditure would imply composition effects, whereas an increase in capital expenditure financed by a higher level of grants with the level of current expenditure held constant would result in level effects. In the latter case, the composition of total expenditure also changes, but note that other elements of the government budget constraint also change—that is, the level of total expenditure and grants in the example just given.

Finally, the studies we consider disaggregate total expenditure in different ways. Typically, they either decompose public spending by function (education, health, transport and communications, and so forth) or by economic type (such as capital versus current spending), or they classify public spending according to its presumed growth impact whereby depending on the paper productive expenditure mostly includes some combination of education, health, transport, communication, energy, and water supply spending as well as spending on public order and safety and is assumed to affect private sector productivity. In contrast, unproductive expenditure that includes spending outside these areas is assumed to not have any effects on private sector productivity.

Summary of the Estimates

Tables 2.2, 2.3, and 2.4 summarize the estimates of the growth effects that arise from various public spending reforms that we extracted from the papers summarized in table 2.1. We include only those specifications that include GDP per capita growth as the left-hand-side variable (one exception is Yan and Gong 2009, who use absolute GDP growth), but we exclude those estimates that, for example, refer to changes in per capita growth. We further exclude specifications that are based on cross-section data without a panel dimension.

Table 2.2   Estimated Growth Effects of Productive Expenditure

Expenditure category	Paper	Offsetting change	Estimates	Fiscal controls	Other controls
Productive expenditure (% of GDP)	Adam and Bevan (2005)	Deficit (< 1.5%)	0.44	Revenue, unproductive expenditure	GDP per capita, investment, annual average population growth
		Deficit (> 1.5%)	−0.06	Revenue, unproductive expenditure	
		Grants	0.1	Residual revenue, unproductive expenditure	
Productive expenditure (% of GDP)	Bayraktar and Moreno-Dodson (2010)	Other expenditure	Low: 0.136; high: 1.102	Unproductive expenditure, revenue, deficit	Private investment, initial human capital, inflation, growth in previous period
Public goods expenditure (% of total expenditure)	Hong and Ahmed (2009)	Nonpublic goods and nondevelopmental expenditure (e.g., administration)	0.434	Total expenditure, developmental expenditure	Investment proxies, landlocked dummy
Public goods expenditure (% of total expenditure)	López and Miller (2007)	Nontax revenue, nonpublic goods, and consumption expenditure	Low: 0.035; high: 0.115	Tax revenue, government consumption	Total investment, initial per capita GDP, inflation, lagged years of schooling, years of democratic stability, corruption, percentage of land in tropical areas, malaria ecological index, regional dummies

Note: GDP = gross domestic product.

Even though it seems plausible that the growth effects of public spending are likely to be nonlinear, there are only a few studies that control for them, such as Devarajan, Swaroop, and Zou (1996); Rocha and Giuberti (2007); and Bayraktar and Moreno-Dodson (2010). To compare the estimates from nonlinear and linear specifications, it would

Table 2.3   Estimated Growth Effects of Capital Expenditure

Expenditure category	Paper	Offsetting change	Estimates	Fiscal controls	Other controls
Capital expenditure (% of GDP)	Bose, Haque, and Osborn (2007)	Nontax revenue	0.151	Tax revenue, deficit, all other expenditure	Ratio of private capital to public spending, black market premium, shocks, openness
	Gupta et al. (2005)	Deficit	Low: 0.567 high: 0.710	Tax revenue, nontax revenue, grants, disaggregated residual expenditure	Labor force, terms of trade, private investment, initial enrollment, initial GDP per capita, lagged per capita growth (some specifications only)
Capital expenditure (% of total expenditure)	Ghosh and Gregoriou (2008)	Current expenditure	Low: −0.250; high: −0.140	Total expenditure (% of GDP), private capital/total expenditure	Black market premium, shocks, openness
	Ghosh and Gregoriou (2008)	Current expenditure	Low: −0.270; high: −0.190	Deficit, tax revenue, nontax revenue	Black market premium, shocks, openness
	Rocha and Giuberti (2007)	Current expenditure	Low: −0.030; high: −0.010	Total expenditure (% of GDP)	Labor force or private investment (some specifications only)
	Devarajan, Swaroop, and Zou (1996)	Current expenditure	Low: −0.059; high: −0.035	Total expenditure (% of GDP)	Continental dummies, black market premium, shocks
	Haque (2004)	Current expenditure	Low: −0.360; high: −0.040	Total expenditure (% of GDP)	Regional dummies, black market premium, shocks
	Gupta et al. (2005)	Revenue	Low: 0.154; high: 0.237	Deficit, disaggregated residual expenditure	Labor force, terms of trade, private investment, initial enrollment, initial GDP per capita, lagged per capita growth (some specifications only)

Note: GDP = gross domestic product.

be necessary to compare growth elasticities for all specifications from all papers. However, most of the studies do not report summary statistics that would be required to calculate the elasticities (typically, this is done at a specific value of the variables, most commonly the mean). We therefore

Table 2.4   Estimated Growth Effects of Current Expenditure Components

Expenditure category	Paper	Offsetting change	Estimates	Fiscal controls	Other controls
Other goods and services (% of GDP)	Gupta et al. (2005)	Deficit	1.417	Revenue, disaggregated residual expenditure	Labor force, terms of trade, private investment, initial enrollment, initial GDP per capita, lagged per capita growth (some specifications only)
Other goods and services (% of total expenditure)	Ghosh and Gregoriou (2008)	Residual expenditure	Low: 0.130; high: 0.170	Total expenditure (% of GDP), private capital/total expenditure	Black market premium, shocks, openness
	Gupta et al. (2005)	Revenue	Low: 0.129; high: 0.149	Deficit, disaggregated residual expenditure	Labor force, terms of trade, private investment, initial enrollment, initial GDP per capita, lagged per capita growth (some specifications only)
Wages (% of GDP)		Deficit	Low: −0.833; high: −0.385	Revenue, disaggregated residual expenditure	
Wages (% of total expenditure)		Revenue	Low: −0.350; high: −0.196	Deficit, disaggregated residual expenditure	

Note: GDP = gross domestic product.

do not include the results from nonlinear specifications in the summary tables. The exclusion of nonlinear effects or, alternatively, the assumption that the effects are linear (which is implicit in most papers) and the fact that elasticities often cannot be computed based on the information provided in the papers represent important limitations of the empirical literature.

Tables 2.2, 2.3, and 2.4 are organized as follows. In the first column, we report the expenditure category to which the estimates refer, and whether expenditure is measured relative to total expenditure or to GDP. Because 1 percent of GDP implies a greater public spending increase than 1 percent of total expenditure, the coefficients of expenditure variables expressed in terms of GDP tend to be larger in absolute terms than are the coefficients of expenditure variables expressed in terms of total expenditure for the same expenditure category. The second column specifies the paper from which the estimates in the fourth column were extracted.

The third column specifies how an increase in the expenditure category (shown in the first column) is offset in the empirical specification. The fifth and sixth columns include all fiscal and nonfiscal control variables that have been included in the specifications. In the fiscal control column, the definition of "residual" expenditure differs by paper and is usually not termed this way. We use the term to refer to total expenditure minus spending in the category of interest (the first column) minus the omitted expenditure variables if any (the third column), or minus the expenditure categories included as fiscal control variables (fifth column), respectively. The nonfiscal controls are typically those suggested by standard growth models or by previous findings reported in the empirical growth literature. Some studies include a shocks variable that typically represents the weighted average of changes in the world interest rate, and the export and import price indexes of each country, in order to capture the effects of external shocks to these economies. The openness variable is the sum of exports and imports as a ratio of GDP.

In the fourth column, we generally provide a range of estimates, indicating that the same fiscal reform has been estimated several times—for example, using different estimators that result in different coefficient estimates. In these cases, we provide the upper and lower ones. However, this range does not reflect estimates that are not significant (the vast majority of estimates seem to be indeed significant), and in some cases we also do not consider estimates labeled "robustness checks" that confirm the main results qualitatively but not quantitatively (in most cases, these are instrumental variable regressions included as a robustness check). Finally, we generally do not consider estimates that are not robust (that is, that change sign) within the same paper.

We group the estimates by type of expenditure. The effects of increases in some type of productive expenditure and of current expenditure are summarized in table 2.2. Adam and Bevan (2005) and Bayraktar and Moreno-Dodson (2010) find that increasing productive expenditure generally entails positive growth effects. Depending on the way the increase is offset, an increase of 1 percentage point in productive expenditure relative to GDP results in an increase in the growth rate of 0.1–1.1 percentage points. Bayraktar and Moreno-Dodson show that the findings are robust to the exact way in which productive expenditure is defined: they use two slightly different definitions of productive expenditure (which they term "productive" and "core") but obtain largely similar results. Adam and Bevan show that, as an exception, productive expenditure has negative growth effects if it is deficit financed and if the deficit is already larger than 1.5 percent of GDP. The expenditure aggregate that López and Miller (2007) and Hong and Ahmed (2009) use differs from the more traditional definition of productive expenditure in the sense that they consider public goods expenditure. They also find that increases in productive expenditure result in higher growth. However, the results of López and Miller (2007) are difficult to interpret because the omitted category is a mix of revenue and expenditure, and in Hong and Ahmed the absence of a sufficient number of control variables that vary across states and time is problematic.[12]

Table 2.3 reports the effects of increases in capital expenditure. The effects seem to depend crucially on the way in which capital expenditure is financed. All studies that estimate pure composition effects find that, contrary to conventional wisdom, reallocating resources from current to capital spending (which typically excludes interest payments) entails negative growth effects.[13]

According to the estimates, a 1 percentage point increase of capital expenditure (in terms of total expenditure) results in a 0.04–0.36 percentage point decline in the growth rate. Although Rocha and Giuberti (2007) use subnational data that overcome some of the problems of cross-country data, their estimates are not necessarily more credible because they include neither sufficient control variables nor time and province fixed effects in the same specification.

By contrast, Bose, Haque, and Osborn (2007) find positive effects of capital expenditure financed by nontax revenue when all other fiscal variables (including expenditure, tax revenue, and grants) are held constant. Because nontax revenue is likely to not have significant and direct negative effects on growth (unlike distortionary taxation, for example), this finding may not be surprising. Gupta et al. (2005) find positive effects of capital expenditure when financed through borrowing as well. However, they do not control for threshold effects in the context of deficit financing along the lines of Adam and Bevan (2005), which may imply that their results hold up only to a certain level of the deficit. Gupta et al.'s finding, that a revenue-financed increase in capital expenditure is growth-enhancing (last line of table 2.3), is also somewhat difficult to reconcile with those studies that consider composition effects and find negative effects of capital expenditure.

Table 2.4 summarizes the effects of two components of current expenditure: wages and spending on other goods and services. It is interesting to note that although Gupta et al. (2005) find negative effects of current expenditure in general, they find positive effects of deficit-financed spending on other goods and services but negative effects of spending on wages. Ghosh and Gregoriou (2008) also find positive effects of spending on other goods and services, but, in contrast to Gupta et al., they consider composition effects.

Table 2.5 summarizes the growth effects of expenditure disaggregated by function or sector, including education spending, health spending, and infrastructure investment. Overall, the results with respect to sectoral expenditure seem to be less robust across and within studies, and it is less likely that they can be generalized compared with the expenditure aggregates considered in the previous tables. Whereas broad expenditure categories are likely to be approximately similar, expenditure categories that are more narrowly defined may differ across countries. This would imply that measurement error is more problematic when estimating the effects of functionally disaggregated expenditures in cross-country studies. However, it is also difficult to compare the estimates because the offsetting category differs across the studies. In this sense, the differences in the coefficient estimates again highlight the importance of considering the government budget constraint. Different public spending categories may also differ in terms of their lag structure. For example, public spending on road infrastructure might affect growth over very different time horizons, when compared with public spending on education (often requiring longer periods of time to show effects). Because there is little robust evidence of the growth effects of particular public spending categories and because public spending lags are usually taken into account by using multiyear averages (as explained earlier), the existing empirical studies are of little value in uncovering the specific lag structure of different public spending categories.

Whereas these estimates refer to the effects of intersectoral expenditure composition, the article by Devarajan, Swaroop, and Zou (1996) is the only one that also investigates the growth effects of intrasectoral composition in the health and education sectors. However, when they include subsectoral expenditure categories in the analysis, they hold neither total nor sectoral expenditure constant, so the offsetting change is unclear. We therefore chose to exclude them from the summary tables.

Gupta et al. (2005) and Yan and Gong (2009) also estimate the effects of additional expenditure categories, including interest payments, transfers,

Table 2.5 Estimated Growth Effects of Sectoral Expenditure

Expenditure category	Paper	Offsetting change	Estimates	Fiscal controls	Other controls
Education expenditure (% of GDP)	Bose, Haque, and Osborn (2007)	Nontax revenue	Low: 0.658; high: 1.582	Tax revenue, deficit, all other expenditure	Ratio of private capital to public spending, black market premium, shocks, openness
	Yan and Gong (2009)	Residual expenditure	−1.972	Total expenditure, infrastructure expenditure, scientific research expenditure, taxation	Private investment, openness, inflation, labor force growth
Education expenditure (% of total expenditure)	Ghosh and Gregoriou (2008)	Residual expenditure	−0.030	Health expenditure, total expenditure, private capital/total expenditure	Black market premium, shocks, openness
	Rocha and Giuberti (2007)	Residual expenditure	0.074	Defense expenditure, transport expenditure, health expenditure (all % of total expenditure), total expenditure (% of GDP)	Labor force or private investment (some specifications only)
Health (% of total expenditure)	Ghosh and Gregoriou (2008)	Residual expenditure	−0.060	Education expenditure, total expenditure, private capital/total expenditure	Black market premium, shocks, openness
	Rocha and Giuberti (2007)	Residual expenditure	0.115	Defense expenditure, transport expenditure, education expenditure (all % of total expenditure), total expenditure (% of GDP)	Some specifications: labor force or private investment
Infrastructure investment (% of GDP)	Yan and Gong (2009)	Residual expenditure	0.899	Total expenditure, infrastructure expenditure, scientific research expenditure, taxation	Private investment, openness, inflation, labor force growth
Infrastructure investment (% of total expenditure)	Yan and Gong (2009)	Residual expenditure	0.072	Total expenditure, education expenditure, scientific research expenditure, taxation	Private investment, openness, inflation, labor force growth
Transport and communication expenditure (% of total expenditure)	Rocha and Giuberti (2007)	Residual expenditure	Low: 0.111; high: 0.127	Education expenditure, defense expenditure, health expenditure (all % of total expenditure), total expenditure (% of GDP)	Some specifications: labor force or private investment

Note: GDP = gross domestic product.

defense, security, and spending on research. The growth effects of interest payments can be thought of as analogous to the growth impacts of deficit financing rather than expenditure per se, and the estimated effects of the remaining categories are either not robust or not significant. We therefore chose to exclude them from the summary tables.

Public Spending for Growth during the Global Crisis

In a first-best world with long-run growth as the only objective of government policy, changes in expenditure policy would be made on the basis of evidence on the long-run effects of fiscal policy. By contrast, major changes in public spending are often triggered by cyclical fluctuations and short-run rather than long-run considerations or requirements.

On the one hand, economic downturns may result in reduced fiscal space, which Heller (2005, 3) defines as "budgetary room that allows a government to provide resources for a desired purpose without any prejudice to the sustainability of a government's financial position." Typically, countries face lower revenue, which may imply that productive public expenditure levels decline. In this case, fiscal adjustment, and in particular the objective of achieving debt sustainability, may be perceived as conflicting with the objective of long-run growth.

On the other hand, during economic downturns governments may equally increase public spending as a means of stabilizing aggregate demand and protecting vulnerable households in those countries where sufficient fiscal space exists. Ideally, such stimulus packages meet several

---

Box 2.1

Fiscal Policy in the Republic of Korea

Korea has achieved a remarkable growth performance since the 1960s. The average growth rate of real GDP per capita was about 6.1 percent between 1965 and 2010. Fiscal policy may have played an important role. Between 1960 and 1970, the average share of central government expenditure of GDP was about 20 percent (Kim 2008). This share dropped to 17 percent on average between 1970 and 2005, placing it lower than those of other fast-growing developing countries, but the share of growth-enhancing expenditure in total public spending was relatively high (Bayraktar and Moreno-Dodson 2010).

(continued next page)

Box 2.1 *(continued)*

During the 2008–09 global crisis, the growth rate of real GDP dropped to 2 percent in 2008 and almost 0 percent in 2009, which triggered a significant fiscal policy response. The Korean government adopted substantial fiscal measures totaling almost 3.6 percent of GDP in 2008, which was well above the average size of stimulus packages in the G-20 countries of about 2.2 percent of GDP within the same period (Horton, Kumar, and Mauro 2009). The total size of the stimulus package between 2008 and 2010, including both revenue and expenditure components, added up to 6.5 percent of GDP. The Korean government was able to introduce such a relatively large stimulus package in part thanks to the country's healthy financial balance before the crisis. Sixty percent of the stimulus package was allocated to public expenditures, and the remaining 40 percent came from tax cuts (Ministry of Strategy and Finance, Republic of Korea 2010). The focus was on stabilizing livelihoods and maintaining and creating jobs. Using a macroeconomic simulation model developed by the International Monetary Fund (IMF), Eskesen (2009) studied the effectiveness of fiscal policy and found that the temporary increase in government spending contributed significantly to short-run output stabilization. In line with this evidence, Korea experienced strong growth in 2010, totaling 6.2 percent, and unlike most other advanced economies, it did not experience a recession in 2009, based on annual growth rates.

In the future, fiscal policy will be shaped by Korea's demographics, because it is experiencing a shift from one of the youngest populations among the OECD countries to one of the oldest, as pointed out in Feyzioglu, Skaarup, and Syed (2008). This change is expected to put tremendous pressure on the pension system and health and long-term care expenditures. Public age-related spending is expected to increase to 13 percent of GDP by 2060 (Feyzioglu 2006), which can significantly threaten fiscal sustainability. In this context, safeguarding productive expenditure will be politically challenging.

Sources: Kim 2008; Bayraktar and Moreno-Dodson 2010; Horton, Kumar, and Mauro 2009; Ministry of Strategy and Finance, Republic of Korea 2010; Eskesen 2009; Feyzioglu, Skaarup, and Syed 2008; Feyzioglu 2006.

policy objectives simultaneously, including short-run output stabilization, protection of vulnerable households, and long-run growth promotion.[14] However, such stimulus packages do not always succeed in reconciling short-run output stabilization with long-run growth. In practice, it has therefore proved difficult to balance the trade-off between demand stabilization and long-run growth (see box 2.1 for how fiscal policy was conducted in the Republic of Korea).

During past crises, the majority of developing countries had to reduce public spending as a result of limited fiscal space. By contrast, prior to the most recent global crisis many developing countries had stronger fiscal positions, including far smaller fiscal deficits and lower debt burdens (IMF 2010), than in previous downturns. These stronger positions allowed many developing countries to implement a countercyclical fiscal policy—indeed, according to the IMF (2010), 81 percent of low-income countries and about 69 percent of emerging market economies increased public expenditure in real terms. Whereas most low-income countries experienced declines in public revenue—the median decline in revenue in all low-income countries amounted to 0.3 percent of GDP and to 2.1 percent of GDP among commodity exporters (IMF 2010)—only a few countries chose or were forced to adjust spending to the revenue shock to avoid unsustainable debt. Low-income countries used domestic sources, external loans, and grants to finance domestic revenue shortfalls (IMF 2010).

In the past, fiscal adjustments have often involved cuts in productive public expenditure, which suggests that there are trade-offs between achieving debt sustainability and promoting long-run growth, depending on public spending composition. Although those cuts may improve the short-term cash flow indicators (deficit and gross debt), they are likely to prove counterproductive in the long run: less productive expenditure may reduce long-run output growth, which then lowers future revenue flows (Easterly, Irwin, and Servén 2007). In this sense, growth-enhancing policies help ensure that government debt is sustainable.

As for the composition of stimulus packages during the global crisis, no systematic information for all countries is available. However, evidence from a limited sample of low-income countries suggests that, in addition to spending on social safety nets, health and education spending and public investment generally increased. For example, several countries implemented labor-intensive public works programs, including Bangladesh, Cambodia, Kenya, Rwanda, Sierra Leone, and Tanzania.

It is possible that the composition of the stimulus packages in some countries was motivated in part by the expected long-run growth effects of public investment and of health and education spending, while reanimating the economy in the short term. However, there are still trade-offs between short-run stabilization and the promotion of long-run growth, even when the composition of public spending changes in favor of those public spending categories deemed productive a priori. Also, the intrasectoral allocation within productive categories and the efficiency of public spending become critical.

The quality of stimulus spending may be low from a growth perspective. First, although public investment is commonly believed to be growth-enhancing, the evidence just presented is mixed at best, and several studies find negative growth effects from reallocating public resources from current to capital spending. Not all capital spending is growth-enhancing—for example, if there is no clear link to private sector productivity, or if, subsequently, operations and maintenance current expenditures are neglected.

Second, even if overall public investment is growth-enhancing, the objective of short-run stabilization often dictates that those public investment projects financed be labor intensive and quickly implementable. Based on existing evidence, it is not exactly clear what types of public investment are financed after a crisis or an exogenous shock, because this also varies by country. However, large and complex infrastructure projects (such as major roads, railways, or electricity generation), which are often required to remove bottlenecks for growth, are more likely subject to long implementation lags and may be less labor intensive—at least in relative terms and with respect to low-skilled labor. On those grounds, these types of projects are unlikely to be part of any stimulus packages, especially if they are not "shovel ready."[15]

Some countries such as Bolivia, Dominica, Malawi, and Senegal increased spending on cash transfer programs as part of stimulus programs after the recent global crisis (IMF 2010). Although spending on social safety nets is necessary to protect vulnerable households in the event of a major crisis, trade-offs with long-run growth objectives may also arise, depending on the extent of the spending and the design of such programs. However, social safety nets may be equally important to safeguarding stability by preventing social turmoil, which is important for private investment.

In addition to the quality of stimulus spending, its efficiency may be low from a growth perspective—even when the spending appears to be socially desirable. Public works programs aimed at short-run employment creation may be specifically designed to be more labor intensive than required, thereby creating inefficiencies even if, in principle, they contribute to long-run growth. In South Africa, for example, public works programs (in general, not necessarily in the context of stimulus packages) are defined as "the creation of public assets using labor intensive methods" (McCord 2002, 24), and performance is measured by the extent to which projects are implemented labor intensively. In addition, although the IMF (2010) finds evidence of higher real spending on health and education, it also shows that spending on goods and services in those sectors slowed. This finding may point to further inefficiencies if operational spending was relatively insufficient in view of the existing labor force in both sectors.

It seems plausible that hikes in public spending in response to recessions should focus on those expenditure categories that enhance long-run growth, but the evidence on the efficiency and quality of stimulus spending for long-run growth is limited. Nevertheless, our discussion suggests that, in practice, the promotion of long-run growth may be difficult to reconcile with short-run output stabilization, because there are trade-offs between quick employment creation in the area of public works and growth over the long term. Reconciling both policy objectives is further complicated by the requirement that implementation lags be short to produce immediate output stabilization.

In addition to "technical" difficulties, in times of economic crisis governments may be tempted to use the stabilization objective as a pretext for implementing fiscal measures that serve special-interest groups and that neither promote long-run growth nor protect the poor.

Directions for Future Research and for Policy Making in Practice

The earlier discussion of existing evidence defined criteria that restricted the sample of empirical studies we reviewed. From this sample, we have extracted estimates of the growth effects of public expenditure and presented them in a way that makes them comparable. Although this selection process and presentation of the estimates might be expected to restrict the range of parameter estimates reported, we observe a fairly high degree of nonrobustness. Some of the differences in the results can be attributed to the differences in the econometric specifications and in the expenditure changes being estimated, but this feature of the literature makes it hard to compare and to verify individual parameter estimates. In addition, using the reported estimates to predict the effects of functionally disaggregated expenditure categories, for example, may be problematic. In this section, we discuss the reasons for this nonrobustness and how these limitations could be addressed in future research to improve the robustness of the results, and we suggest that policy makers use additional information as a means of complementing the existing estimates.

The Quality of Governance

Especially in cross-country studies, unobserved heterogeneity may be one of the reasons why some of the estimates are not robust. In turn, one potential source of unobserved heterogeneity is related to unobserved differences in the efficiency of public spending—that is, the extent to which public spending actually translates into public services (such as teachers performing their duties in school and students learning more) and public infrastructure assets (such as roads being constructed). Ultimately, it is these types of public sector outputs that are critical for the transmission of public spending on growth. Roads, for example, do not simply lower transport costs but also provide access to schools, markets, and hospitals—all factors that contribute to long-run growth.

The efficiency of public spending may reflect both passive waste (such as inefficiency resulting from red tape or poor administrative capacity) and active waste, which directly benefits public decision makers because they use the resources for their own purposes (Bandiera, Prat, and Valletti 2009). However, evidence suggests that in developing countries it is often poor governance that results in low levels of public spending efficiency, implying that active waste may be of greater concern. In turn, the quality of governance is likely to differ among countries and possibly sectors, but it can only be measured imperfectly. This fact gives rise to unobserved heterogeneity in studies that estimate the growth impact of public spending. Bayraktar and Moreno-Dodson (2010) conjecture that the differences in the growth effects of public expenditure between fast-growing and other countries may result from differences in both the composition of public spending and the overall quality of governance. Rajkumar and Swaroop (2008) find that, with respect to social indicators, public spending in the health and education sectors has virtually no effects in poorly governed countries.

These results at the macroeconomic level mirror the results of public expenditure tracking surveys carried out by the World Bank. The surveys examine the efficiency of public spending at the microeconomic level by tracing the flow of public resources from origin to destination and determining the location and scale of anomaly. López-Cálix, Alcazar, and Wachtenheim (2002) reveal major leaks in the flow of resources toward the final beneficiaries of social programs in Peru. Reinikka and Svensson (2004) examine the efficiency of one particular component of education spending in Uganda in the 1990s. They find that the bulk of spending in this subcategory was partly captured by local government officials. Gauthier and Wane (2007) likewise report significant leakage in the health sector in Chad. In these cases, public resources as inputs are obviously a poor predictor of public sector outputs. This suggests that although the efficiency *and* the quality of public expenditure—that is, the composition of public expenditure—determine the growth effects of public spending, it is often low efficiency that is the primary concern of policy makers and the area in which improvements may have greater effects on growth.

However, anyone interpreting the results of econometric studies for policy purposes typically assumes that the efficiency of public spending cannot be addressed, at least implicitly. For example, studies may find that road expenditure has hardly any growth effects simply because the resources are not used for road construction. With low efficiency, these results may emerge even if road infrastructure has a high output elasticity. As a consequence, the policy implications of the studies essentially hold only in a second-best world and may be reversed when the efficiency changes. Similar results could arise in other sectors—for example, when the salaries of "ghost" teachers are diverted for other purposes.

One obvious but imperfect approach to dealing with the efficiency of public spending is to control for the quality of governance. López and Miller (2007) include an indicator of perceived corruption in their regressions, but find that their results do not change qualitatively. They take this as evidence that there is no systematic variation in the efficiency across sectors. However, it is unclear whether these types of governance indicators are a good measure of the efficiency of public spending and whether other indicators such as the Open Budget Index, which, however, is not available for longer time spans, are better measures in principle.

Increased Use of Subnational Expenditure Data

A considerable amount of research has been conducted on fiscal decentralization in developing countries. For example, Bird (2010) reviews the evidence on the most appropriate structure of regional and local taxes in developing countries. But only two studies—Rocha and Giuberti (2007) and Yan and Gong (2009)—use subnational fiscal policy data to estimate the growth effects of public expenditure. In contrast to the literature on fiscal decentralization, these studies exploit variation in subnational fiscal policy data, but they do not include a judgment of whether the system of fiscal decentralization is appropriate.

Although evidence based on subnational expenditure data is still scarce, depending on the number of observations, in many countries it would be possible to complement cross-country estimates with evidence based on subnational data for public expenditure reviews. The use of subnational fiscal policy data offers several advantages. First, country-specific studies are less prone to measurement error if subnational spending data are recorded by the central government (as is often the case) or if expenditure management systems do not differ among jurisdictions. Arguably, with data from one country, unobserved heterogeneity is also less likely to create problems. By contrast, the results of Bayraktar and Moreno-Dodson (2010) suggest that pooling data from heterogeneous countries may be problematic.

Second, in some cases the specific features of fiscal decentralization may offer a natural way to incorporate the government budget constraint in the empirical analysis, thereby allowing the provision of more credible empirical evidence. For example, in South Africa, and to a lesser extent in Bolivia, most taxes are levied by the central government. The rates, the schedule, and the laws for these taxes are identical across all subnational jurisdictions; conversely, many expenditure assignments are decentralized and vary from place to place.

Increased Use of Firm-Level Evidence

The macroeconomic-level growth outcomes of public spending are a consequence of the changes in aggregate investment and productivity that public spending induces. In the theoretical and empirical literatures on growth and development, productivity improvements have long been identified as a central source of long-run growth in the aggregate economy (Solow 1956; Romer 1990; Prescott 1998; Hall and Jones 1999; Easterly and Levine 2001). Such improvements are not only a consequence of fiscal policy but also driven by other factors such as exchange rate volatility, as shown by Aghion et al. (2009).

Ultimately, it is at the level of the individual firm that these improvements in productivity must take place. For example, there is a wealth of evidence supporting the productivity-improving (and -retarding) effects of trade liberalization, of foreign direct investment (whether as spillovers to domestic firms, from acquisition of domestic firms, or from offshoring parts of the production process), and of firms' decisions to export or invest in research and development.[16]

However, it is surprising that there is very little evidence on the effects of public spending at the firm level, especially because firm-level data are increasingly publicly available for many countries. Using productivity data for firms located in different jurisdictions that are subject to different expenditure policies (instead of aggregate growth) as the dependent variable is potentially an interesting avenue for research, especially from a policy perspective. First, the use of firm-level data may increase the robustness of the estimates, notably because there are typically many more observations available. And this is one approach to dealing with econometric issues, such as the simultaneity bias, because public spending can be seen as fully exogenous to the individual firm.[17] A potential disadvantage of firm- or industry-level studies is that they often miss out on any growth effects arising from externalities at the firm or industry level—for example, agglomeration effects, network externalities, or research and development spillovers.

Second, the use of firm-level data potentially offers additional policy-relevant insights. For example, the results from macroeconomic studies may be biased in the sense that the results are driven only by a small subset of firms, which may give rise to misleading policy implications. By contrast, firm-level data allow exploration of the role of firm characteristics in the transmission channels of fiscal policy. This type of information is potentially useful for policy making in practice, when public expenditure reforms can be tailored to firms in a particular jurisdiction.

To date, however, hardly any studies combine firm-level information with public spending data and consider the government budget constraint. The work of Kneller and Misch (2012) is one exception. They implicitly consider the government budget constraint and, using data from South Africa, find that firms with a relatively low capital intensity benefit to a much greater extent from reallocating public spending from unproductive to productive categories.

Use of Internationally Comparable Indicators for Public Expenditure Reforms

The empirical literature estimates the magnitude of the growth effects of various fiscal reforms. However, as a first step policy makers may be more interested in distinguishing growth-enhancing and growth-reducing public expenditure reforms or in rating reform options to identify the ones that are most conducive to growth. In this sense, the empirical literature is of limited help because it identifies only a few reforms (notably, an increase in productive expenditure) that typically seem to increase growth.

Because of these limitations, future research could explore whether economic indicators are potentially useful in evaluating public expenditure reforms ex ante. Examples of such indicators include the World Development Indicators, indicators from the Doing Business database, and data from the World Bank Enterprise Surveys—all of which provide information on the quality of public services, the level of infrastructure, and the tax system of a given country.

However, most of those indicators share a common problem: if they are considered in isolation, they provide little information that is useful for policy. For example, the mere fact that road infrastructure is poor in a given country does not necessarily imply that governments should change public expenditure in favor of public investment in roads; perhaps there also are severe problems in the education and health sectors and the private sector should be more involved in infrastructure projects. In addition, education and infrastructure indicators are measured using different units, so they cannot be compared directly. Future research could therefore address how economic indicators can be used as diagnostic tools to identify growth-enhancing public expenditure reforms.

The World Bank Enterprise Surveys include business executives' perceptions about whether and to what extent a particular issue that relates to fiscal policy represents an obstacle for the growth of the particular firm. The advantage of these indicators is that they measure different constraints on a single scale. Misch, Gemmell, and Kneller (2012) discuss how this type of information can be exploited for public expenditure policy. They show that, although business perception data do not provide reliable information on beneficial directions for policy reform in some cases, they can serve as guides for imperfectly informed policy makers in others.

Conclusion

Public spending is widely seen as central to growth. The empirical evidence generally confirms that both its level and composition affect growth. This chapter has presented policy-relevant estimates in a detailed and comparable way as a tool for policy makers who wish to estimate ex ante the growth effects of public spending reforms.

Yet, in practice, implementing growth-enhancing public expenditure reforms is still challenging. First, our discussion has shown that there is relatively little detailed, robust, and country-specific evidence that could be used as guidance for governments wishing to assess the effects of expenditure reforms ex ante. Second, in reality, changes in public expenditure policy often follow economic downturns—for example, because fiscal adjustments are needed or because governments implement fiscal stimulus packages aimed at smoothing short-run output fluctuations. This practice implies that expenditure reforms are not always motivated by the desire to promote growth.

With respect to the first issue, we have discussed several ideas that future research could address to improve the robustness of the estimates. We have argued in particular that policy-relevant research should tap innovative sources of information as alternative tools for growth-promoting public expenditure policy in practice. With respect to the second issue, we have reviewed country-level evidence from the 2008–09 global crisis. Our discussion suggests that expenditure reforms for short-run output stabilization through employment creation may be difficult to reconcile with the promotion of temporary long-run growth.

Notes

1. There is a large body of literature on the determinants of long-run growth. Other prominent contributions include Sachs and Warner (1995); Krueger (1998); Acemoglu, Johnson, and Robinson (2001); and Sachs (2001).

2. Agénor and Moreno-Dodson (2006) provide a detailed overview of the direct and indirect effects of public spending on infrastructure.

3. We recognize that, in some instances, there is private sector financing (through different agreements such as purchasing power parity or concessions) in public sector investment projects. However, the capital assets built may be considered part of the public sector portfolio when the government is the main owner, partner, or shareholder.

4. See, for example, the criticism by Temple (1999); Rodrik (2005); and Easterly, Irwin, and Servén (2007).

5. On the one hand, Turnovsky (2004), for example, using a simulation model with neoclassical properties, finds that "transitional" output adjustments to fiscal policy changes can take decades. On the other hand, the empirical estimates of convergence by Lee, Pesaran, and Smith (1997) for a panel of approximately 100 countries reveal that convergence to equilibrium may take as little as two to three years.

6. Not all endogenous growth models predict long-run growth effects from fiscal policy. These growth models are sometimes labeled "semi-endogenous" or "nonscale"—see Eicher and Turnovsky (1999).

7. For the purpose of this book, we use the term *public investment* to refer to public capital spending.

8. An example is Albala-Bertrand and Mamatzakis (2001). Time series models for individual developing countries are comparatively rare, largely reflecting the limited availability of suitable data. M'Amanja and Morrissey (2005) examine Kenya using an error correction model.

9. For recent examples, see Mountford and Uhlig (2009), Auerbach and Gorodnichenko (2010), and Beetsma and Giuliodori (2011).

10. The effect of bilateral switches between any two expenditure categories can generally be identified from the set of regressions, including each category in turn.

11. One notable exception is M'Amanja and Morrissey (2005), who use annual data from Kenya.

12. M'Amanja and Morrissey (2005), who use time series data, find that productive expenditure has negative growth effects. However, their finding may result from their definition of productive spending, which excludes any type of public investment.

13. We consider the negative of the estimated effects of increases in current expenditure offset by capital expenditure as equivalent to increases in capital expenditure offset by current expenditure.

14. See chapter 1 for a more detailed analysis and country examples.

15. In developed countries, implementation lags of public investment projects constrain countries' abilities to pursue a countercyclical fiscal policy by increasing public investment. The U.S. government recently recognized that the country has only a few shovel-ready projects and that this situation is causing significant delays in spending the money from the stimulus package. Therefore, given lower administrative capacity, it seems plausible that in developing countries such implementation lags also arise.

16. See the reviews by Tybout (2000), Görg and Greenaway (2004), Keller (2004), and Greenaway and Kneller (2007).

17. This holds as long as firms are sufficiently immobile between different jurisdictions, which is frequently the case because many firms in developing countries heavily depend on local input and output markets, thereby implying a high cost of relocation.

References

Acemoglu, D., S. Johnson, and J. Robinson. 2001. "The Colonial Origins of Comparative Development: An Empirical Investigation." *American Economic Review* 91 (5): 1369–1401.

Adam, C. S., and D. L. Bevan. 2005. "Fiscal Deficits and Growth in Developing Countries." *Journal of Public Economics* 89: 571–97.

Agénor, P.-R. 2005. "Infrastructure Investment and Maintenance Expenditure: Optimal Allocation Rules in a Growing Economy." Discussion Paper 060, Centre for Growth and Business Cycle Research, School of Economic Studies, University of Manchester, U.K.

Agénor, P.-R., and B. Moreno-Dodson. 2006. "Public Infrastructure and Growth: New Channels and Policy Implications." Policy Research Working Paper 4064, World Bank, Washington, DC.

Agénor, P.-R., and K. C. Neanidis. 2006. "The Allocation of Public Expenditure and Economic Growth." Discussion Paper 069, Centre for Growth and Business Cycle Research, School of Economic Studies, University of Manchester, U.K.

Aghion, P., P. Bacchetta, R. Rancière, and K. Rogoff. 2009. "Exchange Rate Volatility and Productivity Growth: The Role of Financial Development." *Journal of Monetary Economics* 56 (4): 494–513.

Albala-Bertrand, J. M., and E. C. Mamatzakis. 2001. "Is Public Infrastructure Productive? Evidence from Chile." *Applied Economics Letters* 8 (3): 195–98.

Arrow, K., and M. Kurz. 1970. *Public Investment, the Rate of Return, and Optimal Social Policy.* Baltimore, MD: Johns Hopkins Press.

Auerbach, A. J., and Y. Gorodnichenko. 2010. "Measuring the Output Responses to Fiscal Policy." Working Paper 16311, National Bureau of Economic Research, Cambridge, MA.

Bandiera, O., A. Prat, and T. Valletti. 2009. "Active and Passive Waste in Government Spending: Evidence from a Policy Experiment." *American Economic Review* 99 (4): 1278–308.

Barro, R. 1990. "Government Spending in a Simple Model of Endogenous Growth." *Journal of Political Economy* 98 (5): S103–26.

Bayraktar, N., and B. Moreno-Dodson. 2010. "How Can Public Spending Help You Grow? An Empirical Analysis for Developing Countries." Policy Research Working Paper 5367, World Bank, Washington, DC.

Beetsma, R. M. W. J., and M. Giuliodori. 2011. "The Effects of Government purchases Shocks: Review and Estimates for the EU." *Economic Journal* 121 (550): F4–32.

Beetsma, R. M. W. J., and H. Jensen. 2004. "Mark-up Fluctuations and Fiscal Policy Stabilization in a Monetary Union." *Journal of Macroeconomics* 26 (2): 357–76.

Bird, R. M. 2010. "Subnational Taxation in Developing Countries. A Review of the Literature." Policy Research Working Paper 5450, World Bank, Washington, DC.

Blanchard, O., and R. Perotti. 2002. "An Empirical Characterization of the Dynamic Effects of Changes in Government Spending and Taxes on Output." *Quarterly Journal of Economics* 117 (4): 1329–68.

Blankenau, W. F., and N. B. Simpson. 2004. "Public Education Expenditures and Growth." *Journal of Development Economics* 73 (2): 583–605.

Bose, N., M. E. Haque, and D. R. Osborn. 2007. "Public Expenditure and Economic Growth: A Disaggregated Analysis for Developing Countries." *Manchester School* 75 (5): 533–56.

Devarajan S., V. Swaroop, and H. Zou. 1996. "The Composition of Public Expenditure and Economic Growth." *Journal of Monetary Economics* 37 (2–3): 313–44.

Easterly, W., T. Irwin, and L. Servén. 2007. "Walking Up the Down Escalator: Public Investment and Fiscal Stability." Policy Research Working Paper 4158, World Bank, Washington, DC.

Easterly, W., and R. Levine. 2001. "What Have We Learned from a Decade of Empirical Research on Growth? It's Not Factor Accumulation: Stylized Facts and Growth Models." *World Bank Economic Review* 15 (2): 177–219.

Eicher, T. S., and S. Turnovsky. 1999. "Convergence Speeds and Transition Dynamics in Non-Scale Growth Models." *Journal of Economic Growth* 4: 413–28.

Eskesen, L. L. 2009. "Countering the Cycle—The Effectiveness of Fiscal Policy in Korea." Working Paper WP/09/249, International Monetary Fund, Washington, DC.

Feyzioglu, Tarhan. 2006. "Long-Term Fiscal Challenges." In *Republic of Korea: Selected Issues.* IMF Staff Country Report No. 06/381. Washington, DC: International Monetary Fund.

Feyzioglu, Tarhan, Michael Skaarup, and Murtaza Syed. 2008. "Addressing Korea's Long-Term Fiscal Challenges." Working Paper WP/08/27, International Monetary Fund, Washington, DC.

Futagami, K. Y., Y. Morita, and A. Shibata. 1993. "Dynamic Analysis of an Endogenous Growth Model with Public Capital." *Scandinavian Journal of Economics* 95 (4): 607–25.

Galí, J., J. Vallés, and J. D. López-Salido. 2007. "Understanding the Effects of Government Spending on Consumption." *Journal of the European Economic Association* 5 (1): 227–70.

Gauthier, B., and W. Wane. 2007. "Leakage of Public Resources in the Health Sector: An Empirical Investigation of Chad." Policy Research Working Paper 4351, World Bank, Washington, DC.

Ghosh, S., and A. Gregoriou. 2008. "The Composition of Government Spending and Growth: Is Current or Capital Spending Better?" *Oxford Economic Papers* 60 (3): 484–516.

Ghosh, S., and I. A. Mourmouras. 2002. "On Public Investment, Long-Run Growth and the Real Exchange Rate." *Oxford Economic Papers* 54 (1): 72–90.

Görg, H., and D. Greenaway. 2004. "Much Ado about Nothing? Do Domestic Firms Really Benefit from Foreign Direct Investment?" *World Bank Research Observer* 19 (2): 171–97.

Greenaway, D., and R. Kneller. 2007. "Industry Differences in the Effect of Export Market Entry: Learning by Exporting?" *Review of World Economics* 143 (3): 416–32.

Gupta, S., B. Clements, E. Baldacci, and C. Mulas-Granados. 2005. "Fiscal Policy, Expenditure Composition, and Growth in Low-Income Countries." *Journal of International Money and Finance* 24 (3): 441–63.

Hall, R., and C. Jones. 1999. "Why Do Some Countries Produce So Much More Output Per Worker Than Others?" *Quarterly Journal of Economics* 114 (1): 83–116.

Haque, M. E. 2004. "The Composition of Public Expenditures and Economic Growth in Developing Countries." *Global Journal of Finance and Economics* 1 (1): 97–117.

Heller, P. S. 2005. "Understanding Fiscal Space." Policy Discussion Paper 05/4, International Monetary Fund, Washington, DC.

Hong, H., and S. Ahmed. 2009. "Government Spending on Public Goods: Evidence on Growth and Poverty." *Economic and Political Weekly* 44 (31): 102–08.

Horton, Mark, Manmohan Kumar, and Paolo Mauro. 2009. "The State of Public Finances: A Cross-Country Fiscal Monitor." IMF Staff Position Note SPN/09/21, International Monetary Fund, Washington, DC.

IMF (International Monetary Fund). 2010. "Emerging from the Global Crisis: Macroeconomic Challenges Facing Low-Income Countries." Public Information Notice 10/148, IMF, Washington, DC. http://www.imf.org/external/np/sec/pn/2010/pn10148.htm.

Keller, W. 2004. "International Technology Diffusion." *Journal of Economic Literature* 42 (3): 752–82.

Kim, Chuk Kyo. 2008. "The Growth Pattern of Central Government Expenditure in Korea." In *Korea's Development Policy Experience and Implications for Developing Countries*, ed. Chuk Kyo Kim. Seoul: Korea Institute for International Economic Policy.

Kneller, R., M. Bleaney, and N. Gemmell. 1999. "Fiscal Policy and Growth: Evidence from OECD Countries." *Journal of Public Economics* 74 (2): 171–90.

Kneller, R., and F. Misch. 2012. "The Composition of Public Spending and Firm Productivity: Evidence from South Africa." http://www.zew.de.

Krueger, A. 1998. "Why Trade Liberalisation Is Good for Growth." *Economic Journal* 108 (450): 1513–22.

Lee, K., M. H. Pesaran, and R. Smith. 1997. "Growth and Convergence in a Multi-Country Empirical Stochastic Solow Model." *Journal of Applied Econometrics* 12: 357–92.

López, R., and S. Miller. 2007. *The Structure of Public Expenditure: A Robust Predictor of Economic Development?* College Park, MD: University of Maryland.

López-Cálix, J. R., L. Alcazar, and E. Wachtenheim. 2002. *Peru: Public Expenditure Tracking Study*. Washington, DC: World Bank. http://siteresources.worldbank.org/INTPUBSERV/Resources/peru.pets.concept.sep9.2002.pdf.

M'Amanja, D., and O. Morrissey. 2005. "Fiscal Policy and Economic Growth in Kenya." CREDIT (Centre for Research in Economic Development and International Trade) Research Paper 05/06, University of Nottingham, U.K.

McCord, A. 2002. "Public Works as a Response to Labour Market Failure in South Africa." Working Paper 019, Southern Africa Labour and Development Research Unit, University of Cape Town, South Africa.

Ministry of Strategy and Finance, Republic of Korea. 2010. "Korea's Fiscal Policy: Countering the Crisis and Rebuilding for the Future." http://www.mosf.go.kr.

Misch, F., N. Gemmell, and R. Kneller. 2012. *Firm-Based Diagnostics for Fiscal Policy Reform*. Mannheim, Germany: Center for European Economic Research. http://www.zew.de.

Mountford, A., and H. Uhlig. 2009. "What Are the Effects of Fiscal Policy Shocks?" *Journal of Applied Econometrics* 24 (6): 960–92.

Nijkamp, P., and J. Poot. 2004. "Meta-analysis of the Effects of Fiscal Policies on Long-Run Growth." *European Journal of Political Economy* 20: 91–124.

Perotti, R. 2002. "Estimating the Effects of Fiscal Policy in OECD Countries." Working Paper 276, Bocconi University and Innocenzo Gasparini Institute for Economic Research, Milan, Italy.

Prescott, E. C. 1998. "Needed: A Theory of Total Factor Productivity." *International Economic Review* 39 (3): 525–51.

Rajkumar, A. S., and V. Swaroop. 2008. "Public Spending and Outcomes: Does Governance Matter?" *Journal of Development Economics* 86: 96–111.

Reinikka, R., and J. Svensson. 2004. "Local Capture: Evidence from a Central Government Transfer Program in Uganda." *Quarterly Journal of Economics* 119 (2): 679–705.

Rocha, F., and A. C. Giuberti. 2007. "Composição do gasto público e crescimento econômico: uma avaliação macroeconômica da qualidade dos gastos dos Estados brasileiros." *Economia Aplicada* 11 (4): 463–85.

Rodrik, D. 2003. "Institutions, Integration, and Geography: In Search of the Deep Determinants of Economic Growth." In *In Search of Prosperity: Analytical Narratives on Economic Growth*, ed. D. Rodrik. Princeton, NJ: Princeton University Press.

_____. 2005. *Why We Learn Nothing from Regressing Economic Growth on Policies.* Cambridge, MA: John F. Kennedy School of Government, Harvard University. http://www.hks.harvard.edu.

Romer, P. 1990. "Endogenous Technological Change." *Journal of Political Economy* 98 (5): S71–102.

Romp, W. and J. de Haan. 2007. "Public Capital and Economic Growth: A Critical Survey." *Perspektiven der Wirtschaftspolitik* 8 (S1): 6–52.

Sachs, J. 2001. "Tropical Underdevelopment." Working Paper 8199, National Bureau of Economic Research, Cambridge, MA.

Sachs, J., and A. Warner. 1995. "Economic Reform and the Process of Global Integration." *Brookings Papers on Economic Activity* 26: 1–118.

Semmler, W., A. Greiner, B. Diallo, A. Rezai, and A. Rajaram. 2007. "Fiscal Policy, Public Expenditure Composition and Growth." Policy Research Working Paper 4405, World Bank, Washington, DC.

Solow, R. 1956. "A Contribution to the Theory of Economic Growth." *Quarterly Journal of Economics* 70 (1): 65–94.

Straub, S. 2008. "Infrastructure and Development: A Critical Appraisal of the Macro-Level Literature." Policy Research Working Paper 4590. World Bank, Washington, DC.

Temple, J. 1999. "The New Growth Evidence." *Journal of Economic Literature* 37 (1): 112–56.

Turnovsky, S. J. 2004. "The Transitional Dynamics of Fiscal Policy: Long-Run Capital Accumulation and Growth." *Journal of Money, Credit and Banking* 36: 883–910.

Tybout, J. 2000. "Manufacturing Firms in Developing Countries: How Well Do They Do, and Why?" *Journal of Economic Literature* 38 (1): 11–44.

Yan, C., and L. Gong. 2009. "Government Expenditure, Taxation and Long-Run Growth." *Frontiers of Economics in China* 4 (4): 505–25.

CHAPTER 3

Public Investment Management Challenges and Tools

James Brumby and Kai Kaiser

Governments usually rely on a diverse portfolio of public assets—roads, bridges, power, telecommunications, schools, clinics, ports, airports, and administrative buildings—to boost social welfare. However, their responses to the recent global crisis worldwide have highlighted their need to more effectively execute public investments so they can achieve their economic and social progress goals. As indicated in chapter 2, from one analytical viewpoint the separation of current and capital public spending is neither straightforward nor desirable in most countries because both types of spending complement each other in triggering an impact on growth and social welfare. The nature of public investment projects and the high share of the budget they represent, especially in developing countries, require special attention, notably in building an adequate institutional capacity for their management.

In addition to economic crises, the frequent natural disasters—floods, earthquakes, tsunamis—considerably affecting developing countries, and the chronic challenge of mitigating and adapting to climate change, point to the need to have adequate physical capital assets to prevent economic and human disasters. Moreover, as indicated in chapter 4, in resource-rich countries, increasing commodity prices, coupled with new resource discoveries, raise the question of whether the value of assets below the ground is being translated into the value of assets above the ground.

When governments are facing crises and other external shocks, public spending generally is an attractive centerpiece for fiscal policy, especially when directed at projects intended to shore up economic stability in the short term while laying the foundation for longer-term growth. However, the significant complexity and institutional demands associated with physical asset creation, maintenance, and utilization[1] indicate that, in fact, in the absence of highly capable administrations, public investment does not always increase the government's stock of physical capital assets.[2]

Although there is consensus around the centrality of public investments to growth and social welfare,[3] in many developing countries deep concerns remain about the inefficiency of public investment projects, the ability of administrations to create value-for-money assets, and the lack of champions to push an agenda to improve public investment management (PIM).

Some estimates suggest that a typical unit of spending in developing countries translates into only half a unit of value of the corresponding physical capital assets (Gupta et al. 2011).[4] These low-efficiency ratios spur ongoing concerns about the ability to address the massive gaps in physical capital assets that exist worldwide, most notably in developing economies (Foster and Briceño-Garmendia 2010). Aggregate levels of government spending have typically been at the center of fiscal policy discussions, including debt sustainability analysis, but now there is a growing empirical and policy focus on the particular challenges of and options for improving public investment and its different management modalities. Those challenges go way beyond those associated with central government investments and include specific challenges associated with megaprojects (Flyvbjerg, Bruzeliua, and Rothengatter 2003), public-private partnerships (Schwartz, Corbacho, and Funke 2008), state-owned enterprises (SOEs), and subnational governments.

It is our contention that although the potential returns to good-quality public investments are high, the challenge to building productive public assets efficiently remains deep seated and pervasive. Presented in figure 3.1, the flash survey of policy practitioners attending a 2011 gathering is indicative of the challenge posed to government administrators by public investments.

The objective of this chapter is to highlight the diverse institutional underpinnings shaping the quality of public investment and to make the case for strengthening PIM. The prevailing era of fiscal austerity and constrained financing facing many governments is exacerbating the challenges associated with *funding, managing,* and *executing* public investments.

Figure 3.1   A Flash Survey of the Public Investment Management (PIM) Challenge

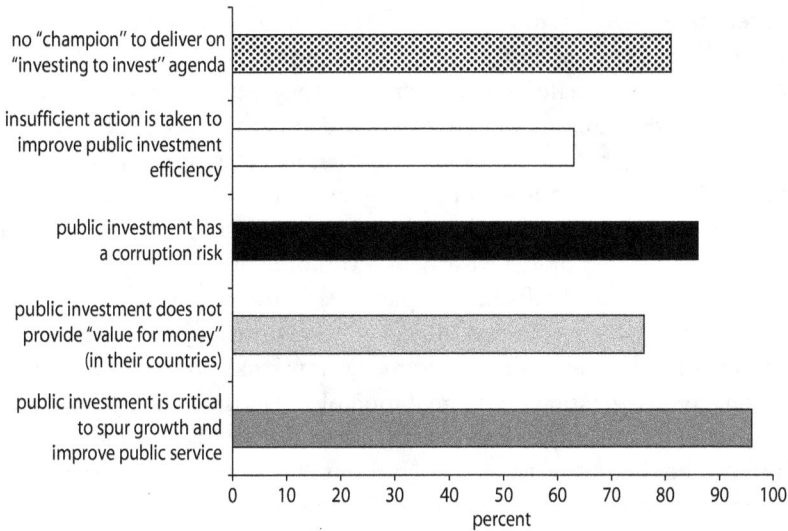

Source: Grant Thornton 2011.
Note: Graph shows percentage of respondents agreeing with the statements.

We present a stylized framework in which to outline the modalities of PIM, notwithstanding the government's roles as manager, financier, and regulator. This framework highlights the various processes associated with public investment. Looking beyond the 2008–09 global crisis, we identify strategies and reform priorities for managing public investment during times of exceptional economic volatility and reducing inefficiencies in public investment viewed from a sector balance sheet perspective.[5]

This chapter has five sections. The first section assesses the diversity of revealed policy measures by governments related to capital spending in the aftermath of the recent global crisis. The second section frames the discussion on public investment around the key objective of improving its efficiency. The third section presents the basic framework by Rajaram et al. (2010) that sets out the key elements for effective management of the project cycle "value chain." It focuses on the results of creating and preserving the productive stock of public physical capital assets. The fourth section offers a selective review of the instruments and entry points available to strengthen the institutional capability for improved PIM.

Public Investment and the Recent Global Crisis

Government investment appears to have been on a steady upward trend across the globe over the last decade.[6] One factor driving this observed trend was governments' recognition that they needed to fill the infrastructure gaps undermining growth and competitiveness. Public investment was a prominent feature of the menu of response options to the recent global crisis both in supporting an initial stimulus and in setting the basis for a future rebounding of growth prospects. Figure 3.2 suggests that the aggregate public investment levels of all income country groups increased significantly after 2008, particularly the high-income group.

The ability of governments to scale-up investments was largely contingent on the availability of "shovel ready" investment projects as well as options for accelerating implementation of the existing investment portfolios, and that ability varied widely by country (Ferris and Thomas 2009). The figures suggest a significant acceleration of government investment after 2008, potentially reflecting countercyclical fiscal policy objectives. Currently, the fiscal position of governments to finance investment continues to be quite diverse by country and region. Several large economies, such as Japan and some European countries, are significantly constrained in resorting to further stimulus, as measured by prevailing debt levels, fiscal sustainability analysis, and debt premiums.[7]

Figure 3.2   Public Investment Trends by Income Group, 1998–2009

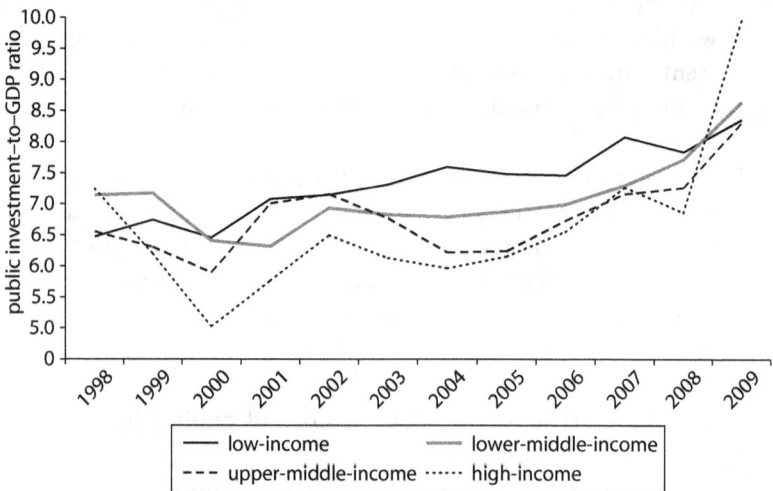

Source: IMF World Economic Outlook Database.

Table 3.1 summarizes cross-country government investment patterns (levels, government contribution to overall investment, and investment as a share of total government spending) and reveals significant diversity as well as outliers.[8] Also, a number of intermediate indicators, such as the Dabla-Norris PIM indicators and the Open Budget Transparency index, provide information about the conditioning institutional environment for public investments. In addition, an infrastructure quality indicator is included. As a component of its Global Competitiveness Index, the World Economic Forum (WEF) (2010) rates a country's overall infrastructure quality from 1 to 7, focusing on transport, telephony, and energy.[9]

A closer analysis of international public investment trends underscores the diversity of revealed responses, while raising questions about the conditioning dynamics behind these observed patterns. Figure 3.3 plots the percentage point change in government investment as a share of investment against initial investment levels for 2008–09. Again, the graph highlights significant dispersion and varying responses. Many of the countries showing very high increases in investment levels, such as

Table 3.1   Selected Country Capital Spending Trajectories and Budget Credibility

	Mean	Min	Max	Sd	Obs
Inputs					
Govt investment (% GDP, 2008)	6.9	1.4	26.4	4.6	152
Govt investment (% GDP, 2008)	7.8	1.3	43.0	5.8	150
Govt investment (% total investment, 2008)	28.6	5.2	93.0	18.2	150
Govt investment (% total investment, 2008)	32.9	4.8	87.3	18.7	148
Govt investment (% govt spending, 2008)	23.7	2.6	126.5	16.8	151
Govt investment (% govt spending, 2008)	24.4	2.6	104.5	16.9	149
Resource rents (per capita, 2008)	1,850	—	85,849	7,752	207
Resource revenues (%, GDP)	35	—	94	32	60
ODA (per capita US$, 2008)	94	—	2,768	261	207
Institutional quality					
Checks and balances (DPI)	3.0	1.0	17.0	1.9	169
Budget transparency (OBI)	42.3	0.0	92.3	24.6	93
PIMI (Dabla-Norris et al. 2011)	1.7	0.3	3.5	0.6	71
Infrastructure outcomes					
Infrastructure quality (WEF 2010)	4.3	2.0	6.8	1.2	135
Other					
Per capita income level (WDI)	13,007	319	91,379	15,356	167

Sources: IMF, World Bank's Database of Political Institutions (DPI), Open Budget Institute (OBI), World Economic Forum (WEF 2010), World Bank's World Development Indicators (WDI).

Note: Table shows summary statistics for observed values. — = not available; GDP = gross domestic product; Govt = government; Max = maximum; Min = minimum; Obs = observed; ODA = official development assistance; PIMI = Public Investment Management Index; Sd = standard.

Figure 3.3   Public Investment Levels and the Global Crisis, 2008–09

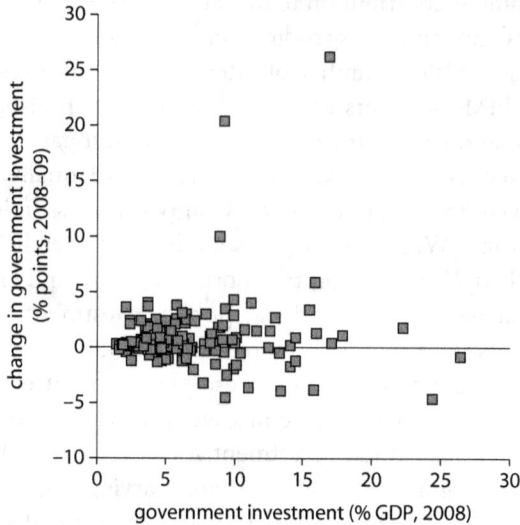

Source: IMF World Economic Outlook database.
Note: Squares represent the change in government investment levels as percentage points of gross domestic product (GDP).

Kuwait and São Tomé and Príncipe, were arguably associated with commodity windfalls, while others, such as the United States, reflect a conscious stimulus decision. Overall, the change in investment volumes was very weakly associated with preexisting stocks. However, this result is driven significantly by a number of outliers. Many of those countries (for example, Iraq, Angola, Libya, and Algeria) are also heavily dependent on oil revenues, and so these results reflect collapsing oil prices and different fiscal adjustments in 2009.

Although the available evidence provides some insights into the observed patterns of public investments and the global crisis, further case studies and systematic econometric analysis could help further elucidate observed patterns.[10]

Since the crisis, there has been a renewed policy interest in creating and maintaining economic and socially productive capital assets across the globe, focusing on both leveraging private sector resources and improving public sector resource allocation and regulatory decision making to fill the remaining gaps. Although previous periods of economic crisis and fiscal adjustment have been associated with public investment volatility, the most recent crisis was overlaid with a sense of previous underinvestment (Easterly, Irwin, and Servén 2008).

From the starting position in 2008, public infrastructure spending was not necessarily well placed as an outlet for fiscal stimulus because of the long lead times associated with developing and implementing good-quality projects through the many ways that projects actually come to fruition. Country experiences with capital spending during the crisis also revealed some of the considerations and trade-offs in using public investment for countercyclical fiscal policy. A number of countries implemented additional capital spending increments of several points of GDP but of a lesser magnitude and with some delays following the initial pronouncements. For example, under the U.S. stimulus plan, US$45 billion was appropriated for infrastructure projects by the U.S. Department of Transportation, but only 62 percent (US$28 billion) had actually been spent by June 2011 (de Rugy and Mitchell 2011). Because of the lags in public investment execution, policy makers need to think realistically about whether capital spending can be used for countercyclical policy and financing a recovery.[11]

The Challenge of Improving the Efficiency of Public Investments

Difficulties are associated with measuring the stock of public investment and the annual flows related to adding to or using up those stocks. Whereas debates about fiscal policy settings have tended to focus on flows of (capital and current) public spending, a comparative international analysis should consider both flows and stocks. Flows reflect the resources devoted to fixed capital formation and the costs associated with its use and maintenance. The most comprehensive international data currently available are from the *World Economic Outlook* (WEO) series published by the International Monetary Fund (IMF). Poor initial asset quality and operations and maintenance practices can reduce the service life of the public capital stock because of premature depreciation (for example, roads washing away in the rainy season) and also diminish the flow of actual service from the asset (for example, schools without books or hospitals without medical equipment) for the period it is in service.[12]

Whereas the ratio of public investment spending to GDP measures the flow of spending, the WEF index is a broad measure of the quality and quantity of the capital stock.[13] Figure 3.4 presents both variables, showing a large degree of international heterogeneity by economy and hinting

Figure 3.4 Government Investment and Infrastructure Quality

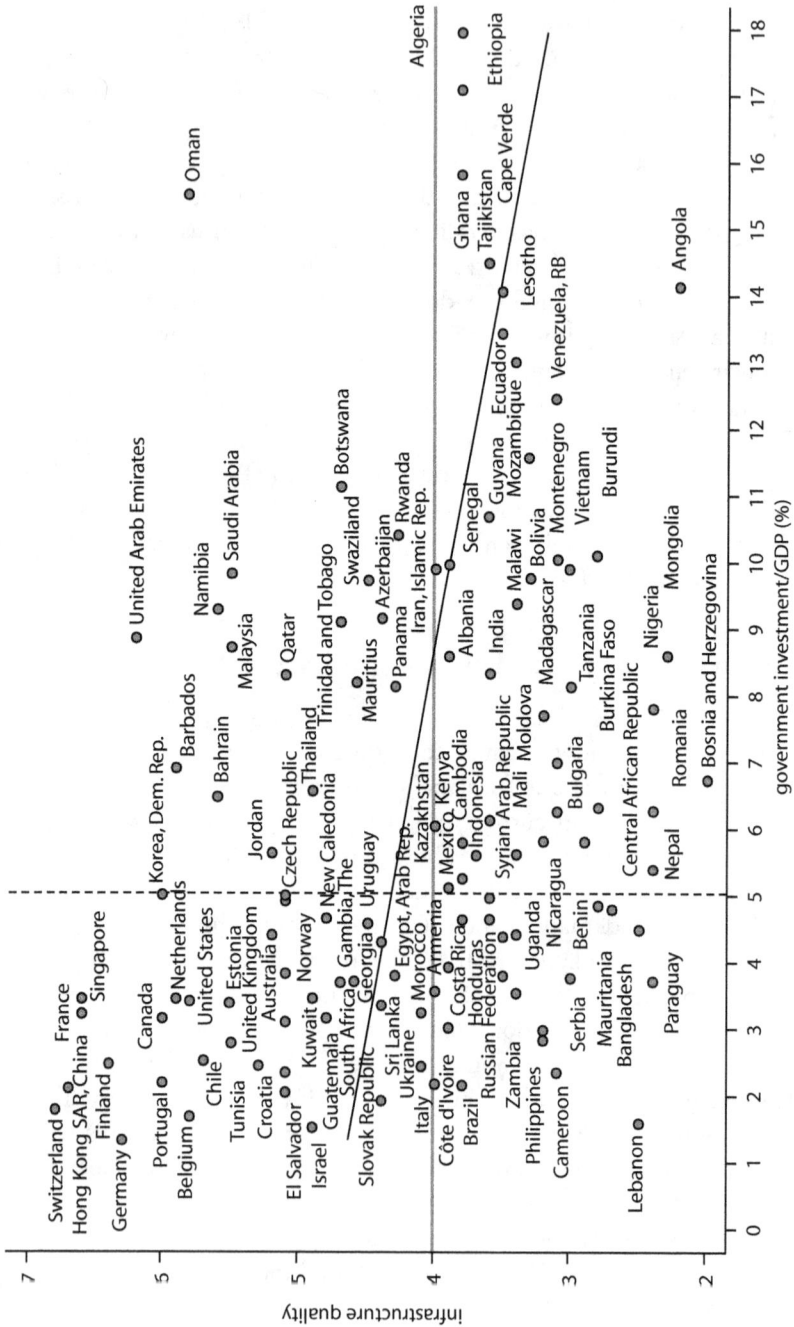

Sources: Quality of overall infrastructure: WEF 2010; government investment/GDP: IMF 2011.

Note: GDP = gross domestic product; vertical and horizontal lines indicate medians.

at the diversity of prevailing initial conditions. As countries attempt to catch up, it is expected that those with poor infrastructure stocks will need to allocate higher levels of public investment. The opposite is true for countries with preexisting large endowments. Figure 3.4 suggests, for example, that Switzerland (in the top left-hand quadrant) has achieved a high stock of physical capital and, as a ratio of its GDP, is devoting lower amounts to additions or replacements of existing investments.

For many developing countries, the infrastructure stock is more limited to start with, and the demand for net additions is likely to be greater, particularly relative to prevailing income. The extent to which governments are efficient in investing and yielding service value from those assets will determine the extent to which they are improving their "real" balance sheet.[14]

Dabla-Norris et al. (2011) have constructed a PIM Index (PIMI) for 71 low- and middle-income countries (LICs and MICs, respectively), drawing on information from 2007 to 2010. The index is based on 17 subindicators used to score four major consecutive phases associated with PIM: (1) strategic guidance and project appraisal, (2) project selection, (3) project management and implementation, and (4) project evaluation and audit.[15] Applying this index further using IMF WEO flow data, Gupta et al. (2011) construct an "efficiency-adjusted" measure of the capital stock, which has a stronger link to output compared with unadjusted measures.[16] Measured over the period 2000–09, efficiency/PIM-adjusted capital stocks are significantly lower: 36.1 percent versus 80.2 percent of GDP for the PIMI sample, 30.1 percent versus 71.0 percent for the LIC subsample, and 44.4 percent versus 93.2 percent for the MIC subsample. The exercise suggests that in the whole sample of developing countries, only about half of the investment effort translates into productive capital stocks.[17]

The efficiency of public investment spending is also likely to decrease as its volume increases (van der Ploeg 2011, 5). This may be true in the context of higher investment stemming from a natural resource windfall or a fiscal stimulus. Drawing on parameters from Gupta et al. (2011), van der Ploeg (2011) finds that a doubling of public investment levels from 6.56 percent to 13.12 percent pushes a (normalized) PIMI down from 0.47 percent to 0.31 percent.

Significant anecdotal evidence suggests that there are massive inefficiencies in public investment because of leakages that channel funds away from their intended purposes. Poor countries with weak institutions and high levels of corruption are especially vulnerable. One strand of the empirical public finance literature suggests that, although weak institutions may skew public spending toward notional public investments, including infrastructure, these sectors may be especially suited or prone to rent seeking. Tanzi and Davoodi (1997), using a 1980–95 panel data set, find that higher levels of corruption are associated with higher levels of public investment, lower levels of operations and maintenance expenditure, and poor infrastructure quality. In the same vein, Keefer and Knack (2007) investigate whether lower levels of checks and balances on governments are associated with higher levels of public investment. Using a 1974–98 averaged cross-sectional data set and an instrumental variables approach, the authors find that public investment is higher in countries with weak governance institutions and more limited checks and balances. Delavallade (2006) conducts a panel analysis of 64 countries from 1996 to 2001 and finds that higher levels of corruption divert spending away from social expenditures (for example, health, education, and social protection) toward other public services such as fuel and energy. The author argues that social sectors may offer less opportunity for embezzlement than those that are more intensive in physical capital. Thus expenditures are skewed away from those sectors.

The cross-country empirical literature provides only indirect evidence of potential leakages in public spending when viewed from the perspective of ultimate asset creation. How large are these impacts? Keefer and Knack (2007) suggest that a decrease of one point in the quality of governance (on a four-point scale) increases investment by 0.286 percent of GDP, after controlling for per capita income. This finding suggests that, under current measures, Uganda will have "excess" investment of over half a percentage point over the Republic of Korea.

Reforms in public financial management (PFM) have sought to overcome a number of weaknesses associated with dual budgeting across capital and recurrent expenditures (Jacobs 2008). These weaknesses include inadequate forward budgeting for making operational use of capital assets (for example, teachers for schools, road maintenance). Although significant progress has been made in promoting more integrated budgeting, there is also a need to appreciate the particular challenges associated with PIM.

Illuminating the "Black Box" of PIM

Projected infrastructure needs over the next decade are massive. Illustrative estimates suggest that for developing countries these could be on the order of US$1.2–1.5 trillion per year in 2015, or 5–6 percent of GDP, and closer to 15 percent in poorer countries.[18] Sub-Saharan Africa will require almost US$98 billion per year, and almost half of that gap is unfunded even in the face of a series of first-order measures (Foster and Briceño-Garmendia 2010). Technological change and associated national competitiveness pressures, as well as growing concerns about climate change and adaptation, are posing new challenges for public and private sectors alike.

Under the banner of "spending for the future" and "investing to invest," policy makers at the country and global levels are increasingly emphasizing the need to strengthen institutional arrangements associated with investment to improve their countries' productive capital stock and to leverage scarce financial resources. Public investment efficiency is influenced by a range of government fiscal and regulatory actions, as well as a diversity of other factors, as highlighted earlier. Moving from left to right, figure 3.5 sets out a basic framework to capture the various modalities of public investment financing, implementation, and outcomes. In practice, the performance of these modalities will shape results in terms of both public capital assets and the liabilities and risks associated with them.

The prevailing and prospective importance of each modality in generating particular types of public capital assets may vary significantly across

Figure 3.5   Public Investment Modalities

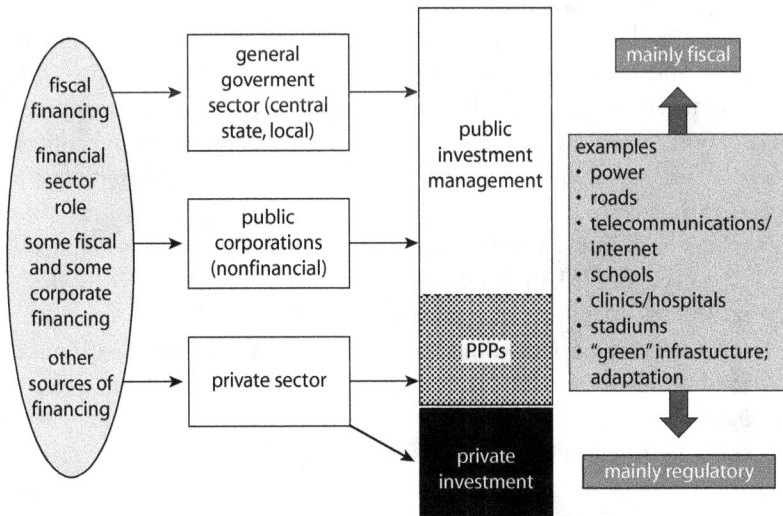

Source: Authors.
Note: PPP = public-private partnership.

country settings. For example, over two-thirds of investments in Organisation for Economic Co-operation and Development (OECD) settings are executed by subnational governments (Bloechinger et al. 2010). Managing PIM across levels of government entails diverse combinations of varying roles and responsibilities across the project cycle and across different segments of the project portfolio. Careful attention must therefore be paid to the institutional arrangements, contexts, and, above all, incentives by which projects are created and maintained.[19] The institutional arrangements associated with a public investment project cycle provide a useful way of unbundling the various potential bottlenecks to its execution but also of thinking about the aggregate challenges of managing a portfolio of diverse projects across a range of different modalities. Rajaram et al. (2010) present eight key steps through which an investment project would ideally pass to yield an economical and social productive public asset (also see chapter 4). This framework allows assessment of the weakest links in the process.

A growing body of contributions by PFM practitioners and policy research has highlighted a number of commonly observed challenges and symptoms associated with translating public finance resources into productive and sustained public assets. Petrie (2010) synthesizes case study evidence from almost two dozen PIM country case studies and develops a country typology covering advanced, emerging, low-income, resource-rich, and fragile settings. These case studies highlight the diversity in existing public capital endowments as a starting point; the available fiscal resources (and associated volatility); and the strength of public finance, political, and bureaucratic institutions and the capacity associated with generating and preserving public physical capital assets. The development of a country's construction industry and access to international contractors also affect the potential cost, timeliness, and quality countries confront in generating public infrastructure. Cutting across all these challenges is likely to be some degree of debate over form versus function in key aspects of PIM, or "good enough" arrangements, notably for developing country settings (Grindle 2007).

Here we briefly review three policy challenges associated with public investment. The first relates to the *optimal assignment of roles and responsibilities* for the creation and preservation of physical capital public assets across different agencies and levels of government. The second relates to striking an optimal *balance between the different stages of project selection and management*—from strategic planning to budgetary allocation, project design and inception, and completion. The third consists of *balancing fiscal resource allocation and execution for capital assets.* Associated with this is the desire to meet fiscal constraints through top-down budget reforms, while providing resources to meet the "bottom-up" challenges of project portfolio prioritization and implementation, typically across decentralized agencies and levels of government.

More in-depth analysis of practice in each of these areas suggests the need for careful attention to institutional design, and in particular to the prevailing bureaucratic and broader political economy considerations. Successful outcomes will ultimately have to be incentive compatible with the prevailing political economy of fiscal policy and the "PIM subsystem."

In the *optimal assignment of roles and responsibilities,* PFM reforms since the 1980s and 1990s have strongly emphasized dismantling the dual budgeting processes (current and capital) in place in many posttransition and newly independent developing countries. A main risk of dual budgeting was that it tended to neglect medium- to longer-term operations and maintenance expenditure needs. There appears to be growing recognition that, because of some of the features of capital spending (discretion, myopia, seesaw effects, and execution transaction costs), special attention should be paid to the institutional arrangements for capital spending and the associated operating expenditures, particularly in developing country settings. A potentially emerging concern is whether many governments have adequate capacity to engage in comprehensive and strategic national public investment planning and execution that are consistent with the rest of the budget over the medium term.[20]

In this context, the assignment of some capital spending to subnational levels of government is relevant. Although such assignment may promise greater responsiveness to local needs through better local information, framing these decisions in the context of limited territorial constituencies can risk generating a fragmented portfolio of suboptimally small projects. From a top-down budgeting and financing perspective, it will be important to determine the actual allocation role played by subnational decision making or whether allocation is primarily determined by higher levels of government (for example, as part of transfer design). Higher levels of government may play a regulatory or direct role in various aspects of the PIM value chain. Mongolia, for example, has recently sought ways to meet the large-scale infrastructure needs associated with the development of its mineral sector versus meeting the needs of individual parliamentary constituencies (Hasnain 2011).

Regarding the *different stages of project selection and management*, significant attention has been paid to enhancing the ex ante appraisal function (see Fontaine 1997), but there is also increasing appreciation of the potential challenges posed by other links in the PIM chain. Well-designed and well-appraised projects are likely to be better implemented. However, a number of factors may lead the initial cost of a project to be underestimated and subsequently inflated. Flyvbjerg (2007) highlights the prevalence of significant cost overruns for megaprojects even in advanced settings and the institutional and political complexity of reforms that could enhance large-scale project implementation (Priemus, Flyvbjerg, and Van Weer 2008). If the ex post costs of a project are quite divergent from the ex ante estimates, appraisal techniques are likely to be seriously undermined, especially if there are significant differences in the costs projected versus the actual costs across sectors or size of projects.[21]

Figure 3.6 presents evidence from a recent sample of cross-country projects in terms of project cost and time overruns compared with the original estimates (CoST 2011b). Inaccurate estimates of the costs of projects may pose significant challenges for ministries of finance in charge of the annual budget preparation and execution vis-à-vis the sectoral ministries executing the budget.[22] Strengthening the initial gatekeeping

Figure 3.6   Cost and Time Overruns, CoST Baseline Sample

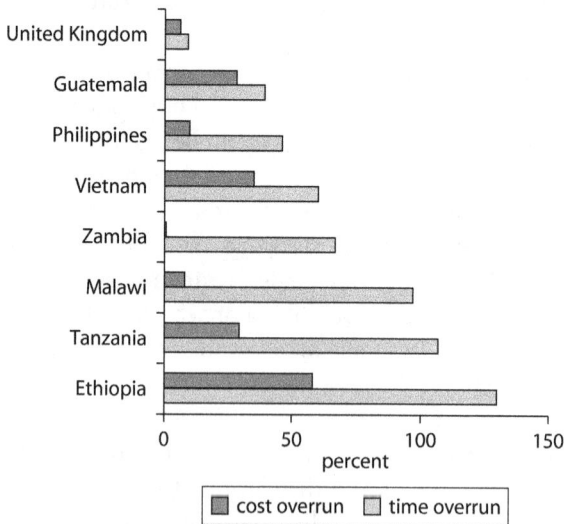

Source: CoST 2011b, 3.

functions for projects entering the budget remains a priority for many countries.

Indicators of time and cost overruns provide one set of evidence-based performance indicators for public investment. A further challenge centers on the adequacy of the operations and maintenance expenditures relative to the existing public capital stock as well as projected capital expenditures. Underspending on operations will lead to suboptimal levels of public capital stock depreciation, beyond the expected "service value" of a project. The literature points to a variety of hypotheses on relative over- or underspending of capital, as well as operations and maintenance expenditures. Suboptimal spending is manifested not only in the public investment levels but also in the excessive volatility and lack of predictability in the budget planning and execution envelopes. Poor and excessively volatile "top-down" fiscal policy for operations and capital in terms of levels and predictability in the context of the annual budget cycle can significantly strain effective PIM and ultimately the creation and operation of productive assets.

Finally, regarding the *allocation and execution of resources for public investments*, project portfolio budget planning and execution are ideally nested in a medium-term expenditure framework (MTEF) that allows linking inputs with outputs and outcomes.[23]

Significant roles for subnational governments in capital spending also add an intergovernmental dimension to budgeting and execution. We seek to address the interplay of both these top-down and bottom-up decentralized processes in capital expenditure realization.

Three factors may make capital spending especially vulnerable to lack of predictability or greater volatility, including relative to other types of expenditure (see box 3.1). First, capital spending could be *discretionary*.[24] Second, politicians that shape government actions may be subject to *myopia* and thus may excessively discount the longer-run growth and poverty reduction impacts of investment. Capital spending can be especially prone to seesaw and ratcheting effects.[25] Third, capital spending is often associated with *high transaction costs*. This means that poor planning and implementation will manifest itself in weak annual execution rates.

Figure 3.7 captures the capital expenditure fiscal policy along the dimensions of spending levels and volatility/lack of annual predictability. Yardsticks for whether country capital spending is too low or too high will depend on country conditions. Developing countries with low capital-to-labor ratios will arguably merit far higher levels of spending relative to GDP, especially if infrastructure has been identified as a binding

Box 3.1

Is Annual Public Investment Too Volatile?

Cross-country analysis of annual public investment spending levels during the global crisis reveals a significant degree of diversity. From a fiscal policy point of view, it is exceptionally difficult to assess the extent to which these flows are optimal. Low spending in the face of large infrastructure gaps might suggest the need for additional spending. Higher spending may imply a significant degree of waste. The pressures of countercyclical fiscal stimulus policies would argue for an upward trajectory of public investment, whereas excessive sovereign debt and risk levels would argue for reining in public investment spending. The experience of Latin America during the 1980s, however, suggests that excessive reductions of public investment due to financial constraints can be self-defeating from a longer-run growth perspective (Easterly, Irwin, and Servén 2008).

Cross-country data suggest that public investment spending is far more volatile than overall spending. This shows the volatility of capital expenditure and of total expenditure in 149 countries during 2000–10. Developed countries experienced less volatility of capital spending than developing countries. Among developing countries, resource-rich countries appear to have more volatility of capital spending. A series of hypotheses can be developed to explain why this is so and what can be inferred from this about the quality of budgeting and budget execution for public investment. These lines of argument suggest different conclusions about the links between observed public investment spending volatility and actual improvements in a country's public infrastructure capital stock.

High year-to-year volatility may be fully consistent with effective fiscal policy. But high annual volatility may also be associated with the lack of predictability at either the budget or cash release stage. Because of the generally longer project preparation, selection, and implementation cycles of infrastructure spending, these sources of volatility might compromise actual physical implementation. Excessively rapid growth of public investment spending might exceed implementation capacity. Rapid cutbacks may defer the completion of otherwise ready projects at high social costs, as line agencies seek to safeguard the overall project portfolio. As such, higher volatility can be seen as a "red flag," suggesting more deep-seated problems with PIM.

The fact that public investment spending is typically one of the most discretionary forms of spending (for example, compared with the wage bill) is likely to

(continued next page)

Box 3.1 *(continued)*

magnify budgetary volatility and make it more unpredictable. For example, in Vietnam the budget allocation rules state that capital expenditures can be funded only after current expenditures are taken into account. Country-level analysis needs to assess whether observed relative volatility measures are consistent with predictable prioritization or whether they are more symptomatic of weak PIM.

Source: Ha Thi Thu Vu.

constraint to growth.[26] Excessive volatility is likely to be especially acute in settings that do not have an adequate MTEF.[27] The fact that the bottom-up life cycle of a project typically stretches beyond a single budget year accentuates the need for more predictable capital budget envelopes at the aggregate and, especially, implementing sector agency levels.

High volatility of capital expenditures may be particularly detrimental to effective PIM for a number of reasons. For one thing, it may be especially disruptive to the actual implementation of a physical project cycle. In practice, this disruption may be associated with stop-and-start implementation. In the face of poor budget predictability, line agencies will be further encouraged to engage in adverse gaming relative to the central finance agencies (CFAs). Knowing that uncompleted projects are likely to receive priority budget allocations, line agencies may initially undercost projects and keep going back for supplementary budgets rather than effectively prioritizing between a new and existing project portfolio pipeline and its maintenance.

At the project portfolio level, governments may pursue various strategies in both changing the composition of the investment portfolio and implementing short-term adjustments and medium-term changes in prioritization around capital spending envelopes. From an annual budgeting perspective, the completion of existing projects will typically be given priority. Table 3.2 provides a further perspective on prioritizing changes in the composition of the investment portfolio over time, in which policy makers may focus on strengthening the PIM value chain (for example, appraisal versus downstream cost control and incentives for on-time execution by sector agencies). Because countries typically maintain public investment portfolios of several thousand projects, good management information systems are likely to be a critical ingredient in the implementation of such prioritization strategies in practice. Although

Figure 3.7   Capital Budgeting and Execution Challenges, 2000–10

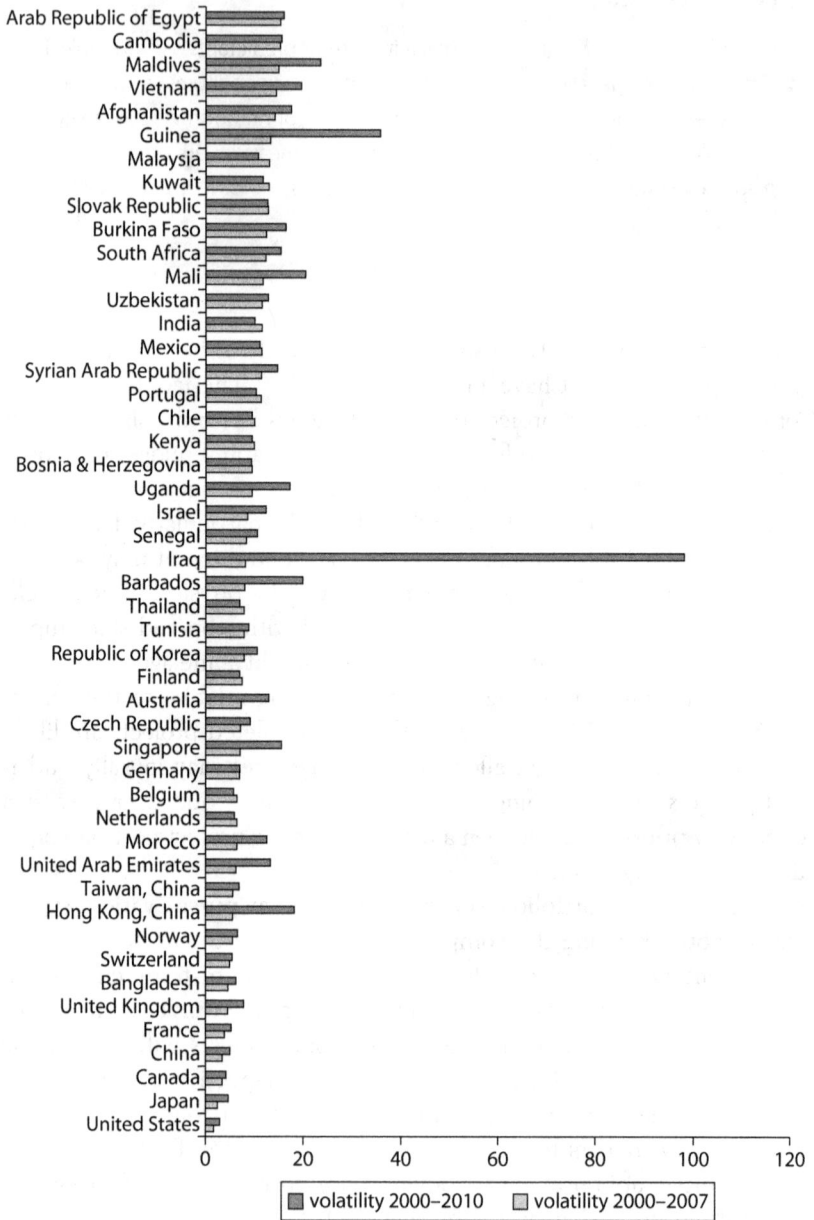

Source: IMF World Economic Outlook Database.
Note: Volatility of government investment is measured as a standard deviation of the annual growth of government investment. Government investment is defined as gross public fixed capital formation. GDP = gross domestic product.

Table 3.2   Project Selection and Execution Challenges

project	Poor implementation	Good implementation
Poor projects		
Good projects		

Source: Rajaram et al. 2010.

technical solutions are available to help implement these types of approaches (see box 3.2), a deeper challenge frequently lies in the decentralized nature of implementing the investment portfolio.

Overarching development and corresponding sectoral strategies will continue to be important instruments in identifying and responding to public investment gaps. These strategies are likely to be driven by the prevailing levels of public services, access, and quality, as well as future demands. Especially in developing countries, ensuring basic access to education, health services, and transport infrastructure are the guiding objectives for defining the best targeting of particular investment projects.[28] Because of the multiyear lag times associated with the likely realization of major investment project portfolios, governments need to respond to projected demand, while striking an effective balance among deliberating, designing, and delivering outcomes.

A perspective that emphasizes the particular challenges of implementing a portfolio of public infrastructure investments also lends itself to an operational risk management perspective on the part of CFAs. These risk management approaches may emphasize project size or proportionality, particular priority programs, types of infrastructure and associated implementation modalities, the extent to which a bank of well-conceived projects exists, or particular institutional procedures and arrangements.[29] The effectiveness of any particular strategy will depend on a good diagnostic of PIM capabilities and potential bottlenecks in the given context. A number of diagnostic tools could be used to assess key aspects of the PIM subsystem focused on capital spending and so could, in principle, provide greater medium-term predictability and effective prioritization of expenditure envelopes.

Tools for Better PIM

Effective fiscal policy for the creation and preservation of physical capital assets needs to be cognizant of these challenges and calibrate potential "good fit" institutional design and implementation to better address these

Box 3.2

Are Ministries of Finance Well Informed about Public Infrastructure Investments?

Implementation of advanced financial management information system (FMIS) and PIM technical capabilities is usually possible after building substantial institutional and technical capacity and gaining experience with core FMIS solutions over several years.

Public investment projects have several characteristics that are likely to exert specific demands on the information system. Investment projects will typically span multiple budget years. Prior to actual approval in the budget, projects may be subject to periods of initial identification, prefeasibility, and appraisal. Projects are therefore typically assigned some unique identification that must subsequently be linked to annual budget information. At a minimum level, a functional system should provide the CFA with a real-time overview of the government's project portfolio. The system should be able to identify the final to initial cost and time estimate of a project. Ideally, it should provide updates of the aggregated forward cost estimates of the existing project portfolio, which would help identify the fiscal space for new projects. Because project implementation is typically decentralized across line agencies, care must also be taken to ensure that updates on both the financial and physical implementation of projects are issued in a timely fashion. Users in key agencies must actually see the information being generated by the system as useful for ensuring sustainability.

A key requirement for successful implementation of FMIS solutions supporting PIM and other advanced PFM functions is *the daily recording and reporting of all financial data* through a countrywide information system. This can be achieved through a reliable ICT infrastructure that connects all line ministries and agencies and provides online access to a centralized Web-based FMIS solution for all system users in order to share reliable and complete information from a central database. Moreover, a unified budget classification, including a detailed program segment capturing all important activities and projects, needs to be developed to ensure collection and analysis of consistent budget data over the years. The information demands of a PIM module are, however, likely to be high, especially if the system is intended to provide measures of financial and physical implementation as well as data assessing the value for money suggested by procurement processes.

Since the late 1980s, the World Bank and other development agencies have been very active in funding treasuries/FMIS projects. Indeed, as of August 2010, the World Bank had financed 94 projects in 51 countries totaling over US$1.4 billion

(continued next page)

Box 3.2 *(continued)*

(55 completed, 32 active, and 7 pipeline projects). Recently, a report titled "The World Bank's Experience in Treasury and Financial Management Information Systems (1984–2010)" was prepared by a group of Bank specialists (it is an updated and expanded version of the draft FMIS review report prepared in 2003) to highlight achievements and challenges observed during the design and implementation of Bank-funded projects since 1984.

According to the findings of this study, a significant number of countries have developed customized software modules for PIM, often as a part of integrated FMIS solutions. Within the 55 completed FMIS projects, there appear to be PIM and MTEF/program-based budgeting components mainly in Latin America (Argentina, Colombia, Ecuador, Guatemala, Honduras, and Nicaragua) as well as in Africa (Burkina Faso). Similarly, other information systems supporting PIM are being implemented in 31 ongoing treasury/FMIS projects in Albania, Ukraine, Mongolia, and Lao People's Democratic Republic.

Source: Dener, Watkins, and Dorotinsky 2011.

challenges in the prevailing country contexts. Beyond the significant resource flows associated with public investments, the long-term fixed and sunk costs pose significant challenges for intertemporal regulatory and political credibility, as well as time inconsistency.[30]

A variety of strategies can be used to address perceived weakness in public infrastructure creation and operation. PIM benchmarking can be used to establish baselines for reform prioritization and capturing of progress over time. Earmarking/hypothecation can under certain circumstances better align resource allocation, notably for more optimal maintenance, whereas shifting the emphasis of financing for subnational governments or line agencies from pure inputs to outcomes can enhance public infrastructure creation performance. Balance sheet and accrual accounting innovations can support improvements in public investment spending over time but require a realistic appreciation of the information and procedural demands for applying these approaches in practice. Finally, there is a growing recognition that transparency and demand-side measures can enhance accountability for effective public infrastructure provision.

The provision of public-private partnership infrastructure may be particularly vulnerable to time-inconsistency challenges and thus may deter either upstream investment or the effective operation and maintenance of this modality of public infrastructure provision. Because the average and marginal costs will diverge once assets have been put in place, ex post pressures by governments will effectively expropriate private investors by pushing them to operate assets at marginal cost or even below.

Benchmarking

The IMF's PIMI provides insight into the general quality of appraisal, selection, implementation, and evaluation based on 17 indicators (Dabla-Norris et al. 2011). In effect, it codifies the must-have features of the project cycle proposed by Rajaram et al. (2010) and depicted in figure 3.8.

The World Bank's Public Sector Group recently developed a diagnostic framework for capital spending (World Bank 2011). This framework is designed as a drill-down tool for the 28 performance indicators of the Public Expenditure and Financial Accountability (PEFA) framework directed at capital spending. In addition to indicators for the project cycle, the tool seeks to capture the broader PFM practices surrounding capital spending in an evidence-based fashion. Because of

Figure 3.8   Steps in the Public Investment Management Value Chain

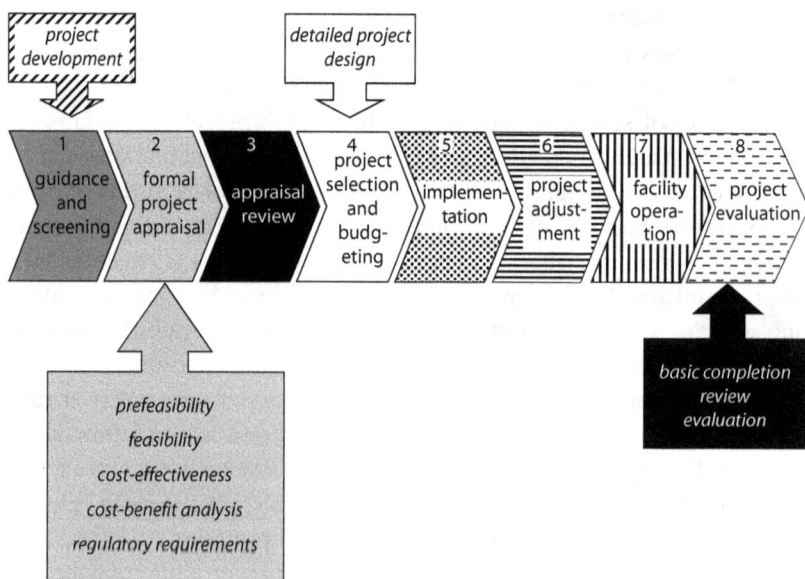

Source: Rajaram et al. 2010.

the data requirements of the PIMI, the tool involves a more in-depth diagnosis.

Both of these tools can be used as a reference point for prioritizing actions to strengthen PIM, but they cannot be applied in a mechanical fashion to enhance the probability that resource flows will translate into productive assets.

Earmarking/Hypothecation

Specific earmarking or parallel institutional arrangements, such as revenue hypothecation for particular areas of government expenditures, are often questioned by economists and public finance specialists because these tools tend to reduce budget flexibility and risk increasing fragmentation. In addition, earmarked channeling of resources may not necessarily generate the intended outcomes. Examples of hypothecation in this sense include the gasoline tax in the United States, which is dedicated to, or "earmarked" for, funding transportation infrastructure. According to Gwilliam and Shalizi (1999), there are two long-term institutional options for reconciling fiscal prudence with asset maintenance: (1) a specialized agency that is operated commercially (subject to the normal oversight of behavior applied to privatized agencies) or (2) a reformed and well-functioning medium-term budget process. Gwilliam and Shalizi (1999) argue that, for example, road funds must be viewed as a provisional, case-specific intermediate step in the direction of one of the long-term solutions. The role and nature of earmarking for specific purposes should be assessed not on general principles but on a case-by-case basis through the analysis of micro- and macroeconomic effects.

The expanding role of subnational governments in the provision or operationalization of investments has put greater emphasis on associated intergovernmental transfers, especially in the case of significant vertical fiscal imbalances. A variety of transfers exists for specific capital creation purposes, although an ongoing challenge is to ensure effective implementation, timely reporting, and maintenance. Earmarking intergovernmental transfers for subnational capital expenditures may generate particular risks of dependence on central transfers. Moreover, subnational governments may be particularly vulnerable to procyclical adjustment, which is then amplified in public investment operations. Central levels of government may look to balance their own budgets by squeezing transfers in times of fiscal stress, whereas the tax base of subnational government levels (for example, property taxation and shared fuel taxes) may be particularly procyclical.

Input-based capital grants have been a prevalent feature of many inter-governmental systems (Bird and Smart 2002), but linking transfers to outputs and outcomes, particularly in infrastructure, is attracting ever-greater attention. For example, Indonesia, with the support of the World Bank, recently sought to enhance the result orientation of specific-purpose capital transfers by focusing on improving the reporting on the actual completion of projects (Ellis, Mandri-Perrott, and Tineo 2011). Such performance-oriented approaches can be effective in promoting a shift in emphasis from investment flows to actual outcomes in stocks/assets. But again, these approaches need to be carefully calibrated to context, including the capability of implementing agencies or subnational governments to deliver to well-specified benchmarks and associated incentives and resourcing (Kaiser 2010).

Accounting Innovation

The growing emphasis on public sector balance sheets is consistent with a stronger focus on asset creation and preservation. Accrual concepts are now central to the two major public sector standards: the IMF's government finance statistics (GFS) framework and those from the International Public Sector Accounting Standards Board (IPSASB). In an accrual framework, there are three main fiscal reporting statements: the operating statement, the balance sheet, and the cash flow statement. It is an integrated package, in which each statement is reconciled with the others. The operating statement of government includes most recurrent spending and other operating expenses such as depreciation—whether or not any disbursement occurs. The balance sheet includes assets, liabilities, and "net worth" (either a negative or positive value), which is the difference between the value of assets (financial and nonfinancial) and the value of liabilities. Cash flow statements are generally organized by major categories of disbursements—that is, operations, investing activities, and financing activities.

In recent times, when much of the fiscal debate has surrounded accessing financing and concerns have been expressed about the liabilities side of the balance sheet (debt and nondebt) and the liquidity position (from the cash flow statements), economists and others have focused on financial assets because they may provide a quick means of realizing financing. Nonfinancial assets (as well as some financial assets held as equity) may involve cumbersome processes for realization, or they may not be considered suitable for sale (such as heritage assets).

Contrary to standard cash accounting, accrual accounting records and reports assets and liabilities that are relevant to fiscal policy, long-term fiscal sustainability, and asset management. When items are not recorded and reported, it is likely that they are also not well managed or are more susceptible to being manipulated or becoming rundown or stolen. Accrual accounting offers a more complete picture of a government's financial performance and position because it provides information not just on debt but also on a government's contingent and other liabilities and guarantees on the liability side, and physical and nonphysical assets on the other side of the balance sheet.

In an accrual world, capital spending does not flow directly into the operating statement and therefore is not counted in measures of the operating balance (although clearly capital spending will add to financing requirements in the cash flow statement). The annual loss of the service potential of physical assets, known as depreciation, is included in the operating statement even though no transaction takes place.[31] This reinforces the need to consider capital spending and asset management more generally in an intertemporal context. Awareness of the balance sheet, operating statement, and cash flow effects may ease undue concerns about the inherently bulky nature of spending on major capital projects, where financing exists.

The ongoing shift to basing government accounting on accrual concepts is one of the defining trends in contemporary PFM (Khan and Mayes 2009; IFAC 2011). Notwithstanding the general direction of the shift, to date only a relatively small number of mostly advanced countries have made the full transition to accrual accounting.[32] About 80 countries have been identified by the International Federation of Accountants (IFAC) as being in various phases of introducing accrual-based accounting and reporting.[33] Some observers have argued that the financial crises, and notably the sovereign debt crisis, have further strengthened the case for governments to redouble their efforts in this direction (Ball and Pfugrath 2012). Although many LICs and MICs have signaled an intention to adopt accruals, the speed of implementation commonly falls short of the original plans. High-capacity countries such as Korea have also slowed down the pace of introduction.

The application of accrual concepts to fiscal policy making is a work in progress. It remains to be seen whether accruals can balance the tendency to have too narrow a focus on the financing aspects of public infrastructure projects in periods of limited government fiscal space, which may threaten longer-term growth prospects (Easterly, Irwin, and Servén 2008). Good valuation techniques should also address whether a dollar or peso of spending on asset creation necessarily translates into a commensurate increase in the real value of a government's balance sheet (Pritchett 2000; Gupta and Verhoeven 2001). Poor maintenance practices can increase the rate of depreciation, which should be identified in valuation exercises.

Coming out of the global crisis, ministries of finance could undertake more systematic efforts to assess the updated value of their existing public infrastructure assets, as well as to realistically cost out the options for meeting their respective binding public infrastructure gaps. Because of the complexity of valuing very heterogeneous public infrastructure assets, it may be practical for such initiatives to focus on particular classes of assets and line agencies such as roads or bridges, where the economic significance may be greater than, for example, valuing school buildings. Accrual accounting practices, whether introduced in full or in part, should not only improve the quality of financial information for all stakeholders (for example, investors, taxpayers, ratepayers, public officials, suppliers, creditors, employees, and the media) but also augment the quality of financial management and reduce the risk of financial reporting fraud.

Transparency and Social Monitoring Initiatives

Transparency is a tool for improving project and public investment performance, particularly when coupled with mechanisms that allow stakeholders to provide decision makers with feedback. Where stakeholders have access to the relevant information, they can assess progress against plans, the quality of investments, and the value for money. They also can identify risks arising from shortcomings in project design or corruption. Stakeholders can include a wide range of actors—civil society organizations, concerned citizens, the users of public infrastructure, and contractors—each with distinct capabilities and perspectives. Feedback from these social monitoring initiatives complements formal reporting and monitoring mechanisms.

The development of information and communication technology (ICT) has greatly enhanced the public sector's ability to generate timely, relevant information and make this information accessible to a wide range of users. Agencies can provide ready access to their public investment programs through Internet portals, allowing users to drill down to the details of projects, including budget and performance indicators and background documentation. Projects can be geocoded and mapped. For example, the recovery.gov website of the U.S. Recovery Accountability and Transparency Board includes details on how the funds of American

Recovery and Reinvestment Act of 2009 (ARRA) are being spent. Mapping is particularly helpful when projects are dispersed and relatively simple, because citizens and communities are well placed to assess and report on progress. Internet applications can also be used to facilitate interaction with users, allowing them to post comments and provide feedback on projects.

Existence of a reliable financial management information system (FMIS), including core functional modules for budget preparation, execution, accounting, reporting, and auditing, is essential for the implementation of advanced PFM reforms in many countries (see box 3.2). Information systems designed for PIM are usually linked with several other software modules supporting the MTEF, program-based budgeting (PBB), and monitoring and evaluation of budget execution performance through specific indicators, in addition to commitment control, procurement, and asset management solutions.

Information technology (IT) can be used to bring transparency to some of the higher-risk areas of PIM, notably the procurement process. IT procurement applications can be used to post procurement plans, consolidate shopping across agencies, advertise bidding, and manage the contracting process. The World Bank has developed Internet-accessible software, SEPA, that provides access to the procurement plans and contracting process for the World Bank Group–financed projects. SEPA has now been adopted by the Inter-American Development Bank and is widely used for projects in Latin America.[34] Such initiatives increase competition and facilitate participation by local and small-scale enterprises by reducing transaction costs. They also reduce the opportunities for corruption by providing public access to information at each stage of the contracting process and allowing competing firms to confirm that the process is fair.

Although the accessibility of information has improved significantly, effective engagement with stakeholders in social monitoring initiatives has proved to be much more challenging. Political support is critical to overcoming resistance from administrations and interests, which may not be served by transparency. For example, the Concerned Citizens of Abra for Good Government (CCAGG) in the Philippines was launched as a civil society initiative to monitor the quality of public investments in highways. The CCAGG identified numerous substandard and incomplete projects, as well as fraudulent activities carried out by the civil servants responsible for managing and monitoring projects. In 2001, the National Audit Commission (CAO) entered into a partnership with CCAGG to monitor projects in Abra Province. Although CAO expressed satisfaction with the results of this partnership, it was eventually discontinued because of privacy concerns about the involvement of CAO in the audit process (International Budget Partnership 2010). Experience suggests that there are tensions between civil society organizations' desire to maintain their independence from public agencies and the continued reluctance of public agencies to integrate independent actors—particularly those critical of the public sector—in their monitoring systems.

Multistakeholder initiatives that bring together the construction sector, civil society, and governments may help resolve some of these tensions. The Construction Sector Transparency Initiative (CoST) is one such multistakeholder initiative that seeks to promote transparency and accountability in public infrastructure, thereby reducing mismanagement, waste, and corruption (CoST 2010, 2011a). The initiative, which has been sponsored by the United Kingdom's Department for International Development (DfID) and the World Bank, recently completed a two-year pilot project in seven countries: Ethiopia, Malawi, the Philippines, Tanzania, the United Kingdom, Vietnam, and Zambia. Under CoST, the cost and quality of public projects are disclosed during the preparation and construction phases. The early results of the initiative are promising. CoST baseline studies demonstrated considerable scope for improvement by discovering cost overruns and significant time overruns (figure 3.7) in many of 145 construction projects reviewed (CoST 2011b). Progress to date is promising but it is too early to provide systematic evidence on the impact of the various country initiatives in enhancing public investment efficiency and their longer-term sustainability.

Conclusions

The recent global crisis—through concerns about fiscal space, countercyclical policy, and the need to fill gaps in public physical capital assets, particularly in developing countries—has given new impetus to efforts to address governments' capabilities to make more effective public investments. In moving beyond a macrofiscal analysis of public capital spending, we have illustrated the significant complexity and institutional demands associated with the creation, maintenance, and utilization of public physical capital assets in terms of both securing adequate financing from governments and ensuring value for money.

The global crisis amplified concerns about effective public investment in many different ways. The prospect of "win-win" forms of fiscal stimulus by means of providing public infrastructure was subject to delays and criticism of waste. Even the most advanced settings faced challenges in scaling up the identification, implementation, and operation of productive physical assets. Low-budget execution rates for capital spending represented one of the most obvious symptoms of this challenge.

Uncertainty about sovereign fiscal sustainability and pressures to de-leverage are raising concerns about building adequate public capital assets in the future. From a political economy perspective, capital spending remains one of the most discretionary forms of spending, and it is still subject to volatility that is detrimental to growth. This chapter has sought to emphasize the complexity of the process by which public resources are actually translated into public capital assets with a positive service value. The quality of PIM is increasingly being appreciated as an important link in enhancing the relationship between fiscal policy and growth.

Elucidating the "black box" of PIM should therefore be of increasing interest to key fiscal policy makers, notably finance agencies. Beyond the potential contribution of selected PIM benchmarking metrics in opening this dialogue, special arrangements for sustaining capital assets through hypothecation, a realistic assessment of accounting innovations, and greater fiscal transparency and public participation can all make contributions.

The diverse time horizons, institutional demands, and political economy associated with PIM indicate that there are no easy short-term fixes to better bridging the quantity and quality of resources dedicated to building public capital assets. PIM requires effective coordination and accountability across oversight/CFAs, line agencies, different government levels and SOEs, and private sector actors. A key message for policy makers seeking to have a tangible impact on a country's physical balance sheet is that it is critical to look at the institutional underpinning to public investment processes and decisions. This requires effective management by both CFAs and regulatory agencies and the respective line agencies for traditional government spending, in collaboration with private sector actors.

Good economic returns may accrue from public investment, but perhaps only after there has been some investment in these institutions— investing to invest. But the quest for good solutions is likely to yield few silver bullets. Like the act of investment itself, "investing to invest" is a long-term project with uncertain rewards, despite its rhetorical and substantive appeal. A more systematic assessment of the project cycle or "value chain" underscores the need to evaluate both the upstream and downstream aspects of project success. In terms of yielding actual results, a pragmatic balance needs to be struck between project "designing versus doing." Although clearly a focus, economic appraisal and screening of projects are a critical priority with potentially significant payoffs. In addition, efforts to enhance the quality of investment need to stress the practical issues of implementation, operation, and maintenance, adjusted to the prevailing contexts (Harberger 2005). Evidence on aggregate public investment flows, provision indicators, and PFM benchmarking indicators must be triangulated to inform potential reform priorities and options. Fiscal magnitudes linked to a result focus on asset creation and preservation can provide some compelling measure of possible "payoffs."

Notes

The authors wish to acknowledge the excellent contributions and data analyses provided by Ha Thi Thu Vu.

1. We focus on public fixed capital formation—that is, assets with a service life of over one year, in which the government has a significant role in the formation or operation and maintenance of these assets. These assets are in turn associated with a benefit stream or "expense" in an accrual accounting framework (IMF 2001, table 4.1).

2. In this analysis, we are not including human capital assets.

3. The literature on the linkages between public investment and growth is wide ranging (see Anderson, de Renzio, and Levy 2006; de la Croix and Delavallade 2009; Fay et al. 2011). A key challenge for this literature remains that of drawing on effective indicators of infrastructure capital stock versus flow indicators (Pritchett 2000), and capturing network efforts associated with infrastructure stocks (Hulten 1996). This chapter emphasizes the processes by which productive infrastructure stocks are generated.

4. Using an international Public Investment Management Index (Dabla-Norris et al. 2011) as a time-invariant index that captures the efficiency of public investment, Gupta et al. (2011, table 2) calculate an efficiency-adjusted per capita stock on the basis of a perpetual inventory method for investment flows for a sample of low- and middle-income countries.

5. Efficiency in capital spending can have various dimensions. These may include allocative efficiency in terms of sectors and project selection, as well as operational efficiency—that is, the value for money of completing selected projects and their subsequent operation.

6. The International Monetary Fund's *World Economic Outlook* (WEO) series captures government investment. It excludes public investments by state-owned enterprises (SOEs) or public-private partnerships (PPPs).

7. Coming into the global crisis, a subset of resource-rich countries had benefited from notable windfalls from higher commodity prices, although the magnitude of additional fiscal revenues was dependent on the prevailing fiscal regimes. Projected surges in investment spending, and the subsequent weakening of commodity prices, invariably raised concerns about sustainability and quality of spending (Ossowski et al. 2008). The fiscal position on capital spending varied significantly, as did the desire and ability of policy makers to prioritize public investments.

8. These figures exclude public infrastructure formation by SOEs and frequently by PPPs. A recent major accounting exercise for Africa has sought to provide more systematic accounting of public infrastructure creation flows (Briceño-Garmendia and Sarkodie 2011).

9. This measure aggregates various classes of infrastructure and is clearly subject to a significant degree of subjectivity. The diversity of international infrastructure is also borne out by more targeted indicators such as access or cost of basic infrastructure services from water to power.

10. Petrie (2010) groups his analysis around a typology of advanced settings: lower-income country, middle-income country, resource-rich, and fragile. Countries such as Vietnam appear to have made a concerted effort to not sustain their already high government investment levels during the crisis period but also to push for reform and strengthening of the underlying PIM systems. The timing of these studies, however, does not yet yield a typology in terms of the relative emphasis governments placed on the quantity of government investments (as observed in figures 3.2 and 3.3) versus efforts to strengthen quality through concerted policy priorities and institutional reforms.

11. On the one hand, turbulence in the international economy is likely to introduce additional uncertainty for the demand planning associated with public investment and thus for governments to get short- and medium-term policies for financing and provision right. The global crisis probably shaved off several points of growth from some economies, and recovery estimates are likely to be subject to some uncertainty. On the other hand, high commodity prices introduce significant gains in terms of trade for some economies, even to the extent of generating booms. These types of dynamics highlight the higher demands for agility and responsiveness being placed on public investment management systems.

12. The use of accrual accounting, with a policy focus on the balance sheet, provides at least a start to focus on the annual service value of an asset and its service life. See the concluding section of this chapter.

13. A number of authors have argued that perpetual inventory methods of estimating the monetary value of a country's physical capital stock are fundamentally flawed because of the high degree of waste and inefficiency assumed in public investment (Pritchett 2000; Gupta et al. 2011).

14. However, infrastructure does not necessarily rely only on public investment spending for its creation. For example, PPPs and SOEs may be significant providers of public infrastructure, but their activities may not be captured in public investment as defined.

15. The aggregate indicators, and those for the four subcategories, are presented in an annex in Gupta et al. (2011). For East Asia, the PIMI does not score high-level investors such as China and Vietnam.

16. The approach amends the perpetual inventory method by incorporating PIMI as a discount factor on investment flows.

17. Gupta et al. (2011) also find that the implementation component of the PIMI appears to be particularly relevant for low-income countries, whereas the appraisal component is more important for middle-income countries.

18. The McKinsey Global Institute (2010) suggests that both private and public capital spending will grow scarcer because of global imbalances and the growing demands from emerging markets.

19. A significant part of the literature has focused on the objectives and issues associated with public infrastructure through SOEs and PPPs.

20. The recent creation of Infrastructure Australia is one example of institutional efforts to address the perceived fragmentation in public investment planning.

21. If the final costs of all projects are underestimated to the same ratio at the time of appraisal, the ranking of projects may remain the same, but their actual returns may decrease.

22. The CoST baseline studies also provided quantitative data on time and cost overruns for 145 sample construction projects, ranging up to US$500 million in cost (CoST 2010). Figure 10 suggests that although cost overruns were significant, time overruns were in all instances higher. A survey of cost markups by the World Bank reveals that in procurement in many developing countries they are frequently in the order of 50–60 percent of likely competitive costs (Messick 2011).

23. For example, as part of the United Kingdom's recent spending review, the government for the first time agreed to capital allocations across the whole public sector over a four-year period, against the backdrop of an overarching four-year U.K. infrastructure plan encompassing both private and public investment (Stewart 2010). The extent to which this plan ultimately proves credible in view of the implementation challenges, financing, and assumptions about private sector contributions remains to be seen.

24. There may, of course, be important lobbies for capital spending. These could include contractors, the private sector, as well as the international development community.

25. Strum (2011) shows that although capital expenditure levels are at least in part deficit financed, large deficits tend to lower capital spending in the

future. At the same time, if the high levels of capital spending envisioned in an annual budget cannot be executed, they may be crowded out by other types of expenditures such as consumption/quick disbursing.

26. For example, Collier et al. (2009) suggest that, contingent on absorptive capacity, resource-rich countries invest more than the traditional permanent income hypothesis would suggest in order to lay the foundation for growth and diversification.

27. In addition to developing MTEFs and fiscal rules to promote enhanced public resource allocation over time, governments also have to make more explicit the possible risks to annual budget execution through fiscal risk statements (Everaert et al. 2009). Risks can have implications for the fiscal space for priority expenditures, including capital spending. The prevalence of underexecution of government investment spending, even when fiscal space is not the primary constraint, suggests that central finance agencies should pay more attention to potential bottlenecks in capital spending execution across implementing agencies.

28. But settings like China demonstrate the challenges of balancing responsiveness to infrastructure needs in typically urban growth poles versus those in more remote regions. These in turn pose particular challenges for sectoral and spatial public expenditure prioritization, including in forecasting medium-term demand in areas such as transport, power, telecommunications, administrative infrastructure, education, and health care.

29. Examples include arrangements of postdisaster infrastructure rehabilitation, including "building back better" (Fengler, Ihsan, and Kaiser 2008).

30. The provision of PPP infrastructure may be particularly vulnerable to time inconsistency challenges and thus may deter either upstream investment or the effective operation and maintenance of this modality of public infrastructure provision. Because the average and marginal costs will diverge once assets have been put in place, ex post pressures by governments will effectively expropriate private investors by pushing them to operate assets at marginal cost or even below.

31. This requires public sector accounting to adequately reflect changes in the rates of depreciation of various public infrastructure asset classes, especially under the various operations and maintenance provisions (Hepworth 2003, 3).

32. Following the leadership of New Zealand, other examples are Australia, Canada, Colombia, France, the United Kingdom, and the United States (Khan and Mayes 2009, 2).

33. The OECD's 2008 International Budget Practices and Procedures Database provides the last extensive survey on this issue (http://www.oecd.org/gov/budget/database).

34. http://www.iniciativasepa.org/sepa_banco_mundial_mapa.asp.

References

Anderson, Edward, Paolo de Renzio, and Stephanie Levy. 2006. "The Role of Public Investment in Poverty Reduction: Theories, Evidence and Methods." Working Paper 263, Overseas Development Institute, London. http://www.odi.org.uk/resources/details.asp?id=1166&title=role-public-investment-poverty-reduction-theories-evidence-methods.

Ball, Ian, and Gary Pfugrath. 2012. "Government Accounting: Making Enron Look Good." *World Economics* 13 (1): 18.

Bird, Richard M., and Michael Smart. 2002. "Intergovernmental Fiscal Transfers: International Lessons for Developing Countries." *World Development* 30 (6): 899–912.

Bloechinger, Hansjorg, Claire Charbit, Jose Pinero Campos, and Camila Vammalle. 2010. "Sub-Central Governments and the Economic Crisis: Impact and Policy Responses." Working Paper 752, Economics Department, Organisation for Economic Co-operation and Development, Paris.

Briceño-Garmendia, Cecilia, and Afua Sarkodie. 2011. "Spending on Public Infrastructure: A Practitioner's Guide." Policy Research Working Paper 5905, World Bank, Washington, DC.

Collier, Paul, F. van der Ploeg, Michael Spence, and Anthony Venables. 2009. "Managing Resource Revenues in Developing Countries." Department of Economics, Oxford University, Oxford, U.K.

CoST (Construction Sector Transparency). 2010. *Report of the Cost International Advisory Group.* Washington, DC: CoST.

———. 2011a. *Briefing Note 1: Overview.* Report of the CoST International Advisory Group, Washington, DC: CoST. http://www.constructiontransparency.org/TechnicalFinancialAssistance/CoSTBriefingNotes/.

———. 2011b. *Briefing Note 5: Baseline Studies.* Report of the CoST International Advisory Group, Washington, DC: CoST. http://www.constructiontransparency.org/TechnicalFinancialAssistance/CoSTBriefingNotes/.

Dabla-Norris, Era, Jim Brumby, Annette Kyobe, Zac Mills, and Chris Papageorgiou. 2011. "Investing in Public Investment: An Index of Public Investment Efficiency." Working Paper WP/11/37, International Monetary Fund, Washington, DC.

de la Croix, David and Clara Delavallade. 2009. "Growth, Public Investment, and Corruption with Failing Institutions." *Economics of Governance* 10 (3): 187–219.

Delavallade, Clara. 2006. "Corruption and Distribution of Public Spending in Developing Countries." *Journal of Economics and Finance* 30 (2): 222–39.

Dener, Cem, Joanna Alexandra Watkins, and William Leslie Dorotinsky. 2011. *Financial Management Information Systems: 25 Years of World Bank Experience on What Works and What Doesn't.* Washington, DC: World Bank.

de Rugy, Veronique, and Matthew Mitchell. 2011. "Would More Infrastructure Spending Stimulate the Economy?" Working Paper 11-36, Mercatus Center, George Washington University, Washington, DC.

Easterly, William, Timothy Irwin, and Luis Servén. 2008. "Walking Up the Down Escalator: Public Investment and Fiscal Stability." *World Bank Research Observer*. 23 (1): 37–56.

Ellis, Peter, Cledan Mandri-Perrott, and Luis Tineo. 2011. "Strengthening Fiscal Transfers in Indonesia Using an Output-Based Approach." Note 40, Global Partnership on Output Based Aid, Washington, DC. http://www.gpoba.org/gpoba/sites/gpoba.org/files/OBA No.40 Indonesia 1-26-11web.pdf.

Everaert, Greetje, Manal Fouad, Edouard Martin, and Ricardo Velloso. 2009. "Disclosing Fiscal Risks in the Post-Crisis World." http://www.imf.org/external/pubs/ft/spn/2009/spn0918.pdf.

Fay, Marianne, Michael Toman, Daniel Benitez, and Stefan Csordas. 2011. "Infrastructure and Sustainable Development." In *Post Crisis Growth and Development*, ed. S. Fardoust, Y. Kim, and C. Sepulveda, 329–82. Washington, DC: World Bank.

Fengler, Wolfgang, Ahya Ihsan, and Kai Kaiser. 2008. "Managing Post-Disaster Reconstruction Finance—International Experience in Public Financial Management." Policy Research Working Paper 4475, World Bank, Washington, DC.

Ferris, Tom, and Theo Thomas. 2009. "Review of Public Investment Management Performance (Pimp) in an Economic Crisis." Global Expert Team (GET) Brief, World Bank, Washington, DC. http://siteresources.worldbank.orgEXTPREMNET/Resources/C11TDAT_193-206.pdf.

Flyvbjerg, Bent. 2007. "Policy and Planning for Large-Infrastructure Projects: Problems, Causes, Cures." *Environment and Planning B: Planning and Design* 34: 578–97.

Flyvbjerg, Bent, Nils Bruzeliua, and Werner Rothengatter. 2003. *Megaprojects and Risk: An Anatomy of Ambition*. Cambridge, U.K.: Cambridge University Press.

Fontaine, E. R. 1997. "Project Evaluation Training and Public Investment in Chile." *American Economic Review* 87 (2): 63–67.

Foster, Vivien, and C. Briceño-Garmendia, eds. 2010. *Africa's Infrastructure: A Time for Transformation*. Africa Development Forum Series. Washington, DC: World Bank.

Grant Thornton. 2011. Instant Participant Survey, Winter Conference of International Consortium on Governmental Financial Management (ICGFM), Washington, DC, December.

Grindle, Merilee. 2007. "Good Enough Governance Revisited." *Development Policy Review* 25: 533–74.

Gupta, Sanjeev, Alvar Kangur, Chris Papageorgiou, and Abdoul Wane. 2011. "Efficiency-Adjusted Public Capital and Growth." Working Paper WP/11/217, International Monetary Fund, Washington, DC.

Gupta, Sanjeev, and Marijn Verhoeven. 2001. "The Efficiency of Government Expenditure: Experiences from Africa." *Journal of Policy Modeling* 23: 433–67.

Gwilliam, Ken, and Zmarak Shalizi. 1999. "Road Funds, User Charges, and Taxes." *World Bank Research Observer* 14 (2): 159–86.

Harberger, Arnold C. 2005. "On the Process of Growth and Economic Policy in Developing Countries." PPC Issue Paper 13 (PN-ADE-081), U.S. Agency for International Development, Washington, DC.

Hasnain, Zahid. 2011. *Incentive Compatible Reforms: The Political Economy of Public Investments in Mongolia.* East Asia PREM. Washington, DC: World Bank.

Hepworth, Noel. 2003. "Preconditions for Successful Implementation of Accrual Accounting in Central Government." *Public Money and Management* 23 (1): 37–44.

Hulten, Charles R. 1996. *Infrastructure and Economic Development: Once More unto the Breach.* University of Maryland; Cambridge, MA: National Bureau of Economic Research.

IFAC (International Federation of Accountants). 2011. *Transition to the Accrual Basis of Accounting: Guidance for Public Sector Entities.* 3rd ed. New York: IFAC.

IMF (International Monetary Fund). 2001. *Government Finance Statistics Manual 2001.* Washington, DC: Statistics Department, IMF. http://www.imf.org/external/pubs/ft/gfs/manual/.

———. World Economic Outlook (WEO) Database. IMF, Washington, DC. http://www.imf.org/external/ns/cs.aspx?id=28.

———. 2011. *World Economic Outlook: Slowing Growth, Rising Risks.* Washington, DC: IMF.

International Budget Partnership. 2010. http://internationalbudget.org/wp-content/uploads/Our-Money-Our-Responsibility-A-Citizens-Guide-to-Monitoring-Government-Expenditures-English.pdf.

Jacobs, D. 2008. "A Review of Capital Budgeting Practices." Working Paper WP/08/160, International Monetary Fund, Washington, DC.

Kaiser, Kai. 2010. "Money for Nothing? Using Specific Intergovernmental Transfers to Buy Local Results." Presentation to World Bank Country Office, Jakarta, September 29.

Keefer, Philip, and Stephen Knack. 2007. "Boondoggles, Rent-Seeking, and Political Checks and Balances: Public Investment under Unaccountable Governments." *Review of Economics and Statistics* 89 (3): 566–71.

Khan, Abdul, and Stephen Mayes. 2009. *IMF FAD Technical Guidance Note.* Washington, DC: Fiscal Affairs Department, International Monetary Fund. http://www.eastafritac.org/images/uploads/documents_storage/Transition_to_Accrual_Accounting.pdf.

McKinsey Global Institute. 2010. "Farewell to Cheap Capital? The Implications of Long-Term Shifts in Global Investment and Spending." Report. http://www.mckinsey.com/mgi.

Messick, Rick. 2011. *Curbing Fraud, Corruption, and Collusion in the Roads Sector.* Washington, DC: Integrity Vice Presidency, World Bank. http://siteresources.worldbank.org/INTDOII/Resources/Roads_Paper_Final.pdf.

Ossowski, Rolando, Mauricio Villafuerte, Paolo A. Meda, and Theo Thomas. 2008. *Managing the Oil Revenue Boom: The Role of Fiscal Institutions.* Washington, DC: International Monetary Fund.

Petrie, Murray. 2010. "Promoting Public Investment Efficiency: A Synthesis of Country Experiences." Paper presented at World Bank Preparatory Workshop, "Promoting Public Investment Efficiency: Global Lessons and Resources for Strengthening World Bank Support for Client Countries," Washington, DC, July 7.

Priemus, Hugo, Bent Flyvbjerg, and Bert Van Weer. 2008. *Decision-Making on Mega-Projects: Cost-Benefit Analysis, Planning and Innovation.* Cheltenham, U.K.: Edward Elgar.

Pritchett, L. 2000. "The Tyranny of Concepts: CUDIE (Cumulated, Depreciated, Investment Effort) Is Not Capital." *Journal of Economic Growth* 5: 361–84.

Rajaram, Anand, Tuan Minh Le, Nataliya Biletska, and Jim Brumby. 2010. "Framework for Reviewing Public Investment Efficiency." Policy Research Working Paper 5397, World Bank, Washington, DC.

Schwartz, Gerd, Ana Corbacho, and Katja Funke, eds. 2008. *Public Investment and Public-Private Partnership: Addressing Infrastructure Challenges and Managing Fiscal Risks.* New York: Palgrave McMillan; Washington, DC: International Monetary Fund.

Stewart, James. 2010. "The UK National Infrastructure Plan 2010." *European Investment Bank (EIB) Paper* 15: 29–33.

Strum, Jan-Egbert. 2011. "Determinants of Public Capital Spending in Less-Developed Countries." Working Paper 200107, CCSO Centre for Economic Research, University of Groningen, Netherlands.

Tanzi, Vito, and Hamid Davoodi. 1997. *Corruption, Public Investment, and Growth.* Washington, DC: International Monetary Fund.

van der Ploeg, Fredrick. 2011. "Bottlenecks in Ramping Up Public Investment." Research Paper 66, Oxford Centre for Analysis of Resource Rich Economies, Department of Economics, Oxford University.

World Bank. 2011. *Strengthening Public Investment Management: Indicator Framework*. PREM Public Sector and Governance Group (Exposure Draft). Washington, DC: World Bank.

WEF (World Economic Forum). 2010. *The Global Competitiveness Report 2010–2011*. Geneva: World Economic Forum.

CHAPTER 4

Fiscal Policy for Sustainable Development in Resource-Rich Low-Income Countries

Kirk Hamilton and Eduardo Ley

This chapter deals with the role of fiscal policy in harnessing nonrenewable resources for development in low-income countries. Extractive activities have several characteristics that make them special from development and fiscal perspectives.[1] Collier (2010a) highlights four generic distinctive features of natural resource extraction:

- Ownership is vested in the country's citizens.
- Extraction is a process of depletion rather than production.
- Investment in extraction requires substantial sunk costs and long payback periods.
- Prices are highly volatile.

In addition, from a development perspective, Collier focuses on distinctive features of low-income countries:

- Time consistency problems are more severe.
- Present consumption and capital are more scarce.

The authors wish to thank Jack Mintz and Blanca Moreno-Dodson for their very useful comments.

- Asymmetric information issues relative to extraction companies are worse.
- The size of undiscovered natural assets is likely to be large.

Several authors have stressed two main aspects of the allocation of the benefits associated with resource rents. The first aspect is the present allocation among the country's broad citizenship and others (including local elites, foreign companies, and so forth). The second aspect is between the present (consumption) and future generations (investment). Too often, the broad citizenship has lost in the first aspect, and future generations have lost in the second aspect (Collier 2010b).

The second trade-off—now versus later—is key to sustainable development. A nation's wealth must be preserved and developed to achieve sustainable well-being. Adjusted investment—that is, investment net of depletion charges and including investment in human capital—is what drives the changes in a nation's wealth. If the social value of adjusted investment is negative, then there is a decline in wealth and in intergenerational well-being (Dasgupta 2001). If natural capital is being depleted and consumed rather than being reinvested in other types of capital, the nation's wealth will decline.

Table 4.1 shows the relative importance of natural capital in the poorer countries' wealth composition. *Natural capital* includes land, forest, and subsoil assets. The first thing to note is how the shares of natural capital in the country's wealth decline with the level of income. At the other extreme, the richer countries' wealth is concentrated in *intangible capital*, which includes human and institutional capital and knowledge.

Table 4.1   Wealth and Per Capita Wealth by Type of Capital and Income Group, 2005

Economy	Population (millions)	Total wealth (US$, billions)	Per capita wealth (US$)	Natural capital (%)	Produced capital (%)	Intangible capital (%)
Low-income	586	3,597	6,138	30	13	57
Lower-middle-income	3,433	58,023	16,903	25	24	51
Upper-middle-income	580	47,183	81,354	15	16	69
High-income, OECD	938	551,964	588,315	2	17	81
World	5,591	673,593	120,475	5	18	77

Source: World Bank 2011, table 1.1.
Note: OECD = Organisation for Economic Co-operation and Development.

This is where the biggest gap among richer and poorer countries lies, especially in human capital.

As noted in *The Changing Wealth of Nations* (World Bank 2011), most countries at the bottom of the economic ladder start out with a high dependence on natural capital. As they move up the economic rungs, they use these assets to build more wealth, especially in the form of produced and intangible capital. Transforming natural capital into other forms of wealth is the path to sustainable development.

Higher-income countries also have higher per capita natural capital—about six times that of low-income countries. The potential for raising low-income countries' per capita natural capital lies in the discovery of subsoil assets and in better management of all types of natural capital. As stressed by Collier (2010a), there is still a substantial discovery potential in low-income countries.

A large body of literature has formed on the "resource curse" (box 4.1). However, this chapter focuses on the role of fiscal policy in harnessing nonrenewable natural capital for development. From a national perspective, the depletion of exhaustible resources should be counterbalanced by an enhancement in the country's productive capacity—that is, in its produced and human capital.

Box 4.1

The Resource Curse

The well-documented *resource curse* refers to the paradoxical observation that countries with an abundance of natural resources—specifically, point source exhaustible resources such as minerals and fuels—tend to experience slower economic growth and worse development outcomes than do countries that are relatively less endowed with resources.

At the macroeconomic level, the main channel by which resource *abundance* may lead to resource *dependence* (thereby damaging development prospects) is the appreciation of the real exchange rate (that is, Dutch disease). The inflow of foreign exchange from resource exports puts downward pressure on the nominal exchange rate and upward pressure on domestic prices, resulting in an appreciation of the real exchange rate. This appreciation of the rate shifts capital away from the nonresource tradable sector and into the nontradable

(continued next page)

Box 4.1 *(continued)*

sector. The nonresource tradable sector (which typically includes other primary commodities, as well as manufactures and service exports) is subject to global competition and is usually the more dynamic sector, generating positive spill-overs (technological change, innovation) that benefit the rest of the economy. When the tradable sector shrinks in a developing economy, future growth is jeopardized. Successful development, almost always and everywhere, requires vigorous industrialization and diversification, which in turn are associated with a dynamic nonresource tradable sector.

A second channel is associated with the volatility of commodity prices, which translates into the volatility of resource revenues at both the country and government levels. If this income volatility is allowed to influence aggregate spending, then it will be transmitted to real exchange rate volatility. That volatility in turn introduces risk and acts like a tax on long-term investment.

A third channel by which resource revenues may compromise development prospects is associated with the political economy of large and unpredictable point source revenues and with its detrimental effects on governance and insti-tutional quality. Tornell and Lane (1999) stress the "voracity effect," which is the race by various government agencies and other economic actors to spend the available revenues before somebody else spends them—an action that inevitably leads to waste.

National Wealth and Extractive Industries

The traditional measure of economic performance, gross domestic product (GDP), is especially misleading in the context of resource-rich countries because it ignores the depletion of natural resources and so may overestimate national savings (Hamilton and Lutz 1996). Because "what gets measured gets managed," there is a strong case in low-income, resource-rich economies for routinely monitoring a more adequate and informative national income aggregate, including deple-tion charges such as the adjusted net national income (defined below).

Sustainable development requires increasing the per capita wealth for future generations (Dasgupta 2001). As the World Bank (2006) explains, national wealth must be conceived broadly to include not only the traditional measures of capital (such as produced and human capital) but also natural assets. Natural capital comprises assets such as land, forests, and subsoil resources. All three types of capital—produced, human, and natural—are key inputs for sustained economic growth.

Because savings and investment play such a central role in the economics of development, Hamilton and Lutz (1996) propose a measure of *adjusted savings*, defined as net national savings adjusted for the value of resource depletion and environmental degradation, with education expenditures treated as investments in human capital. For countries with significant exhaustible natural resources and an important foreign investor presence, adjusted net national income—*a*NNI—is more appropriate than GDP for assessing development progress. Going from GDP to *a*NNI involves moving from domestic production to national income and from a gross concept to a net concept that includes charges for depletion of natural capital.

The key to increasing future standards of living lies in increasing national wealth, which includes both traditional measures of capital (such as produced and human capital) and natural capital. Because increasing national wealth requires investment, national savings—possibly complemented by foreign savings transferred as aid—must be available to finance this investment. Net national income (NNI) is the ultimate source for funding these investments:

- First, national income rather than domestic product is a more appropriate income measure in countries in which largely foreign-operated extractive industries are substantial, because payments to foreign-owned factors are often considerable.
- Second, in resource-rich countries national income must be adjusted by offsetting a part of the credits for resource extraction with the corresponding depletion costs—these are similar to capital depreciation.[2]

After adding net foreign factor income to GDP and subtracting the consumption of fixed and natural capital, we obtain the country's *a*NNI. This is a better measure of the available income that may be consumed or invested to increase the nation's future wealth.

Recognizing that resource depletion and environmental degradation are types of depreciation, whereas education expenditures increase a country's human capital, Hamilton and Clemens (1999) propose a measure of genuine savings. This concept is formalized in the measurement of adjusted net saving (ANS), which subtracts consumption from *a*NNI, adds foreign transfers, and reclassifies all education expenditures as investment. Note that mineral resources are discovered and depleted. Box 4.2 discusses how discoveries are reflected in adjusted measures of income and saving. The policy implications of measuring ANS are quite direct: sustained negative saving leads to decreased national wealth and

Box 4.2

Resource Discoveries in the National Accounts

Mineral and energy resources are depleted each year, but new deposits are also discovered as a result of exploration expenditures by firms operating in the sector, thereby raising the question of how to treat resource discoveries in the national accounts.

Both the *System of National Accounts* (SNA; Commission of the European Communities et al. 2009) and the environmental accounting literature (Hartwick 1993; Arrow, Dasgupta, and Maler 2003) provide guidance on the treatment of natural resource discoveries. The literature suggests that exploration expenditures be treated as investment and that (under reasonable assumptions) adjusted measures of income and saving include discoveries valued as the product of the quantity discovered times the marginal discovery cost. The latter will generally not equal the marginal rental value of a unit of resource extracted.

The SNA differs in some of the accounting details. Exploration expenditures are treated as investment in intellectual property, and the underlying asset is knowledge about the location and extent of the resources discovered. The value of the resource discovered in a given year is not recorded as part of income or saving; instead it is recorded as an "other volume change" that is reflected in the closing balance sheet position of the country in the year of discovery. If each exploration expenditure led to the discovery of new resource deposits, the result of the SNA treatment would be to value resource discoveries at average discovery cost in measures of income and saving. Resource discoveries will generally affect both future income and saving because new reserves will ultimately attract new investments in extraction—and that in turn will affect future measures of resource depletion.

The World Bank measures of aNNI and ANS follow S NA practice. The approach in the literature may be preferred from a theoretical perspective, but data limitations generally do not permit the measurement of marginal discovery costs.

diminished social welfare. The different aggregates discussed in this chapter are defined as follows:

$$NNI = GDP + \text{(net foreign factor income)} - \text{(depreciation of fixed capital)}$$

$$aNNI = NNI - \text{(depreciation of natural capital)}$$

$$ANS = aNNI - \text{(consumption)} + \text{(foreign transfers)} + \text{(education expenditures)}$$

What are the practical implications of all these? Figure 4.1 updates Hamilton and Clemens (1999), showing a persistent downward trend in ANS in Sub-Saharan Africa, with negative rates indicating wealth dissipation through much of the recent resource boom. Total net wealth creation in Sub-Saharan Africa was effectively zero from 1990 to 2007, a period when the population grew by 60 percent.[3]

Figure 4.1 suggests a substantial regional divergence in savings rates, which may drive future regional divergence in income levels. East Asia is increasing national wealth much more rapidly than is Latin America, while Sub-Saharan Africa is becoming poorer in the aggregate. Note, however, that the aggregate for Sub-Saharan Africa is driven largely by dissaving in the oil producers.

Figure 4.1   Adjusted Net Saving as a Percentage of Gross National Income (GNI), Selected Regions, 1970–2007

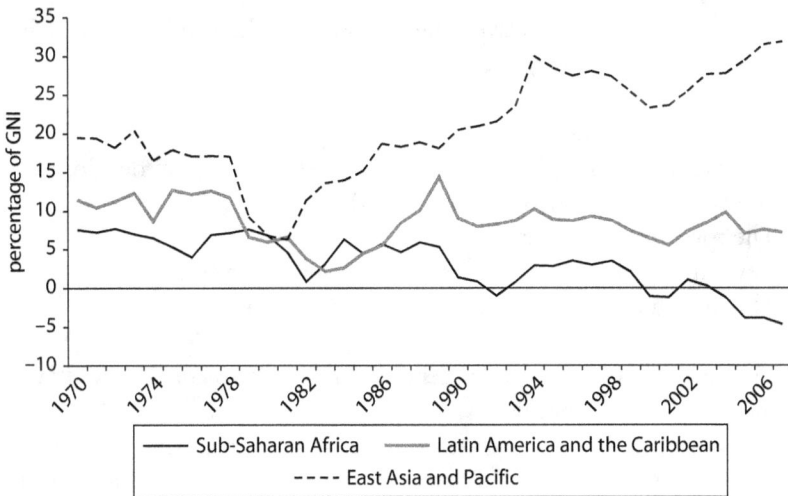

Source: World Bank 2009.
Note: GNI = gross national income.

Many resource-rich countries display very low (and often negative) rates of adjusted savings. In these cases, current macroeconomic trajectories are unsustainable because they imply shrinking national wealth. To reverse this trend, resource-rich countries need to capture an efficient and fair share of the resource rents for the country and invest that share effectively to increase the nation's wealth.

In the context of resource-rich countries, the Hartwick (1977) rule dictates that the rents from natural resources should be invested in reproducible capital to enjoy a constant stream of consumption. The Hartwick rule is a reminder of the old-fashioned obligation to "maintain capital intact." When adjusted savings are negative, however, national capital is shrinking. Atkinson and Hamilton (2003) find that countries that escaped the resource curse used rents as a source of public investment rather than a source of public current expenditure. These countries have been transforming natural capital into produced capital.

To transform natural capital into other forms of capital, the government must capture a fair share of the resource rents. These revenues must be managed properly so as not to destabilize the macroeconomy and must then be invested wisely to increase the country's wealth. The rest of this chapter deals with these upstream and downstream issues.

Upstream Taxation of Exhaustible Resources

From the taxation perspective,[4] the industry of exhaustible resources has several defining characteristics:

- Resources are exhaustible.
- The industry requires substantial investments (mainly at development and when closing down the operation).
- The revenue streams are highly volatile.
- Revenues are large, and concentrated in space and time.
- The industry's environmental impact is significant.

Moreover, this activity often generates few direct economic spillovers to the rest of the economy.

The government plays two fiscal roles: as sovereign tax power and as resource owner. In its role as a sovereign tax power, the government must ensure that the resource sector makes its due contribution to the public finances. In its role as a resource owner, the government must decide on when and how to develop the resource to promote sustainable and equitable economic growth.

Three main parties are involved: resource companies, current government, and future governments. This can be viewed as a principal agent problem in which the government (the principal) gives up a share of the rents to attract the best producer. How returns and risks are divided depends very much on the information and risk tolerances of the different parties. In low-income countries, the asymmetric information problem between firms and government is severe. Another important factor is that the balance of power of each party shifts over time. Before exploration, the power rests on the company side; after the resource has been developed and sunk costs have been incurred, power shifts to the government and the expropriation risk increases. This problem is less severe in more-developed countries, where governments are subject to the rule of law once contracts are developed.

The trade-offs between the amount and timing of revenue, and the issue of risk assignment, imply that multiple fiscal instruments may be required to protect the interests of all parties. The main tax instruments are royalties (at either the production or the export stage), property taxes, standard income taxes, and excess profits taxes. Nontax instruments include fees and rights (often auctioned), production share agreements (mostly in oil), and direct state equity.

Whereas royalties (specific or ad valorem) are simple to administer and may be attractive for the revenue agency, they are unpopular with investors because they are unrelated to costs, they distort incentives because royalties turn ore into waste (for example, the "high-grading" problem), and they must be paid even if operations are incurring losses. A partial solution to this situation is to vary royalty rates by prices, volume of production, and capacity—implicitly "proxying" for cost deductions. Property taxes are uncommon in practice because of the technical complexity in the up-front assessment of the tax base. The last two types of taxes— income and excess profits taxes—are better suited for capturing economic rents, but their administrative cost is likely to be high. Thus there is a need to integrate multiple fiscal instruments in a pragmatic way for a functional and resilient tax regime. The right mix depends on the specific characteristics of the resource, and the capacity of the revenue agency to administer each tax is a crucial factor. As Collier (2010a) reports, even in Chile the reported profits vanish when excess profits taxes are enacted.

Other tax elements specific to these activities are tax incentives for exploration, fiscal stability agreements, and ring-fencing statutes that delineate the taxable entity often defined by projects in a particular area. The first two elements complicate tax administration and should be granted with caution. In particular, generous tax incentives to attract investors should be avoided. The undeveloped resource is not wasted because it can always be developed later, and incentives—typically attached to profit income taxation—are not likely to change firms' behavior at the margin and simply represent the resource transfer from a developing country to the treasury of the investors' countries, especially those with a worldwide income tax system.[5]

In their recent discussion of the topic, Boadway and Keen (2010, 62) follow the convention "to stress that no single resource tax regime will suit all countries and circumstances" and that "it will typically not be optimal to rely on a single tax instrument." Le (2011) and Collier (2010b) stress that the capacity of the revenue administration is the factor determining the appropriate instrument mix in each particular country.

Natural Resource Funds

When resource revenues are flowing into the treasury, downstream issues are the focus of attention. Natural resource funds (NRFs) have long been advocated as a vehicle to partially address the problems associated with macroeconomic imbalances.[6] The NRFs are a particular case of fiscal rules, or, more generally, of rules-based fiscal policy. A *fiscal policy rule* is defined as a permanent constraint on fiscal policy, expressed as a summary indicator of fiscal performance such as the government budget deficit, borrowing, debt, or a major component thereof (Kopits and Symansky 1998). The strongest case for fiscal rules is based on political economy arguments—namely, that the rules correct the deficit bias (the plundering of the future by the present) and that avoiding time inconsistency issues results in significant credibility gains.

This discussion begins with a concrete example of a well-functioning NRF; box 4.3 describes the workings of Chile's Copper Stabilization Fund. The following are its main characteristics:

- Chile's fiscal rule targets a minimum structural budget surplus so that sufficient savings can be accumulated to finance future public commitments. The surplus target consists of a noncopper structural surplus and estimated long-term copper revenues based on a reference price. When copper prices are above (or below) a reference price assumed to reflect

Box 4.3

Chile's Copper Stabilization Fund

The copper sector is a dominant part of the Chilean economy, accounting for about 50 percent of exports and 8 percent of GDP. Public sector revenues from copper have varied between 5 percent and 17 percent of total tax collection. The sector consists of a state-owned company, CODELCO, and private operators, representing approximately 30 percent and 70 percent of output, respectively.

Since 2001, Chilean fiscal policy has been based on the concept of structural balance of the central government. This concept looks at the treasury's balance from a medium-term perspective instead of focusing on its current cash balance. In addition, Chile's fiscal rule insulates the budget from unexpected fluctuations in copper revenues. The rule targets a structural surplus at a certain level; in recent years, the level has been 0.5–1.0 percent of GDP. The surplus target was set so that enough savings can be accumulated to finance future public commitments—particularly, a guaranteed minimum pension and old-age benefit and recapitalization of the central bank. The surplus target consists of a non-copper structural surplus and estimated long-term copper revenues based on a reference price. When copper prices are above (or below) the reference price, which is assumed to reflect a medium-term equilibrium price for copper, revenues are transferred to (or from) the copper fund. (The government is also authorized to transfer 10 percent of CODELCO sales to military procurement.) The reference price and the potential output used for the deficit rule are estimated by independent expert panels. The members represent academia and the financial and mining sectors. For copper, the experts submit their reference price projections for the next 10 years. Those projections are averaged to determine the reference price for the budget each year. The resulting prices have been conservative in light of the commodity boom of recent years, resulting in large savings of about 12 percent of GDP at the end of 2008—even after paying off public debts.

These rules have enhanced transparency and discipline in fiscal policy. Because the effects of automatic stabilizers are small, the fund has enabled Chile to conduct countercyclical fiscal policy in downturns when access to foreign credit is more expensive, as in the global crisis. The fund has been successful in reducing output volatility (Fiess 2002; Rodríquez, Tokman, and Vega 2007; Larrain and Parro 2008) and has made Chile one of the few emerging markets able to pursue strong countercyclical fiscal policies (Perry, Servén, and Suescún 2008).

(continued next page)

a medium-term equilibrium price for copper, revenues are transferred to (or from) the copper fund.

• The reference price and the potential output used for the deficit rule are estimated by independent expert panels. The members represent academia as well as the financial and mining sectors. For copper, the experts submit their reference price projections for the next 10 years, and those projections are then averaged to obtain the reference price for the budget in each year.[7]

Traditionally, NRFs have had three functions: (1) macroeconomic stabilization, (2) budget financing, and (3) savings and investment. The stabilization function aims at insulating the economy from fluctuations in the country's resource revenues. The financing function aims at insulating the budget from fluctuations in public revenues associated with the resource (a "rainy-day fund"). The savings and investment function promotes the preservation of wealth for future generations. In practice, most resource funds have multiple objectives. The stabilization, financing, and savings objectives require accumulating resources in good times. In bad times, however, some dissaving will be required to meet the stabilization and financing objectives.

Another objective of NRFs is to preserve the quality of spending; by setting a "speed limit" on spending increases, they avoid waste in boom times. As noted by Davis et al. (2003), the establishment of NRFs may be justified on political economy grounds because the funds help the government resist spending pressures by formally limiting the resources available to the budget during upswings. In effect, a transparent and well-managed NRF protects resource revenues from the voracity effect and preserves resources for high-quality spending—for example, well-appraised public investment.

However, an NRF should be introduced only if it is judged likely to change the behavior of political actors in ways that reduce the incentives to spend too much too soon (Petrie 2009a). If it does not, an NRF may only contribute to reducing the transparency of fiscal policy by creating a parallel budget or at least making it harder to monitor the government's performance in fiscal management.

Humphreys and Sandbu (2007) suggest three general approaches to designing an NRF that could help improve the incentives for responsible fiscal policy:

1. *Rules-based approach.* The NRF should operate under rules that determine which revenues will be paid into the fund and that limit the discretion of the current government to determine both the size and the allocation of spending from the fund. How "hard" the rules are involves the familiar trade-off between commitment and flexibility.
2. *Broad governance approach.* Governance of an NRF might be broadened beyond the government of the day by involving other actors in its decision making—actors such as the legislature (Norway), members of opposition parties (the U.S. state of Alaska), or new technical bodies that include civil society.
3. *Transparency approach.* Transparent operation of the NRF is critical to its efficacy. Fiscal transparency is a prerequisite for good governance (Kopits and Craig 1998). It should lead to a better-informed public debate about the design and results of fiscal policy and make governments more accountable, thereby strengthening credibility and public understanding of macroeconomic policies and choices.

As for transparency, Collier et al. (2010) argue that one approach is to establish new explicit and transparent decision processes for natural resource revenues linked to a clear vision of long-term development. Although this approach runs counter to the ideal fiscal principle of a fully integrated budget in which all revenues are pooled, Collier et al. argue it might have superior informational properties. By spotlighting the new spending, it may make scrutiny easier and might signal to citizens that the windfall will not be captured by special interests.

Investigation of Natural Resource Revenues and Public Investment Management

The options for use of the NRFs are summarized in table 4.2 (Collier et al. 2010). A transfer of US$1 to the private sector can be spent on consumption (fraction c) and investment $(1 - c)$. Similarly, public spending is divided between public consumption and investment shares of g and $(1 - g)$, respectively. Increased domestic lending could be directed toward private consumption (fraction z) and private investment $(1 - z)$, of which a fraction could be domestic and the rest foreign.

When public investment offers the highest social returns, the second option (minimizing the current component, g) is the best option. However, there is no best option for all times in all places. Even in well-managed public investment management (PIM) systems, there are limits on how fast public investment can be scaled up while preserving quality. A fraction of windfall gains may need to be temporarily held as foreign assets until it can be spent judiciously. Here it is important to be able to uncouple the medium-term to long-term strategy from the short-term policy.

On the design of NRFs, Collier et al. (2010) note that although most of the policy attention to date has been focused on how much to save, the most important question for low-income countries is what assets should be acquired? Collier et al. answer that because low-income countries are capital scarce, the assets should be accumulated by investment within the country. Thus for low-income countries, Sachs (2007) and Collier et al.

Table 4.2   Government Choices for Spending US$1 of Revenue and the First-Order Effects

		Consumption		Investment			Balance sheet	
Optional action	Resource revenue	Private	Public	Private K stock	Public K stock	Foreign assets	Private assets	Public assets
Transfer/tax cut	1	c	0	$1-c$	0	0	$1-c$	0
Public spending	1	0	g	0	$1-g$	0	0	$1-g$
Domestic lending	1	z	0	$\gamma(1-z)$	0	$(1-\gamma)(1-z)$	$-z$	1
Foreign assets	1	0	0	0	0	1	0	1

Source: Collier et al. 2010, table 1.

Note: c = share of consumption from tax cut; g = share of consumption in government spending; z = share of consumption in private response to government debt reduction/lending; γ = share of private investment that goes into domestic capital stock.

(2010) argue strongly for using the natural resource revenues to increase public investment, spending on public assets (human capital and physical infrastructure) with a high social rate of return.

This strategy requires, however, that countries *invest in their capacity to invest*. For public investment to deliver high returns, it must be appropriately appraised and well managed. Countries often encounter managerial and physical bottlenecks when stepping up public investment. At times, avoiding bad investments may be as important as identifying the best projects.

Sachs (2007) also argues that well-appraised public investment can help alleviate Dutch disease. He makes the case that the fear of Dutch disease is a concern mainly if the resource boom is used to finance consumption rather than investment. In many developing resource-rich economies, there is a serious public goods gap. Developing public infrastructure—roads, ports, power, communications, education, health—will raise the productivity of private capital and induce greater private investment. This channel can offset the negative impact of exchange rate appreciation on the tradable sector.

Those planning capital expenditures must adequately project and accommodate the impact of those expenditures on current budgets. This approach implies appropriate operations and maintenance expenditures for all infrastructure projects; it also implies superstructure expenditures associated with schools and hospitals—thus salaries for educational and medical staff.

Unlike in the private sector where bankruptcy eventually takes care of a serial bad investor, a bad PIM system can continue to waste resources without a time limit, thereby causing unlimited economic harm. Harberger (2005) argues that an improved project evaluation system that significantly increases the rate of economic productivity will have a *permanent and continuing* effect on a country's growth rate. This characteristic contrasts with other successful policy reforms (such as trade, tax, and regulatory) that raise the time path of national income but produce one-off effects on the growth rate—that is, just at the time of the reform. An improved PIM system has the potential to permanently increase the country's growth rate.

Decision makers must look at public projects from several points of view simultaneously (Belli et al. 2001):

- *Profitability.* From the country's viewpoint to ensure that projects contribute more resources to the economy than they use.

- *Feasibility.* From the financial and fiscal viewpoints to ensure that the implementing agencies will have the resources to implement projects as designed.
- *Fairness.* From the viewpoint of the people who are most affected by projects to ensure that the distribution of costs and benefits is acceptable to society.

Rajaram et al. (2010) identify a list of the "must-have" features for a well-functioning PIM system (also see figure 3.8). These key features are the bare bones institutional features that would minimize major risks and provide an effective process for managing public investments:

- *Investment guidance and preliminary screening.* At the outset, broad strategic guidance for public investment is often an important way to anchor government decisions and to guide sector-level decision makers. Such guidance may be derived from a national plan or another medium-term to long-term strategic document that establishes economywide development priorities at the highest decision-making levels. A first-level screening of all project proposals should be undertaken to ensure that they meet the minimum criteria of consistency with the strategic goals of the government and the budget classification tests for inclusion as a project rather than as a recurrent spending item.

- *Formal project appraisal.* Projects or programs that meet the first screening test should undergo more rigorous scrutiny of their cost-benefit ratio or cost-effectiveness. The project selection process needs to ensure that projects proposed for financing have been evaluated for their social and economic values. The quality of ex ante project evaluation depends very much on the quality of the analysis, which in turn depends on the capacity of the staff and on their project evaluation skills. Investment in training in project evaluation techniques is an important aspect of an effective public investment system.

- *Independent review of appraisal.* When departments and ministries (rather than a central unit) undertake the appraisal, an independent peer review might be necessary to check any subjective, self-serving bias in the evaluation. Even the worst projects have groups of beneficiaries and promoters, and so it is crucial to kill bad projects before they develop a strong constituency.

- *Project selection and budgeting.* It is important that the process of appraising and selecting public investment projects be linked in an appropriate way to the budget cycle, even though the project evaluation cycle may run on a different timetable. There is clearly a two-way relationship between the budget cycle and the project selection cycle. The fiscal framework and the annual budget need to establish envelopes for public investment (on an aggregate or sectoral basis) so that a sustainable investment program can be undertaken. Efficient investment also depends on whether the recurrent budget adjusts to reflect the impact of the capital projects.

- *Project implementation.* Project design should include clear organizational arrangements and a realistic timetable to ensure the availability of an adequate institutional capacity to implement the project.

- *Project changes.* The funding review process should have some flexibility in the disbursement profile to account for changes in project circumstances. Each funding request should be accompanied by an updated cost-benefit analysis and a reminder to project sponsors of their accountability for the delivery of the benefits. These funding mechanisms can reinforce the monitoring process, making it an active rather than a passive form of monitoring. Governments need to create the capacity to monitor implementation in a timely way and to address problems proactively as they are identified.

- *Service delivery.* Asset registers need to be maintained and asset values recorded. Ideally, countries should require their operating agencies to compile balance sheets on which the value of assets created through new fixed capital expenditure would be recorded. Whether there is accrual accounting or not, agencies should maintain thorough asset registers, including legal title to property where necessary.

- *Ex post project evaluation.* Evaluation of completed projects should focus on comparing the project's outputs and outcomes with the objectives set forth in the project design. Good practice suggests that the project design should build in the evaluation criteria and that learning from such ex post evaluations should be used to improve future project design and implementation.

Petrie (2009a, 2009b) discusses issues pertaining to PIM in resource-rich countries, noting that a PIM system is an open system that affects, and is affected by, the broader political economy of the state (Petrie 2009a). It is increasingly recognized that the key determinants of success for resource-dependent economies are a country's overall governance framework and the political economy of rent extraction and management. Consequently, Petrie (2009b) sets the PIM system within the context of the broader policy issues relating to natural resource extraction and the overall political environment (see box 4.4 on Chile's public investment system).

Conclusion

During the recent commodity boom, the long tradition of using GDP growth as a key performance indicator led to overoptimism in many low-income resource-rich countries. In these countries, aNNI is a better indicator of performance because it accounts both for factor payments abroad and for depletion of natural resources. Moreover, the strongest

---

Box 4.4

The National Investment System of Chile

Chile has managed to promote economic growth and keep discipline in its public finances through the use of transparent cost-benefit analysis for *all* public investment projects.

Every public investment project is subject to the same appraisal discipline under a set of clearly specified methodologies published by the Ministry of Planning. The law mandates that the capital budget sent to Congress by the Ministry of Finance may include only projects within the National Investment Plan (SNI) that have also been favorably assessed by the Ministry of Planning. Among its other qualities, this process screens out "white elephants" and eliminates the possibility of investment projects entering the budget at the congressional stage. The only entry point is the SNI.

The SNI is a coherent system firmly embedded in the public finances and jointly administered by the Ministry of Planning and the Ministry of Finance. It provides methodologies, continuous capacity building, and transparency through a publicly available data bank of projects.

policy messages for resource-rich countries are often linked to the question of net wealth creation, measured either narrowly as the difference between aNNI and consumption or more broadly as ANSs.

The wealth analysis suggests that a range of policies are needed to ensure that mineral wealth is parlayed into sustainable growth. These policies include macroeconomic policies that encourage saving, fiscal policies that capture resource rents, public investment programs that put resource revenues to their best use (including investment in human capital), and resource policies that lead to rates of extraction that are dynamically efficient. Failure to implement sound policies risks the resource curse associated with severely negative growth consequences.

In practice, indicators of economic performance set the stage for the policies that are considered. In resource-rich countries, moving away from GDP growth complacency and focusing on aNNI and adjusted saving measures can improve the focus of the policy discussion. When it is recognized that negative adjusted saving dissipates national wealth and translates into a poorer future, it becomes clear that sustainable growth must be grounded in preserving and increasing national wealth.

Resource-rich low-income countries generally need to capture a larger share of the resource rents and invest them in ways that enhance the nation's productive capacity. An NRF coupled with an effective PIM system has some potential to address the three main problems associated with natural-resource riches:

• The Dutch disease, as public investment increases the productivity of private capital.
• Volatility, as public investment becomes a buffer to absorb fluctuations in revenues.
• Political economy issues, as a transparent, rules-based system discourages mismanagement.

Thus public investment would be the buffer absorbing the volatility of resource revenues.[8]

In summary, a well-designed NRF that successfully transforms resource revenues into national wealth (human and physical capital) could become a key element of the development strategy of resource-rich low-income countries. Such an NRF has the potential to partially, but significantly, address several of the challenges associated with natural resource revenues.

Notes

1. This chapter focuses on *nonrenewable* natural resources and on the effects of depletion on national wealth. Whereas renewable resources (such as agriculture, fishing, and forestry) share some of the fiscal challenges of nonrenewable resources (such as price volatility), depletion is not automatically an issue because sustainable extraction is possible. See Collier (2007) for an analysis contrasting extractive and agricultural commodities.

2. These costs of depletion are now routinely reported in the World Bank's World Development Indicators database. The "About the Data" note to table 3.16 in *World Development Indicators 2010* (World Bank 2010) provides a succinct summary of the methodology used to estimate the depletion of natural resources.

3. Chapter 5 of World Bank (2006) presents per capita wealth accumulation figures in detail.

4. For the most up-to-date summary of the issues, see Daniel, Keen, and McPherson (2010).

5. For example, U.S. ring fencing prevents tax arbitrage and transfer-pricing schemes, and it prevents a company from avoiding taxes by means of new exploration projects.

6. For a comprehensive list of NRFs, see Davis et al. (2003).

7. These copper price projections can be retrieved from http://www.dipres.cl/572/propertyvalue-16158.html.

8. Collier et al. (2010) argue that because investment is already the most volatile part of aggregate output, the cost of some fluctuation in public investment should be quite modest.

References

Arrow, K. J., P. Dasgupta, and K.-G. Maler. 2003. "Evaluating Projects and Assessing Sustainable Development in Imperfect Economies." In *Economics for an Imperfect World*, ed. R. Arnott, B. Greenwald, R. Kanbur, and B. Nalebuff, 299–330. Cambridge, MA: MIT Press.

Atkinson, G., and K. Hamilton. 2003. "Savings, Growth and the Resource Curse Hypothesis." *World Development* 31 (11): 1793–807.

Belli, P., J. R. Anderson, H. N. Barnum, J. A. Dixon, and J.-P. Tan. 2001. *Economic Analysis of Investment Operations—Analytical Tools and Practical Applications*. Washington, DC: World Bank.

Boadway, R., and M. Keen. 2010. "Theoretical Perspectives on Resource Tax Design." In *The Taxation of Petroleum and Minerals: Principles, Problems and Practice*, ed. P. Daniel, M. Keen, and C. McPherson, 13–74. Routledge Explorations in Environmental Economics. New York: Routledge.

Collier, P. 2007. "Managing Commodity Booms: Lessons of International Experience." Paper prepared for the African Economic Research Consortium, Department of Economics, Centre for the Study of African Economies, Oxford University.

———. 2010a. *The Plundered Planet: Why We Must—and How We Can—Manage Nature for Global Prosperity.* Oxford, U.K.: Oxford University Press.

———. 2010b. "Principles of Resource Taxation for Low-Income Countries." In *The Taxation of Petroleum and Minerals: Principles, Problems and Practice,* ed. P. Daniel, M. Keen, and C. McPherson, 75–86. Routledge Explorations in Environmental Economics. New York: Routledge.

Collier, P., F. van der Ploeg, M. Spence, and A. Venables. 2010. "Managing Resource Revenues in Developing Countries." *IMF Staff Papers* 57: 84–118.

Commission of the European Communities, International Monetary Fund, Organisation for Economic Co-operation and Development, United Nations, and World Bank. 2009. *System of National Accounts 2008.* New York: United Nations.

Daniel, P., M. Keen, and C. McPherson. 2010. *The Taxation of Petroleum and Minerals: Principles, Problems and Practice.* Routledge Explorations in Environmental Economics. New York: Routledge.

Dasgupta, P. 2001. *Human Well-Being and the Natural Environment.* Oxford, U.K.: Oxford University Press.

Davis, J. M., R. Ossowski, J. Daniel, and S. Barnett. 2003. "Stabilization and Savings Funds for Non-Renewable Resources: Experience and Fiscal Policy Implications." In *Fiscal Policy Formulation and Implementation in Oil-Producing Countries,* ed. J. M. Davis, R. Ossowski, and A. Fedelino, 273–315. Washington, DC: International Monetary Fund Press.

Fiess, N. 2002. *Chile's New Fiscal Rule.* Washington, DC: World Bank. http://web .duke.edu/~acb8/fsb/fsb_7rev.pdf.

Hamilton, K., and M. Clemens. 1999. "Genuine Savings Rates in Developing Countries." *World Bank Economic Review* 13 (2): 333–56.

Hamilton, K., and E. Lutz. 1996. "Green National Accounts: Policy Uses and Empirical Evidence." Environmental Economics Series Paper 39, World Bank, Washington, DC.

Harberger, A. C. 2005. "On the Process of Growth and Economic Policy in Developing Countries." Bureau for Policy and Program Coordination Issue Paper 13, U.S. Agency for International Development, Washington, DC.

Hartwick, J. M. 1977. "Intergenerational Equity and the Investing of Rents from Exhaustible Resources." *American Economic Review* 66 (5): 972–74.

———. 1993. "Notes on Economic Depreciation of Natural Resource Stocks and National Accounting." In *Approaches to Environmental Accounting,* ed. A. Franz and C. Stahmer. Heidelberg, Germany: Physica-Verlag.

Humphreys, M., and M. E. Sandbu. 2007. "The Political Economy of Natural Resource Funds." In *Escaping the Resource Curse,* ed. M. Humphreys, J. D. Sachs, and J. E. Stiglitz, 94–234. New York: Columbia University Press.

Kopits, G. F., and J. Craig. 1998. "Transparency in Government Operations." Occasional Paper 158, International Monetary Fund, Washington, DC.

Kopits, G. F., and S. A. Symansky. 1998. "Fiscal Policy Rules." Occasional Paper 162, International Monetary Fund, Washington, DC.

Larrain, P., and F. Parro. 2008. "Chile menos volatile." *El trimestre economico* 75 (3): 563–96.

Le, T. M. 2011. "Taxing Resource Wealth: The Political Economy of Fiscal Regimes for Extractive Industries." In *Rents to Riches? The Political Economy of Natural Resource–Led Development,* ed. N. Barma, K. A. Kaiser, T. M. Le, and L. Vinuela, 113–64. Washington, DC: World Bank.

Marcel, Mario, Marcelo Tokman, Rodrigo Valdés, and Paula Benavides. 2001. "Structural Budget Balance: Methodology and Estimation for the Chilean Central Government 1987–2001." Series of Studies on Public Finance, Ministry of Finance, Chile. http://www.dipres.cl/572/propertyvalue-15408.html.

OECD (Organisation for Economic Co-operation and Development). 2009. "Managing the Oil Economy—Can Mexico Do It Better?" In *OECD Economic Surveys: Mexico 2009,* 41–54. Paris: OECD.

Perry, G. E., L. Servén, and R. Suescún, eds. 2008. *Fiscal Policy, Stabilization, and Growth: Prudence or Abstinence?* Washington, DC: World Bank.

Petrie, M. 2009a. "Public Investment Management in Resource-Rich Countries: Overview Paper." World Bank, Washington, DC.

———. 2009b. "Public Investment Management Technical Note as Adapted for Resource-Rich Countries." World Bank, Washington, DC.

Rajaram, A., T. M. Le, N. Biletska, and J. Brumby. 2010. "A Diagnostic Framework for Assessing Public Investment Management." Policy Research Working Paper 5397, World Bank, Washington, DC.

Rodríquez, J., C. Tokman, and A. Vega. 2007. "Structural Balance Policy in Chile." *OECD Journal on Budgeting* 7 (2): 59–92.

Sachs, J. D. 2007. "How to Handle the Macroeconomics of Oil Wealth." In *Escaping the Resource Curse,* ed. M. Humphreys, J. D. Sachs, and J. E. Stiglitz, 173–93. New York: Columbia University Press.

Tornell, A., and P. Lane. 1999. "The Voracity Effect." *American Economic Review* 88 (5): 22–46.

World Bank. 2006. *Where Is the Wealth of Nations? Measuring Capital for the 21st Century.* Washington, DC: World Bank.

———. 2009. *World Development Indicators 2009*. Washington, DC: World Bank.

———. 2010. *World Development Indicators 2010*. Washington, DC: World Bank.

———. 2011. *The Changing Wealth of Nations*. Washington, DC: World Bank.

CHAPTER 5

Analyzing the Distributive Effects of Fiscal Policies: How to Prepare (Analytically) for the Next Crisis

José Cuesta and Jorge Martinez-Vazquez

This chapter reviews the empirical evidence on the distributive consequences of fiscal policies during the 2008–09 global crisis and the methodologies used in the analyses. That review shows, first, that little evidence on distributive impacts exists, and, second, that most of the existing empirical work has focused on aggregated trends of total and social public spending rather than on household-level distributional analyses resulting from such trends. The rest of the chapter assesses the merits and limitations of the available alternative techniques to match analytical demands with available resources and strategic issues against the backdrop of a hard-pressing crisis. Finally, the chapter proposes two simple analytical tools: a follow-up questionnaire and ex ante microsimulations on the impacts of equality of opportunity. These tools complement existing simple aggregate spending trends and sophisticated ex post microsimulation assessments. An illustration based on Liberia shows how ex ante microsimulations can be used to identify fiscal policy response winners and losers and the approximate magnitudes of the effects caused by crisis-related shocks.

Introduction

Poverty and inequality have very complex roots, and so their eradication cannot rely on simple measures. Public finance policy can help, however, by making sure that the tax burdens of the poor are very low and that the composition and direction of public expenditures favor the poor and redress unfair allocations. Implementing these types of policies requires a thorough understanding of the fiscal incidence of government budgets. For decades now, the theory and practice of public finance have been dedicated to conceptualizing and measuring how the revenue and expenditure sides of government budgets affect the distribution of income among households; how equitable these changes may be; and, in particular, how government policies actually help the poor. The main objective of this chapter is to analyze the distributive effects of public spending and revenue-side measures in the context of the global financial crisis.

Because of the limitations of the current methodologies, we propose two specific analytical instruments—(1) a questionnaire on the fiscal decisions made at the sectoral and intrasectoral levels and (2) an analysis of ex ante microsimulations of the impacts on equality of opportunities caused by fiscal policy decisions—as a way to be analytically better prepared for understanding the distributive effects of the next crisis. The analytical discussion is also complemented with two practical illustrations of operational tools, one referring to a crisis sectoral response questionnaire and the other a microsimulation application in a context of severe data limitation (as is the case for Liberia).

Although it is difficult to generalize from the prolific literature, some general patterns emerge from a review of the literature—see Martinez-Vazquez (2008) for an extensive review. First, the higher use of direct taxes tends to make the final distribution of income more equal—that is, direct taxes generally tend to be progressive. The reverse is true for indirect taxes. The higher relative importance of indirect taxes tends to make tax systems more regressive, although this can be automated exemptions (zero rating) of necessities. As a net result, we are likely to find in the typical country that the overall tax incidence may be proportional or mildly regressive for very-low-income groups, proportional over a large range of middle-income groups, and progressive for higher-income groups. It is interesting to note that recent evidence for Latin America shows that the links between spending and taxation are weak (Breceda, Rigolini, and Saavedra 2008). Spending is slightly biased in favor of the rich (that is, it is regressive). Although indirect taxes are paid mostly by higher quintiles of the distribution (for example, they are pro-poor), they are also regressive because the poor pay a higher share of their incomes (with variations across countries). Many tax systems therefore tend to show a proportion to a mildly progressive incidence impact. In general, taxes have not been a very effective means of redistributing income. One reason for the limited redistributional scope of tax policy is the potentially large excess burdens or efficiency losses associated with highly progressive taxation. Second, direct cash transfers and in-kind transfers tend to be more progressive if they are adequately targeted and implemented. And, third, the expenditure side of the budget (including transfers) can have a more significant impact on income distribution. Expenditure programs in the social sectors (education and health) are more progressive as more is spent in relative and absolute terms on those services that are more frequently used by the poor (especially basic education and primary health care).

There are, however, multiple reasons why these general results may vary from country to country. These reasons include other economic and institutional factors such as the level of development of private markets and the degree of decentralization of public finance. For example, the lack of data sometimes leads to the omission of subnational taxes and transfers from incidence analysis. This omission is likely to present a picture of incidence that is more progressive (or less regressive) than is actually the case because regional and local taxes tend to be more regressive than central taxes. Additional factors affecting income distribution are the extent of the underground or informal sector, the distributive effects of other public policies such as monetary policies and price controls on goods and services, minimum wages, foreign exchange rationing, prohibitions on exports and import quotas, interest rate controls on deposits, and other forms of financial repression. These factors may have a significant impact on the overall distribution of tax burdens and public spending, and they may even reverse the final fiscal incidence that we would have reached in the absence of those aspects.[1] For example, price controls on farm products tend to hurt the rural poor and benefit the urban poor and the rich. Financial repression of interest paid on bank deposits tends to hurt the poor more than the rich because of poor people's inability to seek alternative savings vehicles. Foreign exchange rationing and import quotas tend to be quite regressive, and export controls can hurt small traditional crop farmers. As a result, even though our focus is on fiscal incidence, we need to be aware that many other government policies have as large or larger potential effects on the distribution of income and on the welfare of the poor.

In addition, the balance of short- and long-term incidence becomes extremely relevant in a period of crisis. Current or annual income for many individuals is subject to large fluctuations—and more so during crisis periods. Individuals may have low current income simply because they are in a low-income period of their lives (of school age or in retirement) or because they are disproportionately vulnerable to or affected by a crisis. Distributive implications are very different if individuals will pass through these different stages in their life cycles or if the effects of the crisis are transitory. As such, the design of compensatory fiscal policies may need to take these temporality issues into account. In other words, public transfers and tax decisions may contribute differently to short-run vulnerability than to longer-term lifetime vulnerability. In general, what we know from exercises of lifetime incidence, as in Fullerton and Rogers (1991), is that the patterns of lifetime incidence are often quite similar to but less pronounced than those based on an annual income perspective. As shown in the next section of this chapter, evidence related to crises points to efforts to protect public spending that targets the poor, although the extent of this is limited[2] and country specific and is more likely to take place in middle-income than in low-income countries (LICs)—see Arze del Granado, Gupta, and Hajdenberg (2010).

A second important crisis-related consideration from a distributive perspective is that a crisis may generate a cadre of "new" poor or crisis-specific vulnerable groups—typically groups that were not poor in off-crisis periods. This point has been shown by Habib et al. (2010c) in the context of the recent financial crisis, substantiating as well that such vulnerable groups also differ from country to country. A distributive analysis of fiscal policies during a crisis requires identifying those groups; singling them out in the exercise; and capturing the welfare dynamics throughout the precrisis, crisis, and postcrisis periods. Unfortunately, economists have not yet devised adequate methodologies to take into account not only crisis-specific aspects but also more "traditional" considerations (such as a comprehensive or truly *net* fiscal incidence or the integration of the distributional impacts of other government policies). Thus we have a limited view of how government budgets affect the distribution of income, especially that of the poor and vulnerable groups in the context of an economic crisis.

In the next section of this chapter, we review the empirical literature on the distributive effects of public spending and taxation, revenue-side measures, in the context of the recent global crisis. We also review the methodological literature to better understand the merits and limitations of the instruments used to generate such results. That section is followed by a systematic discussion of analytical alternatives and their empirical and operational implications in facing the knowledge demands of a new crisis. The fourth section proposes the use of two specific analytical instruments in preparing for the next crisis: (1) a questionnaire on the fiscal decisions made at the sectoral and intrasectoral levels and (2) ex ante microsimulations of the equity of opportunities-related impacts of fiscal policies as a complement to the traditional (output) indicators of welfare (such as income, expenditure, or wealth). These analytical tools are illustrated in the case of Liberia. The final section presents our conclusions.

Literature Review

What We Know about the Distributive Effects of Fiscal Policies during Crises

The relatively little time elapsed since the onset of the recent global crisis, the scarcity of good disaggregated data, and the unavailability of appropriate analytical tools have limited the number of studies that directly address the impact of the crisis on poor people and throughout the income distribution. Nevertheless, a series of papers directly or indirectly sheds some light on this issue.

Several cross-country aggregate analyses have been conducted on the impact of the global crisis on poverty and income distribution. Chen and Ravallion (2009)[3] estimate that the crisis may have added 53 million people to the 2009 count of people living on less than US$1.25 a day and 64 million people to the number living on less than US$2.00 a day. This means that the global poverty rate would have fallen from 42 percent to 39 percent in 2009, whereas the precrisis trajectory would have brought the poverty rate down to 38 percent. Wan and Francisco (2009) find that the crisis adversely affected poverty reduction, although it should not be expected to lead into an increase in poverty because most developing countries in Asia increased social expenditures in 2009—even in a context of reduced GDP growth.

The International Monetary Fund (IMF) finds that, compared with developed countries, the LICs have been weathering the global crisis rather well (IMF 2010a). Real per capita gross domestic product (GDP) growth has stayed positive in two-thirds of LICs—very much in contrast to the experiences of these countries in previous global crises. The big difference for LICs this time has been the active countercyclical policies these countries have implemented, enabled by policy buffers they worked to build over the last decade. An early account of 15 IMF anticrisis programs indicated that they all included measures protecting the most vulnerable groups (IMF 2009). Yang et al. (2010) also report that 16 of the 19 IMF programs initiated in 2008–09 had budgeted higher social spending during 2009. In addition, spending output data for 2009 suggest that social spending increased by approximately 0.5 percent of GDP in Sub-Saharan Africa countries with IMF-supported programs, which is comparable with the output in nonprogram countries in the region. For 2010–11, the 2010 *World Economic Outlook* projected the real primary spending increases for 86 countries to be on average 3.7 percent a year (IMF 2010b). For a 32-country sample with spending reductions relative to GDP, the real primary spending was still projected to rise, on average, 1.9 percent annually.

The picture painted by the United Nations Children's Fund (UNICEF) is not as optimistic. Using IMF data on fiscal projections for 126 LICs, Ortiz et al. (2010) find that nearly half of these countries (44 percent) are expected to have reduced aggregate government spending in 2010–11 compared with 2000–09, and that 25 percent of the sample countries are expected to have made average reductions of 7 percent in the real value of total government expenditures. In this general expenditure-cutting climate, a publication by the United Nations Research Institute for Social Development discusses the risks of pro-poor social spending being curtailed during the recovery and the potential impacts of further targeting social protection expenditures and reducing subsidies (UNRISD 2010).[4]

Although useful in offering panoramic views on the impact of the crisis on poverty and spending trends in developing countries, the aggregate studies fall short (as openly recognized by their authors) of providing an accurate account of the incidence of such fiscal packages and who the losers are at the individual and household levels. Several recent studies have produced in-depth individual country analyses of the impact of the crisis at the household level. Habib et al. (2010a) use a microsimulation approach for Bangladesh, linking macroprojections with precrisis household data to measure the poverty and distributional impact (by income groups and regions) of the macroeconomic shocks originating in the global crisis. They find that, by comparison to the benchmark case (with no crisis), the average household incomes in 2009 and 2010 are expected to be 0.7 percent and 2.4 percent lower, respectively. Along with the lower incomes, the poverty head count rate and extreme poverty rate are expected to be, respectively, 0.4 and 0.2 percentage points higher in 2009 as a consequence of the crisis; for 2010, those poverty rates are expected to be, respectively, 1.2 and 0.9 percentage points higher. The overall impact of the crisis on aggregate measures of inequality is found to be negligible. But the most striking result of their analysis is that the types of households likely to be poor as a direct result of the crisis are households with characteristics somewhat different from those of the structurally poor, including a higher share of urban and nonagriculture sector workers. Another interesting finding from their approach is that the changes in poverty measures do not tell the whole story about the impact of the crisis. They also find a substantial consumption/income impact in the top half of the income distribution.[5]

Habib et al. (2010b) have conducted a similar microsimulation study on the impact of the crisis in the Philippines. They find that, by comparison with the counterfactual case (with no crisis), the average household income levels in 2009 and 2010 are expected to be 2.2 percent and 3.6 percent lower, respectively. The poverty head count rate is expected to be 1.45 percentage points higher in 2009 and 2.07 percentage points higher in 2010, and the impacts on the poverty gap and severity are expected to be, respectively, 0.71 and 1.02 percentage points higher in 2009 and to go up slightly in 2010. The overall impact of the crisis on aggregate measures of income inequality in the Philippines is also found to be negligible. The microsimulation approach enables the authors to examine how the poverty impact is spatially distributed and what types of households will be most affected. Geographically, the impact of the crisis is expected to be severest in urban centers with a manufacturing base, but even after that is taken into account, the significant regional gaps in poverty and income levels will remain. By gender, the crisis is expected to lead to relatively higher poverty among female-headed households than among male-headed households, even though the poverty rates will continue to be lower among female-headed households. The analysis also reveals differences between the "crisis-vulnerable" or "newly poor" households and the permanently or structurally poor ones. The newly poor households are smaller, have lower dependency, have higher skills, are more urban, and are employed in something other than agriculture. In terms of the distribution of income losses, those in the 70th percentile and above are expected to be less adversely affected in urban areas; the impact is more evenly distributed among rural households.[6]

This cursory literature review is the evidence that most of the empirical work around the crisis has centered on the notion of aggregate impacts; the cyclicality of total and social public spending; and, to some extent, the microeconomic effects across households. However, much less information is available on the specific fiscal decisions made in the context of the crisis. For example, Arze del Granado, Gupta, and Hajdenberg (2010) find that the level of economic development in previous crises was negatively associated with the degree of cyclicality of health and education spending. Brumby and Verhoeven (2010) find that protecting education spending overrides health spending in developing countries, whereas Arze del Granado, Gupta, and Hajdenberg report that spending in health and education sectors tends to be acyclical during economic downturns and procyclical during upswings in developing countries.[7] Yang et al. (2010) find that budgeted social spending in 2009 was higher than in the previous year for 16 of 19 LICs. More interesting, Ortiz et al. (2010) report that approximately 24 percent of the amounts announced in fiscal stimulus packages in developing countries was directed at pro-poor and social protection programs. They also report that numerous governments are considering capping or cutting wage bills, phasing out or removing fuel or food subsidies, and rationalizing or reforming transfers such as social protection; the expansion of wages, subsidies, and social transfers are being contemplated in a smaller number of countries (as discussed in IMF country reports).[8]

Techniques for Distributive Analysis

Despite the relatively scarce attention paid to empirical analyses during the crisis, specific fiscal policy decisions can have important distributive consequences—either deliberate or unintended. Without regard to their primary objectives (for example, economic efficiency or growth), all or practically all fiscal policies have an impact on income distribution and therefore on inequality and poverty. Frequently, however, fiscal policies demonstrate explicit equity goals with more or less political will for redistribution.[9] For decades, a well-developed body of literature has examined the links between fiscal policy and distribution. This literature is reviewed, for example, in Martinez-Vazquez (2008) and Essama-Nssah (2009). The World Bank has produced an important string of contributions in this field, including works by Chenery et al. (1974); Selowsky (1979); Dervis, de Melo, and Robinson (1982); Van de Walle and Nead (1995); Bourguignon and Pereira da Silva (2003); Lofgren (2004); Shah (2005); and Moreno-Dobson and Wodon (2008). Rather than providing yet another review, this section focuses on the merits and limitations of the most commonly used techniques for distributive analysis.

Two critical questions for the distributive analysis of fiscal policies.
There are two fundamental questions that need to be asked and for
which analytical tools are needed:

1. What are the distributive impacts of tax and expenditure policies?
2. What are the capacities of tax and expenditure policies to affect the
   current distribution of income and to reduce the incidence of poverty?

These two umbrella questions can be researched from a *static* perspective, by finding the impact of the entire set of tax and expenditure
policies that make up the budget system. Or they can be researched for
isolated components, such as particular taxes or the entire tax structure,
or for different public spending components. The two umbrella questions also may be researched from a *dynamic* perspective by analyzing
the distributive consequences of fiscal measures in the context of the
financial crisis or in other contexts such as those of changes in expenditure policies or tax reform. In a dynamic context, two sets of results are
compared: those of a counterfactual scenario without the innovation (or
as if the crisis had not taken place) and those arising from the innovation or change.

Available analytical tools. Analyzing the distributive impacts of public
policies has a long tradition in economics, with roots in tax and expenditure incidence analysis going back to classical economists. The actual
quantification of those impacts on the distribution of income and the
incidence of poverty is relatively more recent, dating from the availability
of data sets from individual taxpayer returns and household income and
expenditure surveys over the last several decades. There are different
ways to group the analytical tools available today, but here we will follow
the general practice of distinguishing among (1) conventional tax and
expenditure incidence analysis, (2) the tax-benefit microsimulation
(TBM) model, and (3) the computable general equilibrium (CGE)
model. In terms of calculation and data demands, those three tools largely
build on each other and provide a natural progression in the level of
complexity; however, the TBM model is the newest tool, attempting a
compromise between the simplicity and readiness of conventional incidence analysis and the comprehensiveness and complexity of the CGE
model. We also include ex ante and ex post evaluation techniques, which
(although not specific to fiscal policies alone) may provide useful analyses
on their redistributive consequences.

Conventional tax and expenditure incidence analysis. Incidence analysis is a technique used to estimate how much of a given category of expenditure is received by a particular group in society and how much taxation is borne by each group. The methodology allows for a flexible definition of expenditure and taxation categories, as well as groups (from income groups to others defined by gender, age, or geographic criteria). It aims not only to capture how much a group receives or pays but also to determine how "progressively" it does so—that is, how the share of burdens and benefits decreases and increases, respectively, with incomes. In the case of expenditure incidence, the analysis consists mainly of three steps (Van de Walle 1996):

- Approximating the value to consumers of a public service, typically equated with the cost of providing it
- Ranking the beneficiaries according to some agreed-on measure of welfare distribution across the population
- Assigning the provision—or use—of the public service across the distribution to compute the shares of the services that are allocated to different portions of the population.

Typically, the unit of analysis is the representative household by quintile or decile of either incomes or expenditures (on a per capita basis). In the case of tax incidence, the analysis is carried out on the bases of annual data for income sources and expenditure patterns and of several assumptions on how the different taxes are shifted to households because they are consumers, producers, or owners of factors of production (labor, capital, and land). These assumptions are known in the literature as "shifting or incidence assumptions" that facilitate allocating the burdens of each tax to different income groups.

Two main advantages of this methodology are the simple but powerful set of results it produces and the policy message that can be attached to those results. Results are often presented as the share of expenditures that benefit each considered group or the proportion of each group's incomes represented by taxes paid. When the computational results are compared for two scenarios—for example, before and after a tax policy change across categories of individuals or households—the results directly indicate which group is benefiting most or how the estimated distribution fares with respect to the anticipated distribution.

Several important caveats are associated with conventional incidence analyses. These analyses produce the observed results on the bases of a particular set of assumptions regarding the economic shifting of taxes and of the allocation of benefits from public expenditures. Although most of these assumptions are standard and are supported by a large and well-established body of literature, there is no guarantee that the assumptions actually hold true in different economic environments. In addition, the calculations in conventional incidence analysis rarely incorporate information on how a certain program or policy influences the behavior of individuals (beneficiaries relative to nonbeneficiaries in the case of expenditure programs or labor supplied or commodities purchased in the case of taxes). The analysis does not typically allow for secondary effects or general equilibrium effects. The analysis also equates benefits and costs with budgetary outlays or tax revenues collected, ignoring changes in individual welfare arising from changes in consumer surplus or the excess burden of taxes. Thus conceptually, the incidence analysis rests on several strong operational assumptions: benefits received by individuals equal the costs of providing those benefits; individuals give equal value to transfers received and each dollar taxed away; there is perfect translation of taxes to consumers; and, typically, no evasion or illegal behaviors are taken into account.

TBM models. Conventional incidence analysis may not be adequate when the specific details of policy options or changes in the macroeconomic environment need to be accounted for and incorporated into the analysis. TBMs are a natural extension of computer programs that typically simulate distributions of disposable incomes across a sample of real households—from national microdata sets—after alternative policy scenarios are introduced. The common structure of TBMs for redistribution analysis comprises three elements:

- A microdata set containing the economic and sociodemographic characteristics of a sample of individuals or households
- The rules of the policies to be simulated—such as the budget constraint facing each agent, the tax structure and key parameters, and eligibility for social transfers
- A theoretical model of the behavioral response of agents—see Bourguignon and Spadaro (2006).

In practice, TBMs typically differ in the final element; in fact, not every TBM models behavioral responses of agents. However, static or *arithmetic* models are not necessarily inferior to behavioral models. There may be situations in which policies are expected to have no behavioral effects over the short run. For example, tax deductions associated with children may have no impact on household composition—at least in the short term—and so distributive analyses not concerned with demographic changes may well focus on an arithmetic approach. But if the intervention is expected to affect female labor supply, behavioral models are more appropriate to capture the potential distributional effects through the labor market.

From a distributive standpoint, there are several advantages to using TBMs. First, these microsimulations do not restrict the distributive analyses to representative households—either on socioeconomic levels such as incidence analyses or by some characteristic of the household (perhaps urban or rural) or its head (perhaps skilled or unskilled). These distinctions are harder to achieve in conventional incidence analysis or CGE modeling. Indeed, TBMs are adapted to exploit the heterogeneity of the features and circumstances of real households available in microdata sets. Second, TBMs allow for analyses of policy scenarios that typically offer much greater detail than conventional tax and expenditure incidence analysis (including tax and expenditure rules, conditions, eligibility, and so on). Also, TBMs allow for quite sophisticated reform analyses that incorporate evasion and labor supply decisions.[10]

From the timely standpoint of analyzing the distributional impact of the global crisis, TBMs also offer the advantage of identifying and better fine-tuning the transmission of shocks through trade, credit availability, foreign direct investment flows, changes in migration and remittances, and so forth. Using a TBM approach to establish the distributional impact of the crisis involves several practical steps.[11] First, microdata from household surveys and the like are needed to establish a precrisis baseline. Developing these data may involve creating and calibrating household income generation models (including occupational decisions and earnings) and nonlabor income sources (including capital income from rents, interest, and so on; remittances; and social income). Second, there is a need to generate macroeconomic projections reflecting the impact of the crisis on basic market conditions, including employment, income, prices, remittances, and other transmission mechanisms that are expected to have an impact on the distribution of income at the individual or household level. Third, simulations must be conducted to account for changes in population, aggregate output, employment and earnings, international and domestic remittances, and other changes in nonlabor income sources. These simulations may or may not allow for behavioral responses, as described earlier. The impact of the crisis is established by comparing the predictions from the simulations with the benchmark results, and they can be presented in terms of income distribution; impact on inequality and poverty; or differential effects across regional, gender, age, or other groupings. Profiling those households that are "crisis-vulnerable" may be of particular interest. Those are households that would not have been poor in 2010 had there been no crisis.

Despite the advantages offered, caveats are associated with TBMs. The main caveats refer to the sensitivity of the results to the behavioral modeling and the precision with which fiscal information, on the one hand, and household microdata, on the other hand, can be matched in practice. Typically, it is difficult to develop good behavioral response models from cross-sectional data; national longitudinal series are not often available in developing countries; and income generation information in household surveys is often not very reliable.

CGE models. CGE models have long been used to analyze tax and expenditure incidence, among other things. The general equilibrium approach to tax incidence was pioneered by Harberger (1962).[12] The essence of this approach was in observing the general equilibrium prices in a simplified economy before and after the introduction of taxes. At a later stage, numeric or CGE models were developed to capture in more detail the general equilibrium responses to taxes in the economy, allowing for different demand and production patterns, different resource endowments, and so on. As an example of the many CGE models being constructed, the World Bank in partnership with the United Nations has developed a recursively static, country-level CGE model that builds on standard open-economy models (Dervis, de Melo, and Robinson 1982). Its framework focuses on the fiscal and growth implications of achieving the Millennium Development Goals (MDGs) under current and alternative policies. The resulting CGE framework, known as MAMS (model for MDG simulation), benefits from the intrinsic modeling flexibility regarding structure, closures, commodities and activities, agents, and (specific to fiscal policy) spending and tax categories (see Lofgren 2004). MAMS typically separates investment from recurrent spending, and it includes multiple sectors beyond health and education such as water and sanitation or infrastructure. More important, MAMS is an integrated micro-macro-micro approach, consisting of three parts. First, an initial microeconomic analysis explores the demand and supply determinants of specific outcomes such as education, health, water, and sanitation. Costs associated with

MDG determinants—in line with a cost-effective, basic needs approach—are translated into a traditional economywide framework retrofitted with estimated public expenditures ensuring MDG achievement. Second, MAMS accounts for macro and sectoral impacts associated with MDG achieving spending and compares them with alternative financing scenarios involving foreign financing, domestic debt, or taxation alternatives. Third, a microsimulation model integrates the resulting labor market outcomes obtained from the CGE analysis (in terms of unemployment, employment structure, relative remunerations, and skill composition) with microdata from a household survey. A simulated income distribution is obtained, consistent with such outcomes. From that distribution, a detailed poverty and inequality analysis can be linked with the initial fiscal policies.

From a distributive standpoint, an important advantage of MAMS's integrated micro-macro-micro approach is that it allows capturing externalities and synergies simultaneously arising from public expenditures. Health-related spending may have effects on health status, nutrition, and educational outcomes that partial equilibrium models typically overlook. Also, second-round or indirect effects (in the form of either canceling or reinforcing impacts) are captured, in which, for example, public investment affects private investment, ultimately affecting growth and (potentially) future levels and composition of expenditures. The incidence results also include measures of "excess burdens," thereby allowing total burdens to exceed total taxes paid. All in all, the microsimulation of welfare distributions—consistent with obtained macro scenarios—is clearly superior to distributional analyses based on household data.[13]

Well-known shortcomings are associated with CGE models, and most of those shortcomings are applicable to MAMS. These shortcomings include high sensitivity to modeling assumptions, lack of evidence supporting certain assumptions, outdated national accounting foundations for the economywide modeling, and an inability to capture the institutional dimensions of key sectors. New developments, however, are starting to deal with some of these shortcomings, such as general entropy methods of balancing matrixes and the inclusion of behavior in microsimulation exercises.

Ex ante and ex post evaluations.[14] Experimental and quasi-experimental impact evaluation techniques[15] compare the effects of a program across beneficiaries and nonbeneficiaries. New evaluations of human capital and poverty impacts build on the behavioral benefit incidence literature that typically estimates the distributive (marginal and average) benefits of existing social programs or their scaling. Impact studies—both accounting- and behavior-based exercises—usually assume neither administrative nor delivery costs. They do assume identical valuations and consumption possibilities across households.

Evaluation analyses can be divided into ex ante and ex post behavioral studies, depending on the stage of the program cycle at which impacts are evaluated. For prospective reforms that are not already in place, ex ante simulations are the only feasible ones to assess distributive impacts. Those simulations are rare, however. They require an additional number of assumptions about the way agents choose among different alternatives that are not already established (Bourguignon and Ferreira 2003). By contrast, ex post evaluations typically observe the difference between individuals who are confronted by or concerned with the reforms and individuals who are not (Bourguignon and Spadaro 2006). Ex ante simulations may also take different approaches. General equilibrium models incorporating either static or dynamic behavior have long been criticized for their sensitivity to modeling assumptions—see Cogneau, Grimm, and Robilliard (2003) for a discussion in the context of poverty reduction. Alternative partial equilibrium behavioral microsimulations are rarely used in the analysis of social programs in developing countries, although they are frequently used in tax-benefit models in developed countries— see Creedy and Duncan (2002) and Bourguignon and Spadaro (2006) for reviews. Bourguignon and Spadaro (2006) report that these models are also subject to limitations, such as their specificity to the policy evaluated and the corresponding microdata and the difficulties of testing the assumptions underlying the structural model on which behavior is modeled.

Among the few ex ante behavioral microsimulations in developing countries, Bourguignon, Ferreira, and Leite (2003) and Cuesta and Ponce (2007) analyze social transfer reforms. Bourguignon and Ferreira (2003) argue that, in addition to the technical limitations mentioned earlier, the rare use of behavioral microsimulations to analyze social transfers is a consequence of typically small-size transfer programs and the difficulty in disentangling informal and formal labor-related behavior.

Analytical Preparation for the Next Crisis

The earlier review here of methodological approaches indicates that several analytical alternatives are available for the distributive analysis of fiscal policies. This section proposes how to go, in practice, about choosing among alternatives in a context of crisis. It also provides practical illustrations of specific choices.

Analytical Demands and Supply Issues during a Crisis

Both in off-crisis periods and during crises, a relevant analysis must take into account the following factors: the availability of methodologies, the heterogeneity of analytical demands, and the strategic issues in the policy dialogue. However, crises may shift the relative importance of the factors in this mix. In other words, although a crisis does not change the need to match analytical demands and resource availability, it might change the mix of factors and the priorities of researchers and policy makers. Thus, policy makers are expected to adopt even shorter-term horizons in the buildup to or in the midst of a crisis, with knowledge on overall effects becoming a more urgent demand. A larger interest in impacts across specific groups is expected, identifying the newly poor or quantifying the effects among the traditionally vulnerable groups. Strategic issues very relevant to the distributional analysis in the context of a crisis include the sustainability of an intervention, the transitory versus the permanent nature of a policy, or investments in information collection tools in difficult contexts requiring quick replies.

For example, the analysis by Habib et al. (2010c) of the distributional impact of the financial crisis includes a microsimulation-based comparison of labor and nonlabor incomes across households in crisis and noncrisis scenarios in Bangladesh, Mexico, and the Philippines. Their analysis concludes that the crisis has resulted in a substantial class of newly poor or crisis-vulnerable groups that have characteristics that differ from those of the chronically poor. The authors conclude that anticrisis measures should not only depend on the expansion of the existing safety nets (those targeted to the chronically poor) but also reach out to previously middle-class groups in urban settings—strategically speaking, a relevant group for their expected ability to influence policy choices.

Two different approaches can be taken to matching analytical demands and available resources. The first approach consists of finding an ex ante analytical deal breaker for the exercise. For example, a researcher working in a country where the most recent income-expenditure household survey was conducted five years earlier may consider the lack of updated information to be a critical constraint for a benefit incidence analysis of an ongoing crisis. Although widely used in practice, this approach does not provide objective guidelines across countries or across situations. In fact, another researcher may consider the low quality of the expenditure module, not the age of the survey, the deal breaker. A second approach proposes a two-step strategy. First, all available analytical techniques are compared in terms of some desirable properties that a distributive analysis of fiscal policy should have.[16] Second, the selected template or technique is adapted to include country- or task-specific needs, including those related to the crisis.

Table 5.1 describes how some of the analytical choices discussed in the preceding section fare in terms of a set of desirable properties. It is worth noting that this set of properties is illustrative rather than exhaustive. In addition, there might be multiple views of what a desirable property is in fiscal and redistributive contexts and whether a property should be universal or context-specific. However, although it is acknowledged that a desirable property is a flexible concept, some analytical features are unambiguously preferred over others:

- Low data requirements are preferred over more expansive requirements.
- Generally accepted assumptions are preferred over strong assumptions.
- Fewer assumptions needed to construct the analysis are preferred over more assumptions.
- Approaches that allow for multiple angles (such as incorporating a subnational or regional perspective with a national perspective or allowing for multiple agents based on age, gender, or education rather than representative agents) are preferred over more rigid approaches.
- Rapid-response exercises are preferred over lengthy periods of design, execution, monitoring, evaluation, and capacity building in crisis contexts.

Based on this illustrative list of criteria, the comparison in table 5.1 confirms that there is not one superior technique incorporating all desirable features. It is interesting to note, though, that even simple techniques can provide a meaningful disaggregation by individual features (say, gender or location) and allow one to focus on the most vulnerable groups—something that is critical for a pertinent discussion of distributive issues in a crisis context.

Table 5.1 Taxonomy of Analytical Demands and Potential Responses

Technique	Analytical features	Ex ante/ex post	Questions best addressed	Level of data demands	Strength of underlying assumptions	Incorporation of multiple agents	Speed of implementation
Traditional incidence analysis (arithmetic, behavioral, spatial)	• Partial equilibrium • Flexible enough to include behavior, spatial issues, and multiple groups	Typically ex post	• Are social spending and taxation progressive? • Are they pro-poor? • Are they well targeted?	Low to medium needs (household survey in its simplest version)	• Medium (tax) to low (expenditure incidence) • Additional information if behavioral functions and subnational analyses are included	Typically country- (or subnational-) level distribution	Rapid
TBM	• Typically partial equilibrium • Allows for multiple households and very detailed policy modeling	Ex ante	• Who will be most affected by a change in income tax rates?	Medium to high (household surveys and tax-benefit legislation)	Medium to high (depends on how comprehensive behavioral decisions are included)	Household and individual levels	Slow, unless previous work already exists
CGE	• General equilibrium • Can be designed to focus on specific areas—trade, finance, social	Both ex ante and ex post; static and dynamic (i.e., recursive static)	• What is the total effect in terms of poverty reduction and growth of a planned stimulus package? • What has been the impact of an external or internal shock?	High	High	Macro and sectoral levels, although also micro level (household) if combined with microsimulations	Slow, unless previous work already exists

Note: TBM = tax-benefit microsimulation (model); CGE = computable general equilibrium (model).

Making Sense of the Comparison: The Operational Part

In addition to the trade-offs associated with analytical, data, and strategic policy dialogue demands, this subsection reveals that, in practice, a number of relevant operational aspects are expected to vary from country to country. Once again, the following criteria are an illustrative rather than exhaustive sample of issues:

- *Main objective of the analysis.* Does the analysis have a normative objective or a positive objective? Does the main focus refer to the cost or impact of a prospective reform or anticrisis intervention? Is the focus instead on quantifying how progressive a fiscal intervention is?
- *Circumstances of the analytical demands in terms of timing and preexisting resources.* Is there a recently built CGE? Does a medium-term macroeconomic framework need to be constructed from scratch? Is a panel of data on incomes or expenditures available?
- *Existing capacity.* Does the government want to acquire capacity for its own autonomous analysis? How frequent will be the demand for this type of analysis? Are there possibilities of regional cooperation or economies of scale?

An attempt to triage coherent responses for multiple scenarios determined by these criteria, table 5.2 suggests a set of guidelines that address the operational aspects associated with requests for a distributive analysis of fiscal policies. It also compares those requests within a crisis context.

Table 5.2 substantiates the fact that different questions may call for different approaches, and so it is unlikely that a single approach will address all relevant demands in a crisis context. Rather, a relevant operational road map should look for the approach that bests suits the specific objectives and circumstances of the analytical demand. For example, in analyzing the distributive impact of an anticrisis fiscal intervention, it may be advisable to simply provide a rough estimate of the poverty impact if few details of the intervention/interventions are known. In another case, the most apt response may require a group-specific analysis because the details are already known, and strong opposition may be expected from the group likely to be the most affected. In that case, a TBM may be the best approach. The envisaged advantages of a given methodology may also vary by circumstances within a specific country. Developing a CGE from scratch may appear to require high initial investments, but if the country already has a social accounting matrix

Table 5.2 Decision-Making Guide for Choosing the Appropriate Analytical Tool during a Crisis

Main requirements of the demand for analytical assistance	Suggested analysis	Minimum data requirements	How to start	Capacity-building potential	Crisis relevance
"Quick-and-dirty" snapshots of the magnitude of distributive impacts of fiscal structure	Incidence analysis	Household surveys, expenditure and revenue data, basic understanding of the fiscal system	1. Make sure there are readily available household survey/surveys and expenditure data at national and subnational levels to conduct the impact analysis. 2. Apply the simplest methodological version of the analysis as core work. 3. Expand analysis to cover additional issues such as gender, ethnic disparities, central versus regional decisions, and regional aspects.	Low initial investment and low maintenance cost	Very relevant as a minimum or starting point
Detailed profile of winners and losers in a fiscal policy reform or anticrisis intervention	TBM	TBM software, programmed or available; household surveys and (ideally) administrative data	1. Invest up front in the construction of the TBM software. 2. Think carefully about what kind of behavior (if any) must be included in the analysis.	High initial investment, but relatively low maintenance cost when the model is constructed	Critical to adopt and assess measures
Fiscal policies to reduce distributive gaps in the face of a crisis; also, the growth and efficiency implications of fiscal policies adopted to confront the effects of the crisis	CGE	Social accounting matrix, CGE, sectoral data (for example, on education), macroeconomic sustainable framework, microsimulation model	1. Model the determinants of distributive or sectoral gaps. 2. Model the economy, ensuring fiscal links between sectors and macro aggregates. 3. Decide whether to use a microsimulation model or a simple representative distributive analysis. 4. If necessary, expand the analysis to specific issues: direct versus indirect effects, transmission channels, projections into the future, and so forth.	Medium to high initial investments (depending on decisions on macromicro integration, existence of social accounting matrix, modeling decisions) and medium maintenance costs	Critical for palliative responses to the estimated/expected effects of the crisis

Specific social project or intervention to reduce poverty or inequality	Ex post impact evaluation	Household surveys, beneficiary registries to complete baselines, detailed understanding of the program in question	1. Determine the best type of evaluation, given the circumstances and objectives (experimental, nonexperimental). 2. Ensure a proper baseline against which to estimate the impacts of the intervention. 3. Carefully plan a schedule to follow up the intervention and its effects.	High initial investments and medium to high maintenance costs throughout the lifetime of the project (and sometimes after its conclusion)	Too narrow for a broad perspective under a severe crisis, unless the project or intervention is of sizable magnitude
Prospective analysis of longer-term distributive conseqences of policy reform or anticrisis intervention	Ex ante analysis	Household surveys, main features of policy reform	1. Decide, if possible, to include relevant behavior (consumption or labor modeling). 2. Disaggregate the distributional analysis to the largest extent that household surveys allow.	Low to medium initial investment and low maintenance cost	Typically not the short-term priority in a crisis period, although critical for a consistent longer-term view

Note: TBM = tax-benefit microsimulation (model); CGE = computable general equilibrium (model).

with sufficient disaggregation to inform the CGE exercise, those investments are dramatically reduced. Assessing the specific needs of each demand and the available resources turns out to be critical for selecting an appropriate approach and more so in a crisis context.

Two Analytical Preparation Tools for Practitioners

In what follows, we provide two concrete illustrations of analytical applications to distributive analysis in the context of a crisis.

Tool 1: Fiscal Decision-Making Sectoral Questionnaire

The literature review in the previous sections reveals that most of the empirical work around crises has centered primarily on the notion of the cyclicality of total or social public spending—and much less on the specific fiscal decisions made in a crisis context. For example, what (if any) spending reallocation decisions were made because of the crisis? Did some form of prioritization of existing programs take place, or did spending cuts happen across the board? By contrast, was social spending protected or even increased? Were revenue collection reforms, among other reforms, accelerated or postponed? Although they provide a first critical piece of information, aggregate trends do not provide much knowledge about how fiscal decisions during a crisis are affecting the chronically poor, the newly poor, or (more specifically) the most vulnerable groups. This is true for four reasons. First, aggregate public spending trends say little about inter- and intrasectoral decisions on the spending and revenue fronts. Second, trends in sectoral spending (such as that for health or education) may have different distributional consequences based on the progressivity of their structure and crisis interventions. Third, "priority" pro-poor social expenditures whose changes are expected to have substantive distributional considerations do not have a universally accepted definition, and definitions change from country to country (see Ortiz et al. 2010).[17] Thus an increase in priority spending by some percentage in a given country says little about whether that increase is being directed to specific groups within the priority set, or if instead it is across the board. That will have different implications for both poverty and the distributional impacts of the policy. Fourth, as shown by Habib et al. (2010a), vulnerable groups should be expected to change among and across countries and over time. Ultimately, trends do not permit us to distinguish the distributive effects of the policies adopted to combat the crisis—nor the distributive effects of the crisis itself.

Obtaining information on the specific fiscal measures adopted to confront the crisis must be the first step in understanding the distributive impact of government policy. Table 5.3 provides a simple analytical tool that helps establish priorities, based on the distributive impacts of both spending- and revenue-related measures. The proposed tool is a questionnaire to be completed by government counterparts, country economists, or any other interested and informed actor. It is intended to monitor fiscal decisions regularly, both on their aggregate nature and through inter- and intrasectoral perspectives. If carried out periodically, this tool will allow comparisons between and within crisis periods. The result will be a comprehensive portrait of decisions planned and (effectively) made year by year. Most important, analysts will be able to use information on how adopted measures are expected to target specific vulnerable groups (if any) to link fiscal changes with their potential distributive consequences. An additional quantitative companion questionnaire may complement the qualitative questionnaire.

Tool 2: Ex ante Microsimulations of the Impact of the Crisis on Equality of Opportunities

A second proposed tool belongs to the tradition of ex ante microsimulations presented by Bourguignon and Ferreira (2003); Cogneau, Grimm, and Robilliard (2003); Bourguignon and Spadaro (2006); Cuesta and Ponce (2007); Bourguignon, Bussolo, and Pereira da Silva (2008); and Habib et al. (2010a, 2010b), among others. This section develops the application of ex ante microsimulations to the field of equality of opportunities, as initially developed by Roemer (1998). In contrast to traditional incidence analysis based on the distribution of outcomes (see Van de Walle and Nead 1995), the literature on equality of opportunities focuses on the distribution of opportunities. It also centers on how circumstances and individual effort become responsible for the observed distribution of opportunities, thereby shedding new light on the roles of individuals and the state in equity considerations. Operationally, Molinas et al. (2010) define opportunities as those key goods and services (such as water, basic education, health services, minimum nutrition, and citizen rights) whose access gives a person the chance to advance in society and to live a decent life. In a context of limited resources, an egalitarian allocation of such goods and services toward a goal of universal access is the preferred strategy in terms of fairness and justice.[18]

Suppose that a country whose education sector budget strongly depends on international aid is expected to face financing difficulties as a

Table 5.3   Questionnaire: Fiscal Measures Adopted during the Crisis

	2008		2009		2010 (expected)		Comments
1. What fiscal measures were adopted? *[Please pick all that apply.]*							
a—Total expenditures increased.							
b—Revenue measures were adopted.							
c—Both revenue and expenditures increased.							
d—There was no change in expenditures; however, there were reassignments.							
e—Expenditures were cut.							
f—There was an effort to restructure debt.							
2. What tax policy changes were made? *[Please pick all that apply; put "+" for increase, "–" for decrease, "0" for no change; indicate the change in tax rates in the comments section.]*	Tax rate	Tax base	Tax rate	Tax base	Tax rate	Tax base	
a—Personal income tax							
b—Corporate income tax							
c—Import tax rate							

(continued next page)

Table 5.3 *(continued)*

	Tax rate	Tax base	Tax rate	Tax base	Tax rate	Tax base	
d—Value added tax							
e—Sales tax							
f—Fuel tax							
g—Other excise taxes							
h—Export taxes							
i—Financial transaction taxes							
j—Other taxes *[Please describe.]*							
3. If total expenditures declined or there were reassignments, what was the basis for these decisions? *[Please pick the option that best describes fiscal policy in 2009 and 2010; add comments as necessary.]*							
a—Social spending (defined as health, education, and social protection) was prioritized.							
b—Across-the-board cuts were made.							
c—Generalized subsidies were prioritized (fuel/ gas/electricity or food subsidies).							

(continued next page)

Table 5.3 *(continued)*

	Tax rate	Tax base	Tax rate	Tax base	Tax rate	Tax base	
d—Other (nonsocial) expenditures were prioritized.							
4. If expenditures increased, from what did the increase result? *[Please pick all that apply.]*							
a—Automatic stabilizers (expenditures that increased without the government putting in place any new policy—e.g., a greater number of people qualifying for social assistance)							
b—Expansion of existing programs (e.g., expenditures increased because of government's active intervention: extending expiration dates of existing programs or redefining how beneficiaries qualify, thereby implying an increase in coverage)							

(continued next page)

Table 5.3   *(continued)*

	Tax rate	Tax base	Tax rate	Tax base	Tax rate	Tax base	
c—New programs put in place (i.e., government actively designs and initiates a new program)							

	Name of program		Sector	Targeted/ universal	Effective date (month/ year)	Expiration date (month/ year)	Description of any substantial implemen- tation change
5. If new programs were put in place: a—Give the name(s) of the new program(s); identify the sector(s) (for example, employment, health, pensions, electricity); define the coverage (targeted/ universal); indicate whether specifically targeted to concrete vulnerable groups; and identify the year(s) in which the program(s) began delivering services. *[Please add as many lines as necessary.]*							

(continued next page)

Table 5.3   *(continued)*

	Name of program	Sector	Targeted/ universal	Effective date (month/ year)	Expiration date (month/ year)	Description of any substantial implemen- tation change
b—Provide the date(s) (month/year) when the program(s) became effective and the date(s) (month/year) when the program(s) is/are expected to expire.						
c—Did the implementation change substantially? *[Please describe.]*						
6. Was there political pressure to implement or expand programs in response to the crisis? *[Please pick all that apply.]*						
a—Riots						
b—Large-scale protests/strikes						
c—Heavy criticism of the government by various stakeholders, as disseminated by the media						
d—Moderate criticism of the government by various stakeholders, as disseminated by the media						

(continued next page)

Table 5.3   *(continued)*

	Name of program	Sector	Targeted/ universal	Effective date (month/ year)	Expiration date (month/ year)	Description of any substantial implemen- tation change
e—No visible political pressure, but extensive behind-the-scenes pressure						
f—No political pressure of which you are aware						
7. Was there any international financial institution involvement in the adoption of measures? *[Please pick all that apply.]*						
a—World Bank development policy loans						
b—New World Bank investment loans						
c—Budget support from regional development banks						
d—New investment loans from other regional development banks						
e—IMF conditionality						
f—Other donors						

(continued next page)

Table 5.3   *(continued)*

	Name of program	Sector	Targeted/ universal	Effective date (month/ year)	Expiration date (month/ year)	Description of any substantial implemen- tation change
8. a—Are precrisis and postcrisis household surveys available? [yes/no]	a—					
b—Provide the name(s) of the survey(s) and the years for which it/they is/ are available.	b—					
9. a—Provide the date of the last public expenditure review.	a—					
b—Are there plans for a new public expenditure review in FY11? In FY12? [yes/no]	b—					
10. Do local governments provide reliable accounts of their revenues and expenditures to the central government? [yes/no]						
11. Are local government fiscal data readily available? [yes/no]						

Source: Adapted from questionnaire developed by Gabriela Inchauste and Jose Cuesta.

result of the global financial crisis. What will be the distributional impact of such slashed financing without additional domestic compensation? In addressing this question, a traditional benefit incidence analysis would show how the new (and reduced) monetized educational transfers accrue to the distribution of households ordered by income, consumption, or wealth. It has been argued that these analyses have a very-short-term perspective, require stringent assumptions about household behavior (see also Van de Walle and Nead 1995), and focus on immediate welfare outcomes rather than on longer-term investment consequences in terms of human capital. By contrast, using a logit technique, the proposed tool will, first, determine the probabilities that different groups of individuals who share the same set of circumstances ("types" in Roemer's words) will access a specific opportunity. Second, the exercise isolates the impact of public educational spending on the individual's chance of attending school. Third, the exercise simulates the impact of a crisis-specific shock (for example, public education expenditure cuts following an aid freeze) across population types (defined by sets of circumstances). Fourth, the exercise reestimates the new distribution of probabilities for each type after the financing shock is introduced. By comparing the distribution of probabilities before and after the shock, the exercise identifies winning and losing types (again, based on common sets of circumstances) of individuals and an approximate magnitude of the impact on their chances to attend school.

Before we present the results of the simulation conducted for Liberia (figure 5.1), a few points are in order. First, by focusing on opportunities that will have impacts on individuals' future capacities to lead a decent life, the analysis is able to expand the very-short-run, crisis-specific perspective over a longer-term horizon. Second, results are sensitive to the choice of opportunity, the relevant age group, and the set of circumstances chosen. These are country-specific decisions, but Narayan and Hoyos (2011) reassuringly show that key messages are generally robust to such decisions. Third, the analysis is not intended to provide normative conclusions. Rather, it is conceived as a "constraint" model that assesses the relevance of a number of constraints (the set of circumstances considered) in determining the probability of enjoying an opportunity. In fact, the logit estimation in the first step of the microsimulation does not distinguish among different policy alternatives that are compatible with a given public expenditure; instead, it focuses on the total fiscal cost. Nonetheless, circumstances included in the logit model refer to both demand and supply

Figure 5.1   Effects of Public Education Spending on the Probability of Attending School, Liberia

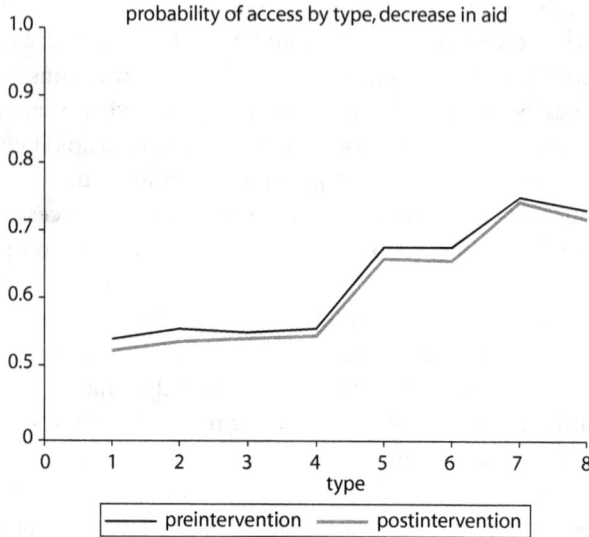

probability of access by type, decrease in aid

— preintervention   — — postintervention

Source: Abras, Cuesta, and Narayan 2011.
Note: See table 5.4 for description of eight types of children.

factors (from individual characteristics to public spending) that are relevant from a policy point of view.

Table 5.4 and figure 5.1 report the results of the microsimulations using 2008 data for Liberia. Information on individual and household characteristics, educational attendance, and private spending on education is from the Liberian Institute for Statistics and Geo-Information Services' Core Welfare Indicators Questionnaire (LISGIS 2007), and information on educational public spending is from the World Bank's Public Expenditure Management and Financial Accountability Review (World Bank 2009). The list of circumstances considered relevant in Liberia includes gender and age of the child, number of children and elderly in the household, location (urban or rural), head of household's gender and education, household wealth, family structure (presence of the parents and orphan status), and region. The opportunity analyzed is access to education among children aged 6–15, whose observed average access is 63 percent. Table 5.4 compares the estimated probability of access to education of eight types of individuals, as determined by three fundamental circumstances: child gender, urban or rural location of the household, and education of the household head. The table shows that

Table 5.4   Distribution of Educational Opportunities in Liberia, 2008

Type ID	Description	Estimated probability of access (%)
1	Rural, female child, head with no primary schooling	53.8
2	Rural, male child, head with no primary schooling	55.4
3	Urban, female child, head with no primary schooling	54.8
4	Urban, male child, head with no primary schooling	55.4
5	Rural, female child, head with primary schooling	67.5
6	Rural, male child, head with primary schooling	67.5
7	Urban, female child, head with primary schooling	74.8
8	Urban, male child, head with primary schooling	72.9

Source: Abras, Cuesta, and Narayan 2011.

the first four types are opportunity vulnerable in that their estimated probability of attending school (given their circumstances) is below the observed access rate—that is, 63 percent. The education of the household head seems to be the most critical factor in the estimated distribution of opportunities: all vulnerable types have parents who have not completed a primary education. For the rest of the circumstances, vulnerable types include children in urban and rural households, female and male children, and male- and female-headed households.

Figure 5.1 compares the estimated probabilities of attending school for the same types of children before and after the crisis-related shock in public financing arising from dried-up aid. The shock consists of reducing about 10 percent of the public education budget that is financed through international aid.[19] Results show that the cut in public education spending causes an average reduction of about 2 percentage points in the probability that the eight types of children will attend school. In terms of the Human Opportunity Index, the simulated shock causes a reduction in the index of 4 percentage points from the original 57 percent (table 5.5). Also, results show that the average effect in the distribution of opportunities is uniform across the board—that is, there are no significant compositional effects among types of children. The reduction in probability among urban and rural children is not very different, a result confirmed by comparing the effects across the eight types of children. In fact, the most affected group is type 6, boys in rural areas whose household head has completed at least a primary education. Members of this group see their probability of attending school reduced by 2 percentage points. In turn, the least affected group is type 7, girls living in urban households headed by an educated individual. The

Table 5.5   Average and Group Effects of Public Education Spending on Probability of Attending School, Liberia

Category/group	Baseline (before shock), %	Aid simulation (after shock), %
National		
Average probability	63.00	61.20
Human Opportunity Index	57.00	53.00
Group probability		
Urban	69.00	68.00
Rural	60.00	58.00
Type 1	53.89	52.20
Type 2	55.41	53.48
Type 3	54.84	53.98
Type 4	55.43	54.36
Type 5	67.53	65.75
Type 6	67.52	65.51
Type 7	74.89	74.23
Type 8	72.96	71.67

Source: Abras, Cuesta, and Narayan 2011.

reduction in their probability of attending school is less than 1 percentage point. Even though the analysis is not intended to identify the most effective sector policy interventions, it is useful for providing an approximate magnitude of the average and of the distributive effects of crisis-related scenarios.

Conclusion

The distributive analysis of fiscal policies seeks to answer two fundamental questions: What are the distributive impacts of tax and expenditure policies? And what is the capacity of tax and expenditure policies to affect the current distribution? These encompassing questions are valid in periods both with and without crisis. The review of empirical work on the effects of crisis shows that much attention has focused on aggregated poverty impacts and spending trends; it has focused to a lesser extent on group-specific impacts and much less on specific within-sector decisions. The findings point to a relatively optimistic aggregated picture of arrested poverty reduction rather than to higher poverty rates. At a more disaggregated level, scarce evidence points more pessimistically to the emergence of newly poor groups of people who differ from the structural poor. The review of analytical tools shows that in terms of desirable features, there is no superior technique. Rather, we find a trade-off between

(1) the simplicity of data, analytical assumptions, and readiness to implement and (2) the comprehensiveness and richness of results to guide policy making.

Both in off-crisis and crisis periods, there is a fundamental need to match analytical demands, available resources, and strategic issues to properly explore the distributive consequences of fiscal policies. What a crisis period may change, however, are the priorities of such a match, with considerations of the newly vulnerable population, the magnitude of the impacts, and the need for rapid responses becoming even more urgent. This chapter develops a two-stage approach to square such considerations in an effort to plan for the next crisis. The approach is based on a set of preferred properties leaning toward analyses that have lower data requirements and fewer strong assumptions, need lower analytical installed capacity, and are disaggregated in nature. Based on those criteria, the assessment of methods shows that (1) there are multiple techniques for analyzing the distributive consequences of fiscal policies before and during a crisis; (2) there is a fundamental trade-off between the simplicity of these tools and the richness and detail of the analysis; and (3) no single universal technique is likely to address the key questions and specific strategic shifts that may happen during a crisis.

Instead of providing a universally preferred distributive technique, this chapter proposes two useful tools in preparing for the next crisis—that is, two simple analytical tools that, if used regularly and frequently, will contribute to a better understanding of the distributional implications of crises. The first tool is a simple qualitative questionnaire on fiscal decisions implemented at the sectoral level in a given period. This information is intended to complement, not substitute for, aggregate spending trends and more sophisticated ex post microanalyses. The second tool is ex ante microsimulations focusing on opportunities rather than on outcomes in the hope that the traditional short-term analysis of welfare outputs may be complemented with a discussion of longer-term effects addressing how to remove critical obstacles to an egalitarian society (in the sense of equal opportunities, regardless of circumstances) with universal access to key services.

For example, the illustrative ex ante microsimulation exercise conducted for Liberia identifies the winners (for example, those types of children who lose comparatively less than the rest of the children) and losers (for example, those children who lose the most) in an economic shock produced by a reduction in public spending on education resulting from an aid cut. It shows that, beyond moderate average effects in the probability of attending school across all types of children (defined by their circumstances), there are no significant redistributive effects of these probabilities because the impacts of the shock are uniformly distributed. These results should contribute to the design of more effective policy responses to a crisis.

Notes

1. See Shah and Whalley (1991) for an initial argument along these lines.
2. Ortiz et al. (2010) report that approximately 24 percent of the amounts announced in fiscal stimulus packages in developing countries was directed at pro-poor and social protection programs.
3. The basic assumptions of the analysis by Chen and Ravallion (2009) are that economic growth tends to be distribution neutral, on average, and that the burden of the crisis will be proportional to initial income, leaving relative inequality unchanged within a given country. Paci, Rijkers, and Seinaert (2008) review the evidence from the previous macroeconomic crisis, suggesting that relative inequality in income distribution is as likely to increase as to fall during those crises.
4. In the area of subsidies, Arze del Granado, Coady, and Gillingham (2010) review the evidence of the impact of fuel subsidy reform on household welfare in developing countries. They find that, although on average its burden is neutrally distributed across income groups, the impact can be quite substantial: a US$0.25 decrease in the per liter subsidy results in a 6 percent decrease in income for all groups, with more than half of this impact arising from the indirect impact on prices of other goods and services consumed by households. (It should be noted that, in absolute terms, the top income quintile receives six times more subsidies than the bottom quintile.) However, the distributional impact of fuel subsidy reform will depend on how the savings are spent—see, for example, Nicholson et al. (2003) for Mozambique. Of course, the same is true for tax policy reform, as Sehili and Wodon (2008) find in the case of indirect tax reform in Niger. Also see Berg et al. (2009), who advocate fiscal stimulus policies for Sub-Saharan Africa countries and an expansion of social safety nets to cushion the impact of the crisis on poor people.
5. An important side benefit of the analysis by Habib et al. (2010c) is the identification of several potentially good real-time "early-warning" indicators for the poverty and distributional impacts of the crisis. Among these indicators are (1) changes in remittance flows from abroad, (2) movement of prices (including food prices), (3) movement of wages by sector, and (4) loss of labor income in the industry sector. These indicators may be easily obtained and

measurable, are sensitive to changes in economic conditions, and correlate with changes in poverty and income distribution.

6. Habib et al. (2010b) summarize the results for Bangladesh and the Philippines and report similar findings for Mexico. For that last country, the authors also report increases in both the level and the depth of aggregate poverty, with income shocks relatively large at the bottom parts of the income distribution. They find that the households made newly poor by the crisis have different characteristics than the chronically poor households.

7. The Lewis and Verhoeven (2010) and Brumby and Verhoeven (2010) samples are identical and cover 131 developing and transitioning countries between 1995 and 2007. The Arze del Granado, Gupta, and Hajdenberg (2010) sample covers 150 countries, both developing and developed.

8. Ortiz et al. (2010) report that most of the decline in public spending in Sub-Saharan Africa—expected for about half of countries in the region—appears to be driven mainly by a substantial decline in expected revenue in 2010–11 compared with 2008–09. Also, apparently the region is unable to secure new financing, reflecting its relatively high initial debt burden and limited access to capital markets. This contrasts with the Latin America region's capacity to maintain public spending (although heterogeneously within the region, with Central America and Caribbean countries having difficulties sustaining expenditures).

9. This is the political will that may turn societies into minimalist welfare states (Breceda, Rigolini, and Saavedra 2008) or, in stark contrast, may use fiscal policies to redress breached social contracts in conflict-affected and polarized societies (Addison, Chowdhury, and Murshed 2004).

10. A recent example of this is presented by Wilkinson (2009, 2010). He uses the South African tax and benefit microsimulation model (SAMOD) and the South African 2006 Income and Expenditure Survey to analyze the poverty-reducing distributive impacts of a wide array of policies such as a child support grant, care dependency grant, disability grant, personal income tax, value added tax, and excise duties. Another example is the estimation of the distributive impact of environmental taxes (Elkes 2007). See Abramovsky et al. (2011) for a recent application to tax reform in Mexico.

11. Here we follow Habib et al. (2010c).

12. Mieszkowski (1969), McLure (1975), and Bovenberg (1987) are expansions on Harberger's (1962) model.

13. Recent evidence provided by a regional MAMS exercise in Latin America (Sanchez et al. 2010) shows that synergies are likely to be important. The compositions of spending and its financing matter and fiscal effects are typically nonlinear, decreasing their effectiveness as welfare levels increase.

14. This subsection is based on Cuesta and Ponce (2007).

15. Experimental and quasi-experimental impact evaluation techniques differ in the way that control and treatment groups are formed: randomized before the implementation of the program in the experimental approach, and somehow "matched" after the implementation of the program in the quasi-experimental case.

16. See Cuesta (2011) for an illustration in the context of the global food crisis.

17. Ortiz and colleagues (2010) report that their reading of recent IMF country reports also suggests that a wide variety of spending categories (such as electricity; judiciary; and, in some cases, defense-related spending) were included in the priority social spending to be protected under country programs. These approaches raise the question about the effectiveness of priority setting in safeguarding those areas of social spending that are most essential for directly supporting vulnerable populations. The United Nations and its Children's Fund have a multidimensional approach to child well-being. The Convention on the Rights of the Child (United Nations 1990), which was ratified by 192 countries, clearly states the need to invest in eradicating all child deprivations. Children have a right not only to education and health but also to food, clean drinking water, sanitation, shelter, and other necessary investments for their families (including those related to basic livelihoods).

18. See Molinas et al. (2010) for a detailed explanation and application to the Latin America region.

19. Using data from World Bank (2009), we estimate that a 10 percent reduction in international aid accruing to public education is equivalent to reducing about 70 percent of the own-resource public education transfers to households with children in primary and secondary schools.

References

Abramovsky, L., O. Attanasio, C. Emmerson, and D. Phillips. 2011. *The Distributional Impact of Reforms to Direct and Indirect Taxes in Mexico. Analytical Report and Results*. London: Institute of Fiscal Studies.

Abras, A., J. Cuesta, and A. Narayan. 2011. *Human Opportunities in Liberia*. Washington, DC: World Bank.

Addison, T., A. Chowdhury, and M. Murshed. 2004. "The Fiscal Dimensions of Conflict and Reconstruction." In *Fiscal Policy for Development: Poverty, Growth, and Reconstruction*, ed. T. Addison and A. Roe, 260–73. London: Palgrave.

Arze del Granado, J., D. Coady, and R. Gillingham. 2010. "The Unequal Benefits of Fuel Subsidies: A Review of Evidence for Developing Countries." Working Paper 10/202, International Monetary Fund, Washington, DC.

Arze del Granado, J., S. Gupta, and A. Hajdenberg. 2010. "Is Social Spending Procyclical?" Working Paper 10/234, International Monetary Fund, Washington, DC.

Berg, A., N. Funke, A. Hajdenberg, V. Lledo, R. Ossowski, M. Schindler, A. Spilimbergo, S. Tareq, and I. Yackovlev. 2009. "Fiscal Policy in Sub-Saharan Africa in Response to the Impact of the Global Crisis." Staff Position Note 09/10, International Monetary Fund, Washington, DC.

Bourguignon, F., M. Bussolo, and L. Pereira da Silva. 2008. "Introduction: Evaluating the Impact of Macroeconomic Policies on Poverty and Income Distribution." In *The Impact of Macroeconomic Policies on Poverty and Income Distribution*, ed. F. Bourguignon, M. Bussolo, and L. Pereira da Silva, 1–23. Washington, DC: World Bank.

Bourguignon, F., and F. Ferreira. 2003. "Ex ante Evaluations of Policy Reforms Using Behavioral Models." In *The Impact of Economic Policies on Poverty and Income Distribution: Evaluation Techniques and Tools*, ed. F. Bourguignon and L. Pereira da Silva, 123–43. New York: Oxford University Press.

Bourguignon, F., F. Ferreira, and P. G. Leite. 2003. "Conditional Cash Transfers, Schooling, and Child Labor: Micro-Simulating Brazil's Bolsa Escola Program." *World Bank Economic Review* 17 (2): 229–54.

Bourguignon, F., and L. Pereira da Silva. 2003. *The Impact of Policies on Poverty and Income Distribution: Evaluation Techniques and Tools*. Washington, DC: World Bank.

Bourguignon, F., and A. Spadaro. 2006. "Microsimulation as a Tool for Evaluating Redistribution Policies." *Journal of Economic Inequality* 4 (1): 77–106.

Bovenberg, A. L. 1987. "Indirect Taxation in Developing Countries: A General Equilibrium Approach." *IMF Staff Papers* 34 (2): 333–73.

Breceda, K., J. Rigolini, and J. Saavedra. 2008. "Latin America and the Social Contract: Patterns of Social Spending and Taxation." Policy Research Working Paper 4604, World Bank, Washington, DC.

Brumby, J., and M. Verhoeven. 2010. "Public Expenditure after the Global Financial Crisis." In *The Day after Tomorrow: A Handbook on the Future of Economic Policy in the Developing World*, ed. O. Canuto and M. Giugale, 193–206. Washington, DC: World Bank.

Chen, S., and M. Ravallion. 2009. "The Impact of the Global Financial Crisis on the World's Poorest." http://www.voxeu.org/index.php?q=node/3520.

Chenery, H., R. Jolly, S. Montek, S. Ahluwalia, C. Bell, and J. Duloy. 1974. *Redistribution with Growth: Policies to Improve Income Distribution in Developing Countries in the Context of Economic Growth*. Washington, DC: World Bank.

Cogneau, D., M. Grimm, and A.-S. Robilliard. 2003. "Evaluating Poverty Reduction Policies. The Contribution of Micro-Simulation Techniques." In

New International Poverty Reduction Strategies, ed. J.-P. Cling, M. Razafin-Drakoto, and F. Roubaud, 340–70. London: Routledge.

Creedy, J., and A. Duncan. 2002. "Behavioral Micro-Simulations with Labor Supply Responses." *Journal of Economic Surveys* 16 (1): 1–39.

Cuesta, J. 2011. "A Qualitative Analysis of Policy Making on the Food Price Crisis in the Andean Region: Preparing for the Next Crisis." *European Journal of Development Research* 23 (1): 72–93.

Cuesta, J., and J. Ponce. 2007. "Ex-Ante Simulations of Direct and Indirect Effects of Welfare Reforms." *Review of Income and Wealth* 53 (4): 645–72.

Dervis, K., J. de Melo, and S. Robinson. 1982. *General Equilibrium Models for Development Policy*. New York: Cambridge University Press.

Elkes, O. 2007. "Tax-Benefit Microsimulation Models in Eastern Europe." *International Journal of Microsimulation* 1 (1): 54–56.

Essama-Nssah, B. 2009. "Assessing the Redistributive Effect of Fiscal Policy." Policy Research Working Paper 4592, World Bank, Washington, DC.

Fullerton, D., and D. L. Rogers. 1991. "Lifetime Versus Annual Perspectives on Tax Incidence." *National Tax Journal* 44 (3): 277–88.

Habib, B., A. Narayan, S. Olivieri, and C. Sanchez-Paramo. 2010a. "Assessing Ex Ante the Poverty and Distributional Impact of the Global Crisis in a Developing Country: A Micro-Simulation Approach with Application to Bangladesh." Policy Research Working Paper 5238, World Bank, Washington, DC.

———. 2010b. "Assessing Poverty and Distributional Impacts of the Global Crisis in the Philippines." Policy Research Working Paper 5286, World Bank, Washington, DC.

———. 2010c. "The Impact of the Financial Crisis on Poverty and Income Distribution: Insights from Simulations in Selected Countries." *Economic Premise* 7: 1–4.

Harberger, A. C. 1962. "The Incidence of the Corporate Income Tax." *Journal of Political Economy* 70: 215–40.

IMF (International Monetary Fund). 2009. "Review of Recent Crisis Programs." Strategy, Policy, and Review Department, IMF, Washington, DC. http://www.imf.org/external/np/pp/eng/2009/091409.pdf.

———. 2010a. "Emerging from the Global Crisis: Macroeconomic Challenges Facing Low-Income Countries." http://www.imf.org/external/np/pp/eng/2010/100510.pdf.

———. 2010b. *World Economic Outlook 2010: Rebalancing Growth*. Washington, DC: IMF.

Lewis, M., and M. Verhoeven. 2010. "Financial Crises and Social Spending: The Impact of the 2008–2009 Crisis." *World Economics* 11 (4): 79–110.

LISGIS (Liberian Institute for Statistics and Geo-Information Services). 2007. "Core Welfare Indicators Questionnaire." LISGIS, Monrovia, Liberia.

Lofgren, H. 2004. "MAMS: An Economywide Model of MDG Country Strategy—Technical Documentation." World Bank, Washington, DC.

Martinez-Vazquez, J. 2008. "The Impact of Budgets on the Poor: Tax and Expenditure Benefit Incidence Analysis." In *Public Finance for Poverty Reduction: Concepts and Case Studies from Africa and Latin America*, ed. B. Moreno-Dobson and Q. Wodon, 113–57. Washington, DC: World Bank.

McLure, C. E., Jr. 1975. "General Equilibrium Incidence Analysis: The Harberger Model after Ten Years." *Journal of Public Economics* 4 (2): 125–61.

Mieszkowski, P. M. 1969. "Tax Incidence Theory: The Effect of Taxes on the Distribution of Income." *Journal of Economic Literature* 7: 1103–24.

Molinas, J., R. Paes de Barros, J. Saavedra, and M. Giugale. 2010. *Do Our Children Have a Chance? The 2010 Human Opportunity Report for Latin America and the Caribbean.* Washington, DC: World Bank.

Moreno-Dobson, B., and Q. Wodon, eds. 2008. *Public Finance for Poverty Reduction: Concepts and Case Studies from Africa and Latin America.* Washington, DC: World Bank.

Narayan, A., and A. Hoyos. 2011. *The 2011 Human Opportunity Report for Africa.* Washington, DC: World Bank.

Nicholson, K., B. O'Laughlin, A. Francisco, and V. Nhate. 2003. "Poverty and Social Impact Analysis: Fuel Tax in Mozambique." World Bank, Washington, DC.

Ortiz, I., J. Chai, M. Cummins, and G. Vergara. 2010. *Prioritizing Expenditures for a Recovery for All: Rapid Review of Public Expenditures in 126 Developing Countries.* New York: United Nations Children's Fund.

Paci, P., B. Rijkers, and A. Seinaert. 2008. *Crunch Time in the Developing World Too? Policy Options for Dealing with the Potential Poverty and Distributional Impact of the Financial Crisis.* Washington, DC: Poverty Reduction Group, World Bank.

Roemer, J. 1998. *Equality of Opportunity.* Cambridge, MA: Harvard University Press.

Sanchez, M., R. Vos, E. Ganuza, H. Lofgren, and C. Diaz-Bonilla, eds. 2010. *Public Policies for Human Development: Achieving the Millennium Development Goals in Latin America.* New York: Palgrave Macmillan.

Sehili, S., and Q. Wodon. 2008. "Analyzing the Potential Impact of Indirect Tax Reforms on Poverty with Limited Data: Niger." In *Public Finance for Poverty Reduction: Concepts and Case Studies from Africa and Latin America*, ed. B. Moreno-Dodson and Q. Wodon, 345–70. Washington, DC: World Bank.

Selowsky, M. 1979. *Who Benefits from Government Expenditures?* Washington, DC: World Bank.

Shah, A., ed. 2005. *Public Expenditure Analysis.* Public Sector Governance and Accountability Series. Washington, DC: World Bank.

Shah, A., and J. Whalley. 1991. "Tax Incidence Analysis of Developing Countries: An Alternative View." *World Bank Economic Review* 5 (3): 535–52.

United Nations. 1990. "Convention on the Rights of the Child." General Assembly Resolution 44/25, New York, November 20, 1989. http://www2.ohchr.org/english/law/crc.htm.

UNRISD (United Nations Research Institute for Social Development). 2010. *Combating Poverty and Inequality: Structural Change, Social Policy and Politics.* Geneva, Switzerland: UNRISD.

Van de Walle, D. 1996. "Assessing the Welfare Impacts of Public Spending." Policy Research Working Paper 1670, World Bank, Washington, DC.

Van de Walle, D., and K. Nead, eds. 1995. *Public Spending and the Poor: Theory and Evidence.* Washington, DC: World Bank.

Wan, G., and R. Francisco. 2009. "How Is the Global Recession Impacting on Poverty and Social Spending? An Ex Ante Assessment Methodology with Applications to Developing Asia." Sustainable Development Working Paper 8, Asian Development Bank, Manila.

Wilkinson, K. 2009. "Adapting EUROMOD for Use in a Developing Country— The Case of South Africa and SAMOD." EUROMOD Working Paper EM5/09, Institute for Social and Economic Research, University of Essex, U.K.

———. 2010. "The Impact of Taxes and Transfers on Child Poverty in South Africa." PowerPoint presentation, Centre for the Analysis of South African Social Policy, Oxford, U.K.

World Bank. 2009. *Liberia—2008 Public Expenditure Management and Financial Accountability Review.* Washington, DC: World Bank.

Yang, Y., P. Dudine, E. Kvintradze, P. Mitra, N. Mwase, and S. Das. 2010. *Creating Policy Space in Low-Income Countries during the Recent Crises.* Washington, DC: International Monetary Fund.

CHAPTER 6

Fiscal Policy Lessons in Sub-Saharan Africa from the 2008–09 Global Crisis

Kathie Krumm and Chandana Kularatne

This chapter assesses the fiscal response to the 2008–09 global crisis in low-income countries (LICs) in Sub-Saharan Africa and identifies key lessons. The crisis required short-term responses, but it also magnified the medium- and long-term challenges for growth and poverty reduction. This review of fiscal policy adjustments made during fiscal 2009/10 is placed in this longer-term context.

When the global crisis hit in 2008, African LICs were building on a base of improvements in fiscal performance. The overall fiscal stance had changed significantly during the 1990s, with positive primary fiscal balances in 72 percent of all countries in Sub-Saharan Africa by 2008, compared with 28 percent in the early 1990s (IMF 2009). Similarly, fiscal space for pro-growth expenditures had grown since the early 2000s. For

The authors would like to thank Doreen Kagarama and Toru Nishiuchi for their support on data. This chapter benefited from policy discussions on earlier papers presented at the African Development Bank's African Economic Conference, held in Tunis, Tunisia, in October 2010, and the High-Level Workshop on Africa Fiscal Policy for Growth in Light of Crisis, held in Maputo, Mozambique, in December 2009.

example, spending on infrastructure in African LICs had been higher than previously thought, amounting to US$25 billion a year when budget and off-budget spending (including state-owned enterprises and extrabudgetary funds) were taken into account. Over half of this overall spending was domestically sourced by the African taxpayer, including US$8 billion in oversight and monitoring and US$5 billion in public capital expenditures (World Bank 2009a).[1] This spending complemented the considerable pro-poor expenditure increases directed to health, education, water, and other public services.

This improved base notwithstanding the global crisis threatened to undermine the gains in growth and poverty reduction in African LICs. The region had already been hit by the first wave of food and fuel price increases, and limited formal safety net programs were in place in African LICs to reduce transitory poverty, in part because of the challenge of targeting when nearly half of the populations are poor and more near poor. A global financial crisis followed, affecting the region less directly.

Then the global economic crisis hit. To varying degrees, most of the impact of the global crisis was transmitted via the real economy. The crisis slowed economic growth through several interrelated channels by lowering demand for exports of goods and services—especially traditional exports—compounded by the slowdown or decline in capital inflows (foreign direct investment [FDI], portfolio inflows, and remittances). Overall, economic growth in Sub-Saharan Africa fell to 2.0 percent in 2009 (negative in per capita terms) from over 6.5 percent in 2007 and 5.1 percent in 2008. African LICs grew by 4.9 percent in 2009 or nearly 1 percent less than in 2008.[2] Although growth for 2010 is estimated to have strengthened slightly to 4.8 percent overall and 6.3 percent for LICs from the reduced levels projected at the peak of the crisis, growth prospects for the medium term are closely linked to the uncertain pace of global recovery and continuing economic crisis in parts of the world (World Bank 2011)—see figure 6.1.[3]

Yet the impact of the 2008–09 crisis appears relatively short-lived. Although economic cycles in developing countries remain closely correlated with those in developed countries, the growth trend in developing countries had become substantially higher than that in advanced economies since the early 2000s: there arguably had been a decoupling in the underlying trend rates of growth. Developing country growth averaged only 0.8 percentage points higher than that in advanced countries in the 1990s, but this gap widened to 3.5 points in 2000–08. Is the growth premium of the 2000s mainly a payoff for the better macroeconomic,

Figure 6.1   Crisis Impact on Sub-Saharan Africa, 2003–10

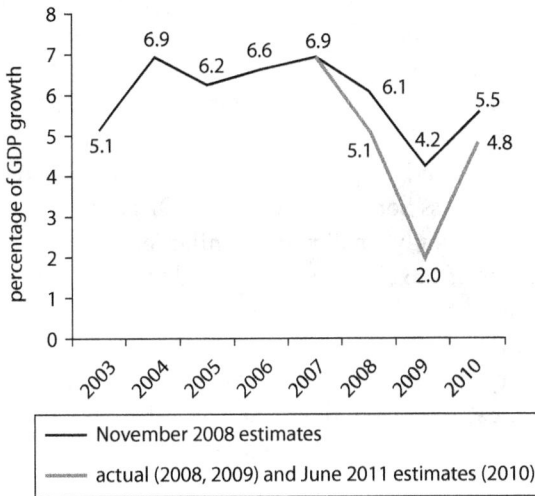

Sources: World Bank 2009d, 2011.
Note: GDP = gross domestic product.

structural, and other policies adopted by developing countries, including many African LICs over the last couple of decades? In this case, we would expect to see it persist in the medium term, despite the shock of the crisis. Or was it mostly temporary because of favorable "bubble" conditions? One piece of evidence: developing countries continued to grow much faster than developed countries in 2009—the expected trough of the crisis—and all major forecasters expect the growth premium to continue over the next few years (Canuto and Giugale 2010). Accordingly, it is possible that African LICs may be able to sustain this growth premium in the years following the 2008–09 crisis, albeit depending on the evolution of the global economy.

How did fiscal policy in African LICs respond to the shocks from the 2008–09 global crisis in the immediate 2009–10 postcrisis period? How should they have responded in order to sustain medium-term growth and poverty reduction prospects postcrisis? Many factors enter into the decision making on the fiscal policy response in addition to the disparate initial country conditions. These include the precrisis fiscal and balance of payments positions, the availability and terms of official aid and private capital, the impact of the crisis on vulnerable segments of society, and the ability of governments to adjust fiscal policy expeditiously to effectively respond to the changing external environment (in particular, the ability to protect growth-oriented and pro-poor expenditure programs). The objective of this chapter is to assess the fiscal policy responses to the 2008–09 crisis by policy makers and glean the lessons from those experiences.

The analysis focuses on 15 low-income Sub-Saharan African countries: Burkina Faso, the Democratic Republic of Congo, Ethiopia, Ghana, Guinea, Kenya, Mali, Mozambique, Nigeria, Rwanda, Senegal, Sudan, Tanzania, Uganda, and Zambia. These economies account for over 85 percent of the gross domestic product (GDP) of Sub-Saharan African LICs and exclude mainly smaller and conflict economies.

The remainder of the chapter is organized as follows. The first section compares the adjustments in overall fiscal stances of this set of African LIC economies with precrisis fiscal plans. The second section reviews how the majority of these countries that chose not to fully adjust financed the increased fiscal deficit and the impact on debt sustainability. The third section examines the adjustments in composition of spending in response to the crisis.

Adjustments in Fiscal Stance in Light of the Crisis

This section compares the adjustments in overall fiscal stances of the selected set of African LIC economies during 2009–10 with their fiscal plans prior to the 2008–09 global crisis. Notably, it finds a close relationship between the presence of fiscal space and low risk of debt distress, and the extent of short-term fiscal stance adjustment.

Fiscal Adjustment, Accommodation, or Stimulus?

The conceptual framework outlined in this section is constructed to facilitate evaluation and comparison of the adjustments in the overall fiscal stances of the selected set of African LICs from precrisis fiscal plans. Its assumptions are chosen to illustrate the common conditions prevailing in African LICs, notwithstanding the diversity in their precrisis circumstances. Unlike high-income countries and many medium-income ones, most African LICs do not maintain formal social insurance programs for which spending automatically rises when output and employment fall. Indeed, employment in the formal sector is generally a small fraction of the labor force. Moreover, few countries implemented changes in tax policy in response to the crisis. Thus the principal fiscal shock from the crisis is a loss in revenue strictly due to changes in the economic environment, and the principal potential fiscal response tool is an adjustment in discretionary government spending.[4] Fully adjusting spending to the revenue loss is defined as full adjustment; maintaining spending despite the revenue loss is defined as no adjustment or accommodation; and increasing discretionary spending notwithstanding the revenue decline that further widens the fiscal deficit beyond the net loss is defined as stimulus (based on Krumm, Dhar, and Choi 2009).

What mix of adjustment, accommodation, or stimulus should African LICs have used? This section provides a framework for comparing and contrasting that recommended mix with the actual responses. A number of factors pertinent to the current crisis are worth highlighting:

- Prior to the 2008–09 crisis, many African countries benefited from a sustained period of stronger growth, rising foreign investment, and debt relief, which together created greater fiscal space. Even a commodity importer not benefiting from debt relief such as Kenya was able to reduce public debt from over 70 percent of GDP in the mid-1990s to just above 40 percent prior to the crisis. However, the decline in debt was driven, at least in part, by higher economic growth and real exchange rate appreciation—trends that have been temporarily reversed in some countries.

- Aid flows may have remained stable immediately following the crisis or even risen, in part reflecting front-loading of multiyear aid programs as practiced by the International Development Association. However, aid flows over the medium term could decline, constrained by persistent fiscal pressures in donor countries. Increased lending from the International Monetary Fund (IMF) and the World Bank may offset these declines in some cases.

- Net private capital flows diminished sharply in 2008–09 and could not be assured of recovering in 2010 and beyond—in fact, by 2011 they had yet to recover to 2007 levels, with FDI largely confined to the mining sector (World Bank 2011). After the onset of the acute phase of the crisis, incipient access to global capital markets was effectively cut off by the prohibitively high interest rate spreads. For example, Kenya had to forgo a US$500 million bond issue planned for fiscal 2008/09.

The thinking on the appropriate response for African LICs in 2008–09 shared both similarities and differences with that going on in the rest of the world. A first approximation of the trends just described was that there would be no net increase in external finance in response to the crisis, although country experiences undoubtedly varied. This reasoning was used as an argument against anything but full adjustment to the external shock under the assumption that an increase in the fiscal deficit must be matched by a parallel decline in the private investment–saving deficit, given no change in external financing. If this were the case, allowing the fiscal deficit to increase would mean squeezing private spending, and no increase in aggregate demand would result. Moreover, displacing private spending with government spending would be bad for growth in the long run.

But private investment, consumption, and saving would also be affected by the shock, independent of fiscal policy. For example, investment might fall because of weaker export prospects. Consumption might decline if output and employment declined. Saving could also increase because of the weaker prospects. So, as was argued in other parts of the world, allowing the fiscal deficit to increase need not cause an increase in net private saving; the latter might rise as a result of the external shock, thereby providing a rationale for a larger fiscal deficit to ease the shock. This suggests that, for some countries, no adjustment would be an appropriate response. At the same time, it is worth emphasizing that for any fiscal stimulus to work, it must create domestic demand that will quickly trigger the employment of otherwise idle resources. The little evidence available on the impact multiplier from fiscal stimulus in the LICs in Sub-Saharan Africa suggests it might be quite limited (see box 6.1), and even more limited than in other parts of the world.

Adjustments in Fiscal Plans in LICs

The methodology used to assess the fiscal response to the crisis across countries focuses on changes in expressions of policy intent before and after the crisis. The standard methodology is to assess changes in fiscal policy over time. The choice of the methodology for this chapter was motivated by the desire to assess adjustments within a shorter time frame. The approach also draws on the framework just provided, assessing diversity of responses across countries relative to the differences the framework would suggest. As noted, for comparability purposes the revenue channel is used as the starting point.

Loss in revenue. As discussed in the previous section, the principal fiscal shock from the 2008–09 crisis was likely to be a loss in revenue from changes in growth and the external economic environment. Almost all countries examined here showed declines in revenues as a share of GDP in the 2009 or fiscal 2009/10 budgets, compared with both earlier projections and previous fiscal years (see annex 6A). In those cases of absolute

Box 6.1

Accommodation versus Stimulus? Limited Impact of Additional Spending? Evidence from Fiscal Multipliers— and Evidence from Kenya

The impact multiplier for high-income countries has been estimated at about 0.24 and the cumulative long-term multiplier at 1.04. In other words, an additional dollar in government spending will deliver 24 cents of additional output in the quarter in which it is implemented. After the full impact of a fiscal expansion is accounted for, output will have essentially risen by only slightly more than the initial level of government consumption. For developing countries, the impact multiplier has been measured at close to zero with a cumulative multiplier of 0.79. In the long term, an additional dollar of government consumption crowds out some other components of GDP (investment, consumption, or net exports) by 21 cents.

The impact of expansionary fiscal policy on the output gap may be limited in Sub-Saharan Africa. Because commodities account for a large share of GDP, the demand in noncommodity sectors needs to rise in order for fiscal policy to effectively reduce the output gap. In view of the structural constraints faced by noncommodity sectors, the increase in output may be marginal. In addition, higher levels of imports lead to a leakage of fiscal impact to the rest of the world. In Sub-Saharan Africa, as trade shares have increased in line with economic openness and integration, the impact of the fiscal multipliers would have become smaller because of greater import leakage. The impact of fiscal expansion on the nontradable sectors also may be limited because of constraints. In the formal labor market, it is far from clear that those who are unemployed because of falling demand in contracting sectors possess the mobility or skills demanded elsewhere in response to fiscal policy. In addition, Sub-Saharan Africa has a relatively large informal economy facing structural constraints, and a growing government expenditure may have fewer positive knock-on effects on the informal sector. However, this remains an empirical question worthy of further analysis.

To assess the effect of random discretionary fiscal policy (fiscal innovations that are purely unpredictable) on Kenya's economy, a small vector autoregressive model was constructed and analyzed (see figure B1.1). The highlights of the analysis are that a discretionary fiscal response has a small impact on output: 0.1 percent for any 1.0 percent change in cyclically adjusted primary balance (as shown in panel c). The impact persists for nine quarters positively, but then moves in a negative direction (as shown in panel b); however, this finding should be

(continued next page)

Box 6.1 *(continued)*

Figure B6.1   Estimated Impact of Fiscal (Discretionary Policy) Shock in Kenya

Impulse response of cycle-adjusted primary balance to

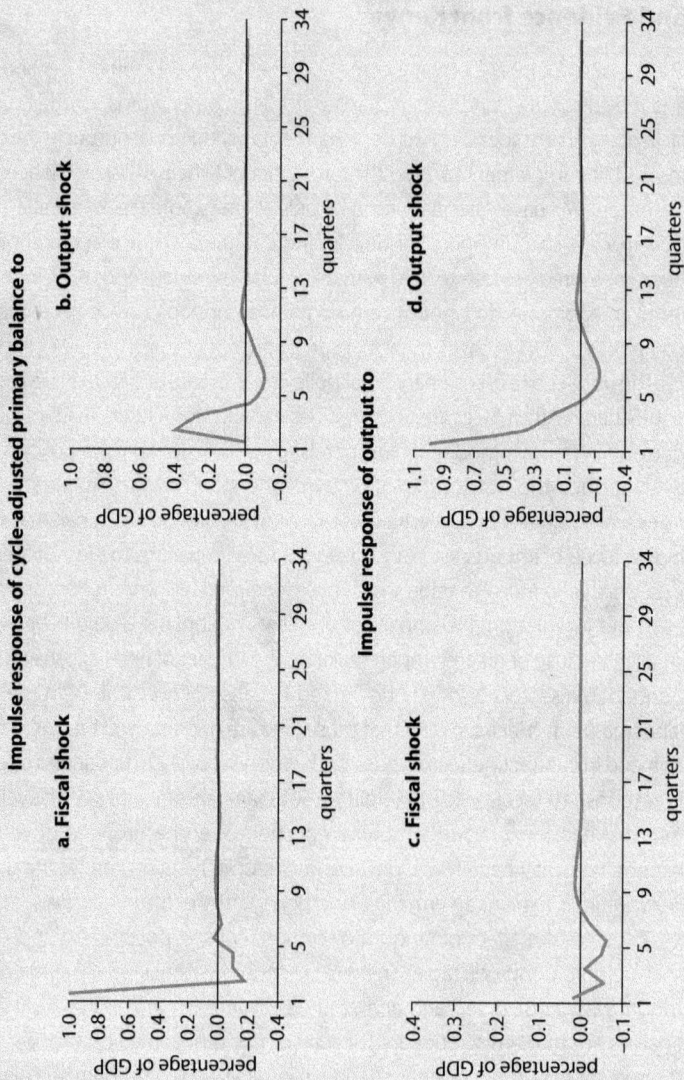

a. Fiscal shock

b. Output shock

Impulse response of output to

c. Fiscal shock

d. Output shock

Source: World Bank 2009f.

Note: GDP = gross domestic product.

(continued next page)

Box 6.1 *(continued)*

interpreted with caution. Two other fiscal policy components are (1) systemic discretionary policy, which is routine responses to changing economic situations;
and (2) automatic policy, governed by rules and laws such as the tax code. A full
assessment of the impact of overall fiscal policy on GDP needs to take all three
components into account, and further research is needed in this area.

Source: Itzetzki, Mendoza, and Vegh 2009.

declines in GDP, a measure of revenues as a ratio of GDP understates the
significance of the revenue decline.

The most pronounced declines were in countries highly dependent on
commodities such as oil and minerals (see figure 6A.1 in annex 6A, comparing the panels for non-commodity-dependent countries with the panel
for dependent countries). In Sudan, for example, the revised total revenues
for the Government of National Unity (GNU) were 27 percent less than
the budgeted levels in April 2009, reflecting lower oil inflows (57 percent
less than the budgeted levels). However, they had steadily improved relative to the first three months of 2009.[5] In Zambia, the sharp contraction
of copper prices nullified any increase in revenues from new mining tax
legislation implemented in April 2008. Revenue from oil in Nigeria was
expected to decline because of both lower global prices and the declining
output resulting from the continued restiveness in the Niger Delta.[6] The
impact was only more muted in certain postconflict countries such as the
Democratic Republic of Congo and Guinea.[7]

Other LICs also projected a revenue impact, such as Senegal, Uganda,
and Ghana. For Uganda, there was a further shortfall in actual revenues
beyond projections equal to 0.5 percent of GDP. In Mozambique, the
2010–12 medium-term expenditure framework prepared in mid-2009
prudently estimated a substantial fiscal contraction as a result of the
global crisis.

It is notable, however, that several countries—among them, Burkina
Faso, Mozambique, and Tanzania—continued to set ambitious revenue
targets regardless of the potential crisis impact. Meanwhile, many of the
countries in Sub-Saharan Africa that had fiscal space prior to the 2008–09
crisis tried to simultaneously increase revenue collection and increase
spending. One rationale was that, although strong revenue performance
would keep automatic stabilizers small, any lower targets would have the
unintended consequence of reducing the administrative effort that had

been the focus of much of the revenue strengthening in the last few years.[8] In fact, Mozambique and Burkina Faso achieved those more ambitious targets. In Senegal, revenue collection was strong through the first semester of 2010 (World Bank 2010d). Nonetheless, while imperfect, we use projected revenue declines as a proxy for crisis impact for a comparison of fiscal responses.

Fiscal response. The fiscal response is examined by looking at the fiscal stance of countries in mid-2009 relative to plans made a year before the full extent of the global crisis was known. The range of responses was evident in African LICs—from stimulus to full adjustment, even fiscal tightening. There is a close relationship between the presence of fiscal space and low risk of debt distress, and the extent of short-term fiscal stance adjustment (figure 6.2). Details on the individual country cases appear in annex 6B. We use the change in plans rather than year-on-year changes, which distinguishes our analysis from others in the literature. A similar story tends to emerge when describing the fiscal stance relative to the previous budget year, albeit less powerfully.

A few countries instituted fiscal stimulus packages, with plans to increase discretionary expenditures beyond the revenue shortfall. As expected, these were mainly countries with the available fiscal space. The most recent joint debt sustainability assessments by the IMF and the World Bank had judged Kenya, Nigeria, Tanzania, and Zambia as having low risk of debt distress.[9] Resource-rich countries such as Nigeria that

Figure 6.2   African LICs with Low Debt Vulnerability

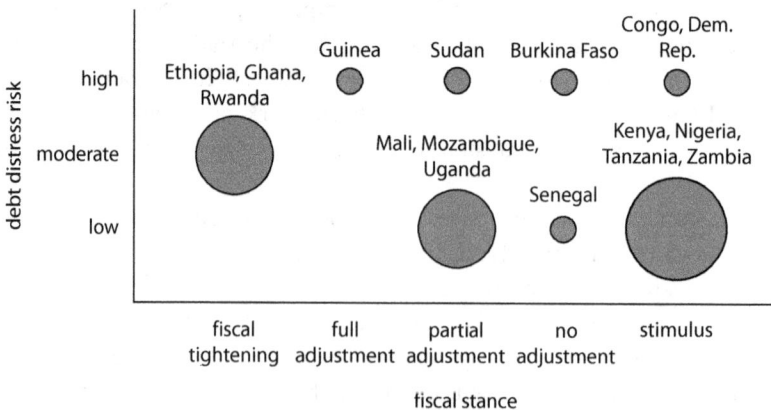

Source: Joint IMF–World Bank debt sustainability analysis, various countries.
Note: The size of the circle is proportional to the number of African countries in a specific category.

had managed the commodity boom relatively well were able, in principle, to introduce fiscal stimulus packages, despite the sharp decline in commodity prices. By and large, these countries had been experiencing relatively strong, stable growth over the last decade.[10]

Several countries planned to adjust little or only partially to the shock—that is, projected public expenditures were reduced, albeit to a lesser extent than the revenue shock. These countries included those such as Mozambique and Uganda that had the macroeconomic space for a more expansionary stance should they have wanted it. Countries such as Burkina Faso already were at high risk of debt distress before the 2008–09 crisis. These countries also had experienced relatively high stable growth over the last decade—notably, Mozambique and Uganda had grown on average more than 7 percent per year.

At the same time, a handful of countries planned to adjust fully to the shock or engage in tighter fiscal policies than originally envisaged. This group included Ghana and Ethiopia, whose macroeconomic tensions and moderate risk of debt distress in fiscal 2008/09 predated the crisis.[11] Sensitive to macroeconomic concerns and with a fiscal stance more expansionary than in the previous year, Rwanda reduced the extent of its expansionary fiscal stance (called tightening for purposes of the methodology in this chapter) and did not plan to expand spending in response to its higher than anticipated revenues. In fact, growth in these countries had sharply increased in 2008, and so a sustained growth path would not necessarily be vulnerable to a temporary slowdown.[12] The fully adjusting countries also included those with serious debt sustainability issues, as suggested by the relevant debt sustainability assessment ratings. For example, Guinea was assessed as having a high risk of debt distress, compounded by weaker management of resources during the commodity boom period.

Financing and Debt Sustainability

We now focus more narrowly on the subset of African LICs that planned countercyclical fiscal policy responses to the crisis. What were the options for financing these adjustments in fiscal plans? What has been the impact on debt sustainability? Official bilateral and multilateral transfers (grants) and concessional lending generally play an important role in LIC government financing. For aid-dependent countries, flows largely remained stable during 2008–09, with evidence of front-loading by multilaterals.[13] However, as noted earlier, several donor countries are facing their own growing fiscal pressures. There is a clear case for—and commitment to—an increase in official flows, but the fiscal adjustment pressures in key bilateral donor countries give rise to some doubts about sustaining current levels of financing, let alone increasing future financing (bilateral Overseas Development Assistance to Sub-Saharan African countries declined in 2011 in real terms).

Because African LICs traditionally have had limited access to external private finance, Ghana had tapped into international bond markets, and a number of others had aspirations to do the same. However, during the crisis, as international investors sharply cut back their lending and reshaped their portfolios, Africa was also affected. With prohibitively high interest rate spreads in international markets, incipient access to global capital markets was effectively cut off. Countries such as Nigeria, Kenya, and Zambia postponed Eurobond offerings. But this trend was only temporary. It has changed postcrisis for African LICs with lower interest rate spreads, similar to the pattern for Latin American and East Asian sovereigns.[14] However, international markets were not very accessible during the 2008–09 crisis period under consideration.

Thus, to the extent that significant additional financing was needed for a more proactive fiscal stance, and in contrast to the earlier shocks hitting African LICs, international financing has not been enough; domestic financing has become an important source.

What are the options for domestic financing other than raising taxes? Countries can borrow domestically, monetize part of the deficit, or accumulate arrears. The latter two options are not advisable or feasible for long, so the focus here is on domestic borrowing. In many cases, African LIC governments could reliably turn to local financial markets to balance dwindling sources of external funding. Domestic government securities markets had been developing steadily, and the African financial sectors were in the middle of a pronounced growth phase when the global crisis hit. During the preceding decade, the domestic financial market depth had increased significantly in African LICs, as reflected in the persistent increase in the ratios of both liquid liabilities to GDP and private credit to GDP across African LICs (Beck et al. 2011). Private credit as a share of GDP increased from an average of 12.1 percent in 1999 to 17.9 percent by 2009; liquid liabilities as a share of GDP also increased by over 5.0 percentage points to 32.0 percent on average by 2009.[15]

Figure 6.3 reveals that domestic borrowing was expected to play a major role. By contrast, most countries, whether greatly aid dependent or not, did not intend to rely more heavily on external financing for their budgets (excluding grants).

Figure 6.3   Shift to Domestic Financing in Crisis Response, African LICs

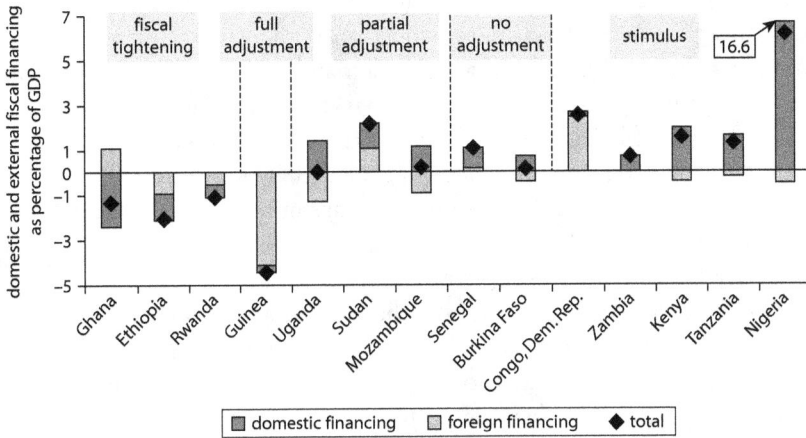

Source: IMF reviews.
Note: Change of projections for calendar year 2009 or fiscal 2008/09 (fiscal year countries: Ethiopia, Kenya, Rwanda, Tanzania, and Uganda).

For domestic borrowing, three sets of issues should be considered: crowding out, debt sustainability, and balance of payments impact. In addition, there is the critical question of reversibility and the importance of an exit strategy.

Crowding Out
A perennial concern about government borrowing is that it diverts resources from the private sector where they may be used more productively. But again it is important not to take a static view. The external shock is likely to affect private demand for funds, as well as banks' perceptions of the risks of lending to the government and private sector. Unless government credibility is low or its debt high, bank risk perceptions are likely to shift in favor of lending to the government in a climate of greater risk and uncertainty. Private demand for bank borrowing from creditworthy borrowers could decline as investment plans become more conservative, opening the space for greater borrowing by the government and in the process providing banks with a source of income when private loan demand declines.[16]

At the same time, there is a risk that governments could abuse the temporary windfall from lower domestic borrowing costs by reinforcing the shift to risk aversion—thereby diverting credit from worthy private borrowers—or by jeopardizing longer-term debt sustainability concerns (considered shortly). If there is recourse to more domestic borrowing when private demand is low, the government needs to remain alert to changing market trends—in particular, the reemergence of private sector demand. Thus the best guidance may be to pay close attention to market signals—that is, consider additional domestic borrowing only if interest rates are more attractive than in the precrisis situation, the yield curve is not unusually steep, and bank liquidity is not a systemic concern.

Preliminary evidence suggests that in Sub-Saharan African LICs crowding out was not an issue in the short-term crisis response period. This needs to be seen in the context of significant financial market deepening in the years leading up to the crisis (see Beck et al. 2011).[17] Higher risk aversion on the part of commercial banks and slower economic growth hindered the increase of credit to the private sector. Even though policy and treasury rates were reduced significantly, bank lending rates in many countries did not follow (see Fuchs and Losse-Mueller 2010). In Kenya, for example, the private sector's share of commercial bank lending in 2009 was below the historical level of 80 percent, and the rate of credit increase to the private sector continued to slow down. Tanzania also experienced a slowdown in credit demand by the private sector. From October 2008 to the end of 2009, growth slowed to 0.9 percent a month, compared with the 3.2 percent increase in the previous two years, well before the government began heavy net borrowing from the banking sector in mid-2009. In fact, banks were so liquid that the government was able to borrow at negative real interest rates in the second half of 2009. In Zambia, because of the rising levels of nonperforming loans on the books of commercial banks, credit to the private sector tightened. There was a widening gap between interest rates on government securities that had been dropping and commercial bank lending rates that remained stubbornly high.[18] In Nigeria, after the crisis began, concerns about banks' balance sheet risks led to a breakdown in the interbank market and higher lending rates. Thus evidence suggests that the slowdown in credit to the private sector was not caused by crowding out.

Debt Sustainability

The 2008–09 global crisis could adversely affect debt sustainability projections through several interrelated channels:

- More external and domestic borrowing that leads to faster buildup of public debts
- Slower real GDP growth
- Lower exports because demand for traditional exports has fallen
- Scaled-back fiscal revenue because of slower GDP growth and the decline in trade.

The advisability of assuming additional debt in this environment will depend on the country's existing debt burden, its medium-term debt sustainability outlook, and the effectiveness of the additional borrowing in generating incremental government revenue or foreign exchange. Risks to debt sustainability also relate to the strength of recovery and the ability of countries' transition to a sustainable fiscal policy. To the extent that the additional borrowing finances investment leading to higher growth, it is important to incorporate this factor into the analysis—in addition to the adverse impact of the increased borrowing on public debt and debt service.

The evidence suggests that the proactive fiscal responses in the subset of countries of interest here have not adversely affected debt sustainability to date. Countries' ratings in the World Bank and IMF debt sustainability analyses have remained unchanged or improved (as shown in figure 6.4).[19]

It will be important to monitor the situation to assess the extent to which debt and fiscal sustainability indicators are stabilizing. Nonetheless, when one looks at the change in indicators through 2010—debt-to-GDP, debt-to-revenue, and debt service–to–revenue ratios, for example—any worsening in indicators was initially modest. Key in this regard is the exit strategy from the countercyclical fiscal stances discussed earlier (figure 6.5).

Balance of Payments Impact

Even if debt sustainability and crowding-out concerns do not constrain a widening of the fiscal deficit, the balance of payment position may constitute a binding constraint—slower exports, remittances, and tourism, and a negative net trend for private capital flows. Declining import demand may offset these trends at least partially, but because of low reserves and large current account deficits, a number of African countries cannot afford to ignore the impact of larger fiscal deficits on the balance of payments.

Looking forward on domestic financing, the major concern is whether there will be enough depth in domestic markets—something key to the

Figure 6.4   Countries in Which Countercyclical Policy Did Not Worsen Debt Distress Risk Ratings, 2009 and 2010

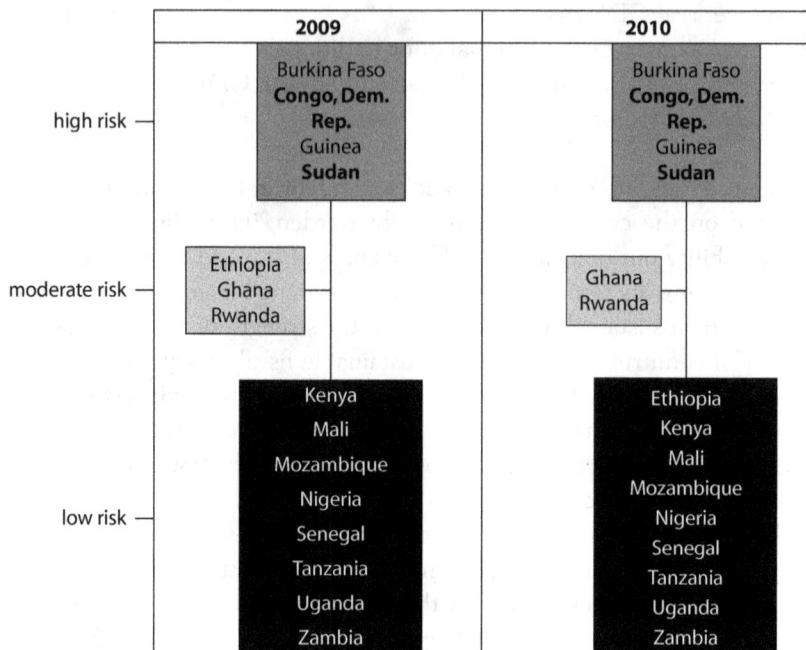

	2009	2010
high risk	Burkina Faso **Congo, Dem. Rep.** Guinea **Sudan**	Burkina Faso **Congo, Dem. Rep.** Guinea **Sudan**
moderate risk	Ethiopia Ghana Rwanda	Ghana Rwanda
low risk	Kenya Mali Mozambique Nigeria Senegal Tanzania Uganda Zambia	Ethiopia Kenya Mali Mozambique Nigeria Senegal Tanzania Uganda Zambia

Source: Joint IMF–World Bank debt sustainability analysis.
Note: Countries that followed countercyclical fiscal policy are indicated in boldface. The five measures of debt distress are (1) public sector debt to gross domestic product (GDP); (2) present value (PV) of public sector debt to GDP; (3) external public and public guaranteed debt to GDP; (4) PV of external public and public guaranteed debt to GDP; and (5) PV of external public and public guaranteed debt to exports. The improvement in Ethiopia's debt profile from moderate to low stems largely from the inclusion of remittances

first round of fiscal stimulus—if a second round of fiscal stimulus is appropriate (in the likelihood that the global economy experiences a W-shaped or double-dip recession). Vulnerabilities related to foreigner holdings of domestic debt are also a concern among Sub-Saharan African countries. The issue of nonconcessional external borrowing for viable projects remains a complex topic because the appropriate institutional frameworks and capacity are generally still being put in place.[20]

Reversibility and Exit Strategy

Today, the crisis has passed, and it is critical that governments move back quickly to a sustainable fiscal path. Maintaining credibility is key. Many African LICs worked hard over the past decade to establish the credibility of their macroeconomic management, including prudent fiscal policy.

Figure 6.5   Debt and Fiscal Sustainability Indicators, 2009 and 2010

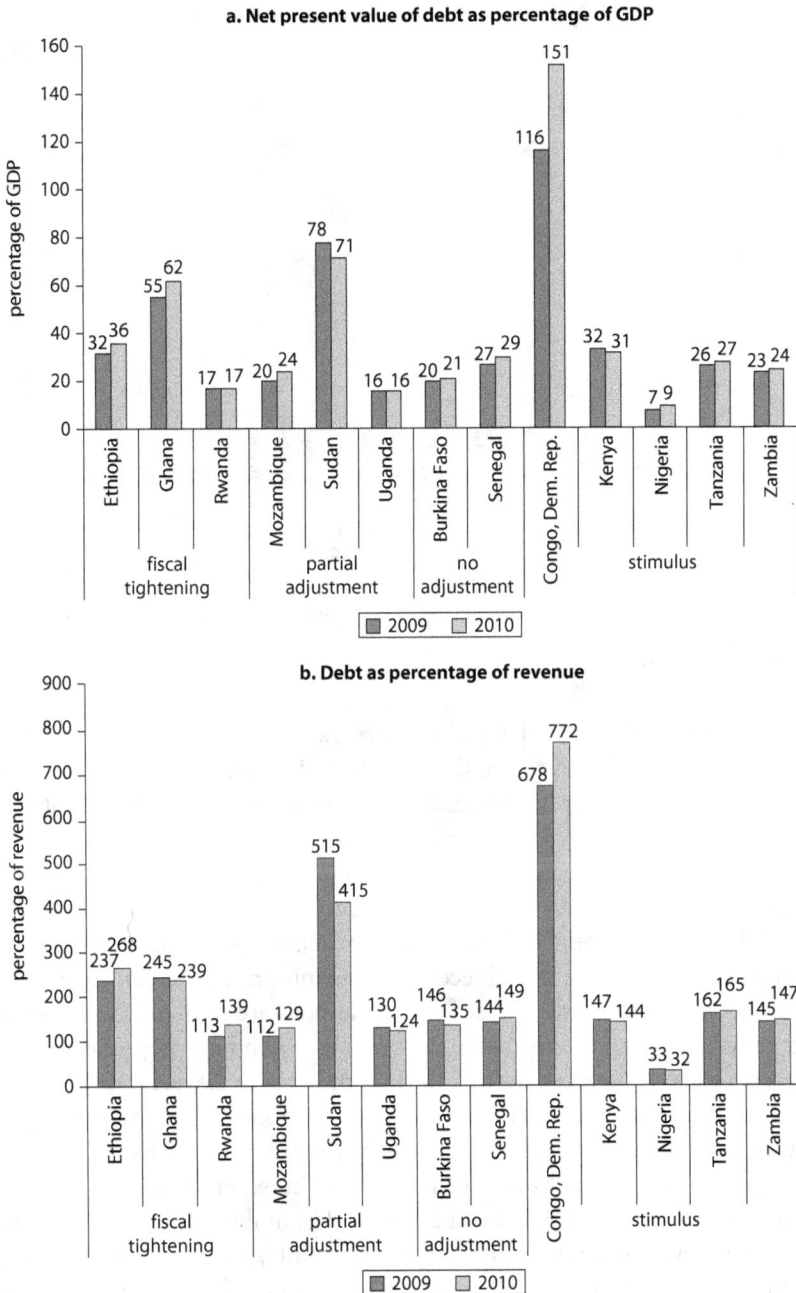

a. Net present value of debt as percentage of GDP

b. Debt as percentage of revenue

(continued next page)

Figure 6.5   *(continued)*

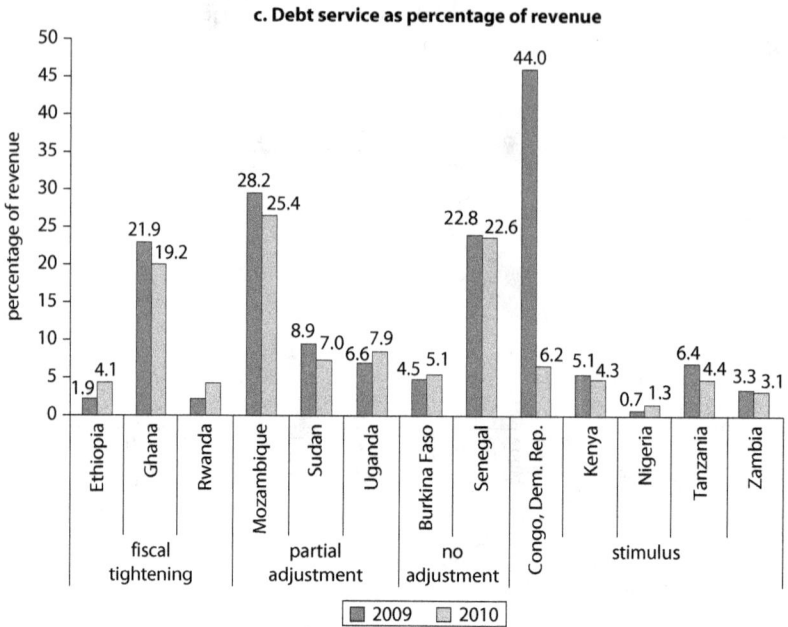

c. Debt service as percentage of revenue

Source: Joint IMF–World Bank debt sustainability analysis.
Note: GDP = gross domestic product.

For example, Kenya had a public debt ratio that declined from over 70 percent of GDP in the mid-1990s, to just above 40 percent prior to the crisis, and then up to 47 percent by the end of 2010—slightly above the target range of 45 percent, albeit with a lower cost and longer maturity profile (World Bank 2010b). Tanzania's and Zambia's public debt ratios crept up slightly but remained at relatively low levels consistent with low debt distress. Although countercyclical fiscal stances as part of the fiscal response were not necessarily inappropriate, the evidence from other parts of the world is that fiscal expansions are difficult to reverse. If governments commit to unsustainably large spending programs during recessions as a countercyclical device, these may be very difficult to reverse when times improve, affecting expectations and threatening fiscal sustainability in the long run. In Tanzania, for example, the fiscal 2010/11 budget (as presented) had a further increase in expenditures beyond the earlier stimulus package of fiscal 2009/10. The ambitious assumptions on revenues and financing sources imply the country will be underfinanced, and thus a major in-year adjustment is needed in order to maintain credibility (World Bank 2010f).[21]

Composition of Spending

How is the impact of the crisis expected to affect the composition of spending among African LICs? Historical experience suggests that expansionary discretionary spending has not been an especially effective stabilization tool for most developing countries; that mistimed interventions can be counterproductive; and that spending increases, if feasible, should concentrate on areas in which the spending either is reversible or is likely to increase long-term growth (see Kraay and Servén 2008 and chapter 2 of this book). Designing discretionary spending in times of crisis is even more difficult when there are no safety nets (to cope with income support) and factor markets do not work very well (to cope with lower consumption). In view of these considerations, how did the onset of the crisis affect the budgeted composition of spending?

Public Capital Investment

Financing of preappraised projects is preferable to embarking on untried projects that may be wasteful or result in unanticipated recurring costs and rents for the few suppliers available.

Before the 2008–09 global crisis, several African countries had been expanding their infrastructure programs with a growth objective in mind. Protection of this expansion has been a key objective in the fiscal response to the crisis. In Tanzania, for example, the allocation to roads in the fiscal 2009/10 budget represented 3.5 percent of GDP, compared with 3.3 percent in fiscal 2008/09 (although the rural road program allocation declined), and 1.1 percent of GDP to water in fiscal 2009/10, compared with 0.9 percent in fiscal 2008/09 (World Bank 2010f). Resource-rich economies that managed resources well during the boom also made plans to protect public investment. In Nigeria, the 2009 budget capped recurrent spending (expected to decline by 1.3 percentage points of nonoil GDP) while allocating higher amounts for capital spending in sectors that represented major growth bottlenecks. Capital expenditure was budgeted to increase by 2.5 percentage points of nonoil GDP in 2009, mostly in the areas of public works projects, housing, agriculture, transport, and power (World Bank 2009k). In Zambia, the total expenditures for 2009 were to rise 0.9 percentage points, reflecting an increase of 1.2 percentage points of GDP in capital spending (about half of which depended on external financing). In Senegal, capital expenditure was set to increase 30 percent in the first semester of the 2010 budget, while current expenditure remained unchanged (World Bank 2010d).

By contrast, countries that were seriously consolidating their fiscal positions and cutting expenditures usually reduced investment expenditures. In Sudan, development transfers from federal to northern states (which are mainly capital spending) were 88 percent less than budgeted in 2008 (with total transfers to northern states' shares declining from 24 percent of the budget plan to 19 percent actual). Expenditure cuts in the initial 2009 budget for Senegal mainly affected investment spending in sectors other than health and education (World Bank 2009l). In Liberia, the reduction in revenues from slower growth stemming from the global crisis may have forced the government to eliminate its already anemic capital spending (World Bank 2009m). Thus countries with fiscal space could focus on protecting growth expenditures in contrast to those with less fiscal space (figure 6.6).

Natural resource–rich countries face particular challenges. Because a significant share of resource-related revenue flow usually remains in public hands and does not directly affect private citizens, fiscal policy can be at the heart of economic mismanagement in the wake of resource booms (busts) when spending levels are adjusted sharply in response to increased (decreased) revenues (see Gelb and Associates 1988 and chapter 4 of this book).

There are ways to manage this volatility—such as a separate (extrabudgetary) natural resource fund—that can position natural resource–rich economies to respond effectively to other external shocks (as in the Great Recession). In Nigeria, for example, the oil price–based fiscal rule attempts to break the link between public spending and oil prices, and it created an oil savings cushion of 15 percent of nonoil GDP as well as foreign reserves that peaked in September 2008 at 16 months of imports (World Bank 2009k). Figure 6.7 contrasts the public investment space for natural resource–rich countries such as Nigeria that had saved during the oil price boom and those such as Sudan (North and South Sudan) that had failed to do so.

However, these public investment budgets were just plans. Limited state capacity to implement quality public investment programs is one of the main challenges facing African LICs. A review of implementation in the crisis period suggests that many governments were unable to absorb the public investment budget allocations. As shown in figure 6.8, actual expenditures continued to lag planned capital expenditures. For example, Uganda and Zambia spent less than planned, although execution of the capital budget was higher than in 2008.[22]

Figure 6.6   Changes in Budgeted Expenditure Composition

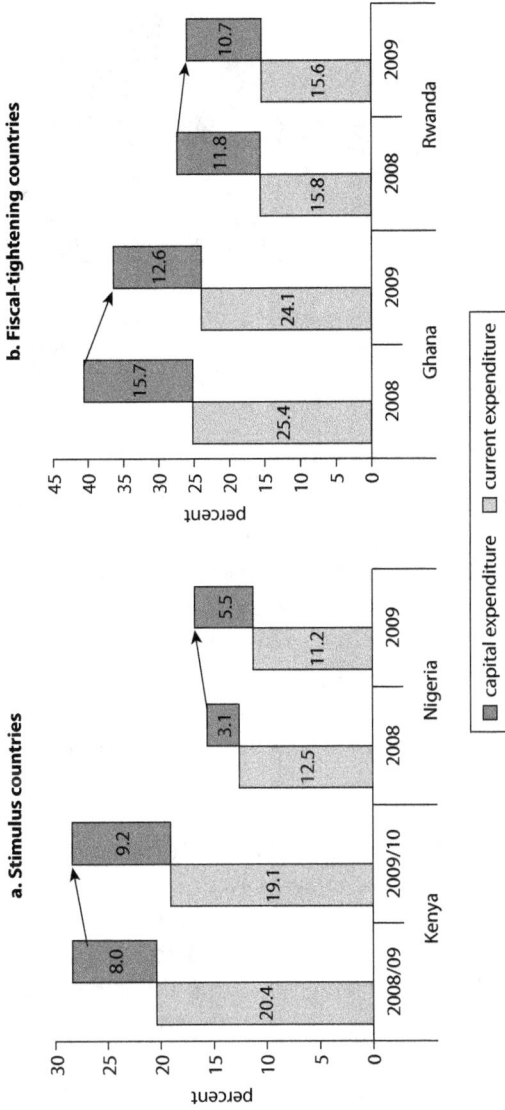

a. Stimulus countries

b. Fiscal-tightening countries

■ capital expenditure   □ current expenditure

Sources: World Bank 2009h, 2009k, 2010b.

233

Figure 6.7   Managing the Natural Resource Boom: Nigeria and Sudan, 2008 and 2009

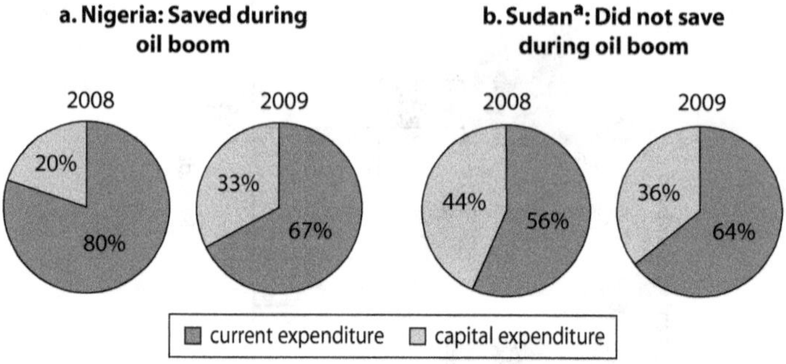

Sources: World Bank 2009k, 2010h.
Note: Shift in capital expenditure budget share of select oil-exporting countries in response to shock.
a. Capital and current expenditures of Sudan are calculated on the basis of the International Monetary Fund's projections as of July 2009. Capital expenditure consists of (1) capital transfers to northern states, (2) all transfers to south, and (3) net acquisition of net foreign assets.

The lesson is to accelerate the institutional strengthening of public investment management (see chapter 3 of this book). Measures to improve public investment management also ensure that any improved budget execution translates into high rates of return and avoids the systematic misallocation of resources through spending on low-return investments.[23]

There are domestic supply constraints as well. For example, an extensive public infrastructure expenditure may not occur because of a lack of skilled workers and domestic construction firms, the inability of unemployed labor to move from the commodity-exporting sector to work in infrastructure development, a poor transport network for materials, and poor logistics, to name a few.[24] These factors dilute the effectiveness of African LIC governments to design and implement effective public investment programs in normal times, let alone ensure execution during crises when an ongoing fiscal impulse is needed to sustain economic activity.

For the donor-dependent settings that characterize many African LICs, weak project management capacity induces donors to set up multiple implementation units that cut across and negatively affect in-line capacities and systems. These units often lack mechanisms for project adjustment (in this case, accelerating spending) and review when they are off track—in particular, for domestically financed

Figure 6.8   Capital Expenditure: Planned versus Observed

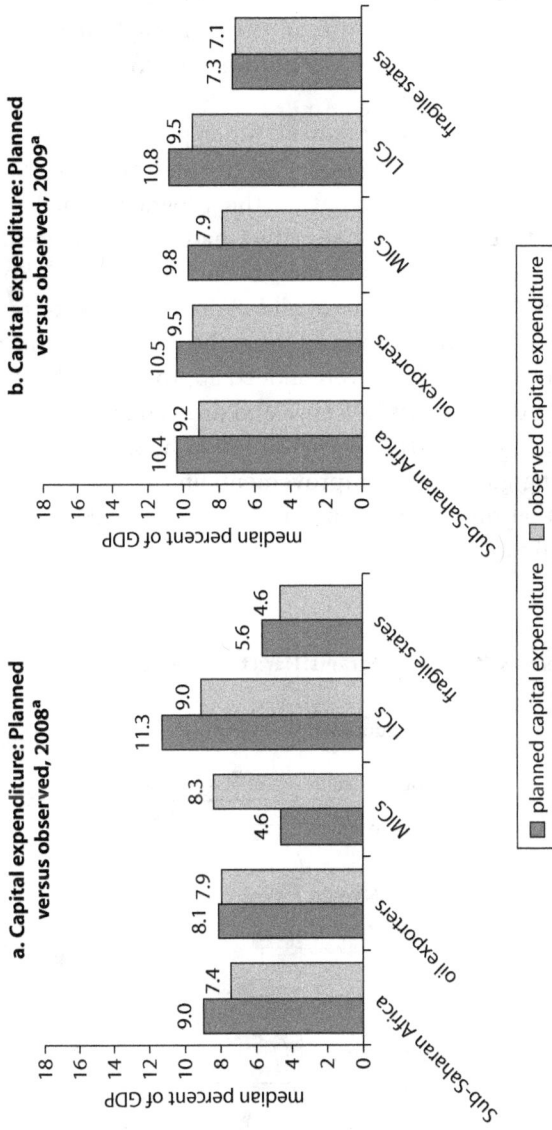

a. Capital expenditure: Planned versus observed, 2008[a]

b. Capital expenditure: Planned versus observed, 2009[a]

■ planned capital expenditure   ☐ observed capital expenditure

Source: IMF 2010a.
Note: GDP = gross domestic product; LIC = low-income country; MIC = middle-income country.
a. Excludes Eritrea, Guinea, and Zimbabwe.

235

projects—because of their heavy reliance on donors to trigger such reviews. Strategic guidance has been at a level of generality that limits the extent to which it can provide a basis for screening of projects, let alone a pipeline of projects that could be accelerated as part of a countercyclical fiscal policy. For postconflict and fragile states, this extends to almost complete reliance on donor systems for implementation and adjustment (Petrie 2011).

Other stimulus programs showed other problems related to implementation. In Kenya, for example, by the end of the third quarter of fiscal 2009/10, only 57 percent of the program aimed primarily at supplements to district-level spending had been disbursed, and it is unlikely that the full stimulus will be implemented.[25] Some of the problems can be attributed to addressing medium-term structural issues, including delays stemming from the need to put in place anticorruption measures, which were indeed appropriate—for example, for education sector programs in Kenya and drug and water investments in Uganda (World Bank 2010e). This situation highlights the importance of accelerating governance improvements in public expenditure management so that programs can be implemented quickly without fear of corruption (figure 6.9).

Figure 6.9   Kenya's Stimulus Programs: Hard to Be Timely

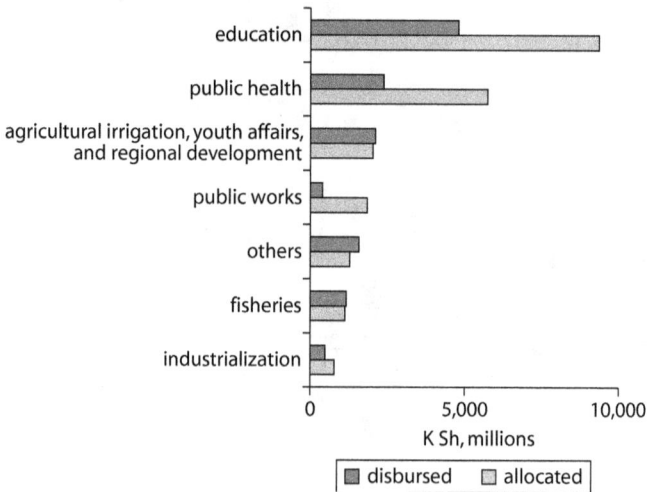

Source: World Bank 2010b, based on the Ministry of Finance.
Note: Fiscal stimulus fiscal 2009/10: 57 percent implementation through the third quarter.

Protecting the Vulnerable

Those most adversely affected directly by a global economic crisis are likely to be workers in exporting industries—particularly, miners, farmers whose crop prices have fallen, workers in construction or tourism, and households relying on remittances. Moreover, households relying unduly on remittances, who may also be poor, may not be easily identifiable and may be regionally dispersed. These factors suggest that creating new government programs to target groups impacted adversely by the crisis may not be a widely applicable strategy. Instead, scaling up existing programs that protect the vulnerable may be the most promising avenue for providing relief, for attracting additional donor financing, and for maintaining social stability, which is also critical to sustained growth and poverty reduction.

Among the programs worth considering are those supporting household income via public transfers and self-targeted public works programs. Cash and in-kind transfers have been an important mechanism for safeguarding minimum levels of consumption in times of crisis (and during regular times) in other parts of the world, but in African LICs their use has been limited and poorly coordinated. Knowledge and methodologies for identifying and reaching households affected by shocks are scarcer than, for example, those for the chronic poor and food-insecure households, both geographically and at the household level.[26] Efforts to reduce transaction costs for remittance payments by exposing intermediaries to more competition can be effective in countering declining remittances—and an important medium-term objective as well. Finally, the permanent losses associated with temporary household descent into poverty can also be prevented. For example, reducing school or health care fees can help keep children in school and support family health, mitigating the impact of declining household incomes.

A number of African LICs encouraged and supported by donors are seeking to develop long-term, sustainable safety nets that ideally could be scaled up in times of crisis and scaled back in better times (DelNino 2009). For those countries that already had programs that aimed to protect the vulnerable, scaling up was a common response to the crisis. For example, Ghana further extended its cash transfer program (Livelihood Empowerment against Poverty) to new beneficiaries. The government also initiated a public works program in the northern region of the country (World Bank 2009h). In Burkina Faso, the authorities expanded programs introduced in 2008 through cash transfers in two major cities and through school lunches (World Bank 2009i). In Tanzania, the government increased its allocation to the Tanzania Social Action Fund (TASAF) that supports community-based public works, and it has started pilot conditional cash transfers. In Kenya, the government introduced a youth workfare program, Kazi Kwa Vijana, in fiscal 2008/09 and later expanded it.

Countries without existing programs were highly constrained in their ability to respond and faced potentially high costs of inaction. Part of Mozambique's looser fiscal stance during 2009 was the introduction of a fuel subsidy at the pump in mid-2009—arguably to avoid civil unrest during the crisis and in the run-up to the elections. The government started phasing out fuel subsidies through price increases for gasoline in mid-2010. However, diesel subsidies, which represent the larger share of fuel subsidies, remained in place after the social unrest of September and were associated with water, electricity, and bread price increases (World Bank 2010c).[27]

This situation highlights the importance of thinking about such programs in noncrisis times, especially in view of the severe challenges in developing interventions that are efficient and well targeted within the African LIC context. What is notable is the complex targeting problem, including the difficulty in defining the target population when nearly 50 percent of the population is poor; the need to avoid negative incentives and moral hazard (households restructuring to fit the targeting criteria); and the need to avoid reshuffling where the recipient households become richer than the nonrecipient households (see DelNino 2009).[28] The other challenge is low administrative capacity, requiring empirical work to inform design and piloting of easy-to-implement methods robust enough to resist influence by pressure groups on program participation. Several years would likely be required for a strong program to run effectively.

Although they were often not among the poorest or most vulnerable, there were more direct pressures to support workers and farmers adversely affected by the crisis. These pressures included support for marketing boards to cover the difference between falling commodity prices and producer prices at previous levels and to protect parts of the domestic financial sectors heavily exposed to domestic commodity exporters. In Burkina Faso, the government put together an emergency package to respond to the sharp decline in cotton prices, with a focus on immediate measures to save the coming crop campaign (fiscal 2009/10). Direct budgetary expenditures added up to US$23 million (0.3 percent of GDP)—see World Bank (2009i). In Mali, the 2009 budget included a transfer to Compagnie Malienne pour le Development des Textiles (CMDT, public cotton monopoly) of CFAF 3.7 billion (0.1 percent of GDP) to pay arrears to cotton co-ops and farmers (World Bank 2009j).

Likewise, in Tanzania both cotton and coffee buyers were seriously affected by the sharp drop in both prices and orders during the 2008–09 crop season, threatening farmers' access to crop finance in the coming season. In response, authorities financed a banking package, including a loss compensation facility, a rescheduled loan guarantee facility, and a working capital financing facility. Direct budgetary expenditures were expected to add up to T Sh 144 billion (0.5 percent of GDP) for the severely impacted subsectors (World Bank 2010f). Evidence suggests that the majority of cotton farmers in these countries are poor. However, although features have been put in place to mitigate the risk of moral hazard and to promote farmers' access to crop financing, the benefit is likely to accrue partially to the intermediaries as well as to farmers who are not from the poorest or most vulnerable segment.

Recurrent Expenditures

Another option in responding to crises is to direct incremental spending toward areas that tend to be chronically underbudgeted in African LICs and address preexisting structural deficits such as operations and maintenance of existing infrastructure or facilities.[29] Such maintenance can be an important element of maintaining fiscal policy for growth in response to the crisis. There may also be reasons to direct incremental spending toward the nontradable sector, reinforcing the advisability to spend more for maintenance than for import-intensive capital goods, or to increase the budget for health and education workers rather than spending to import more drugs. This could occur, for example, if export demand has fallen relative to domestic demand or if balance of payments constraints are more acute than fiscal constraints. However, those relationships may be difficult to establish in practice. In several countries (such as Senegal), there have been sizable increases in road maintenance expenditures. Authorities in Burkina Faso used the crisis as an opportunity to clear domestic payment arrears on maintenance spending, which were outstanding at the end of 2008.

Increases in the public wage and salary bill could serve a similar purpose, but only in cases in which the levels were previously inadequate. In Uganda, it is not clear that the across-the-board increases included in the fiscal 2009/10 budget were consistent with enhanced service delivery, and likely other expenditures could have provided a similar fiscal impulse while making a greater contribution to growth. In Burkina Faso, the government implemented salary adjustments agreed on with labor unions after the 2008 social unrest (IMF 2010b).[30] These recurrent spending categories may also have the disadvantage of being more difficult to reverse. In fact, failure to reverse them might end up forcing sharp reductions in productive nonsalary public expenditures postcrisis in line with macroeconomic goals, thereby worsening efficiency relative to precrisis findings.

Finally, the crisis could provide opportunities to trim wasteful or corrupt spending as well as implement complementary policies that ensure a higher supply response from existing public goods.[31] For example, Mozambique approved measures to rationalize expenditures for nonpriority sectors and limit the cost of internal and external travel (World Bank 2010c). Uganda responded to unanticipated revenue shortfalls with cuts in some nonessential expenditures (World Bank 2010e).

Budget Execution Gap

Although most countries with the requisite fiscal space designed a fiscal policy response to protect (if not enhance) expenditures, only a subset of countries were successful in this regard. As shown in figure 6.10, most governments' actual expenditures were lower than the corresponding budget. As a result, several countries had more contractionary fiscal stances than intended when the fiscal policy response for growth was designed in the face of crisis (see IMF 2010a). The lack of timely implementation is a challenge in developed countries because of lack of shovel-ready projects in the capital budget and even more so in developing countries and African LICs.

In addition, fiscal policy works with a variable lag effect because of structural factors, the type of instrument used, coordination of policy, and complementarities of private sector decisions. Thus, the lag effect of fiscal policy likely delays the impact of the stimulus as well. Although the evidence is limited, it is likely that the multiplier in most African LICs is relatively small, thereby reducing the impact of any stimulus package that could be implemented (as laid out in box 6.1). This observation reinforces the imperative to move back quickly to a sustainable fiscal policy position, as discussed earlier. Evidence from other parts of the world is that fiscal expansions prove difficult to reverse. It will be important that African LICs learn from those experiences and only attempt countercyclical fiscal policy if there is the political will and technical ability to reverse it as required.

Link with Medium-Term Growth Strategy

Although the spending responses to the crisis by African LICs were motivated initially by short-term demand management considerations,

Figure 6.10   Budget Execution Gap: Difference between Planned and Actual or Latest Expenditure Projection, Fiscal 2008/09 and 2009/10

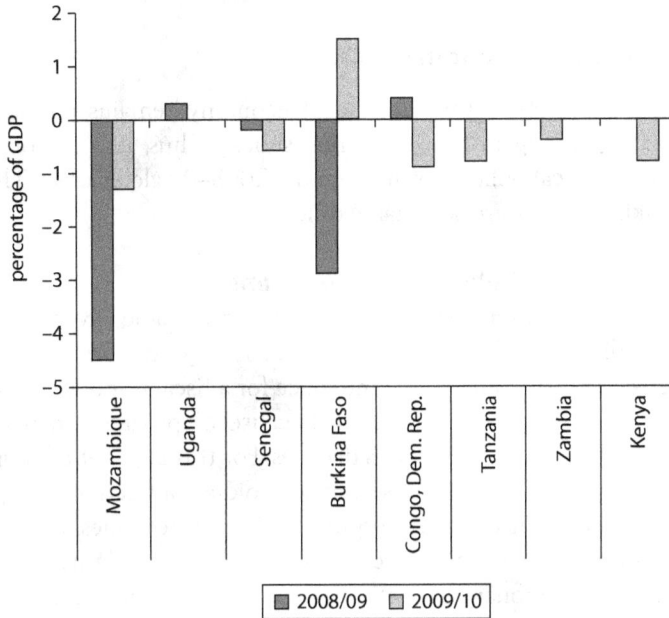

Source: IMF, Articles of Agreement, various Article IV documents.

these countries also assessed the trade-offs between spending that might use otherwise idle resources for a demand response and spending (mainly investment) that would be good for growth in the long run. In most countries, the assessment was that protecting growth-oriented public spending had sufficient aggregate demand properties to serve both objectives. This avoided the fiscal consequences that have often proven disastrous in other parts of the world when the focus has been solely on non-growth-oriented expenditures to stimulate demand in the short run (see Commission on Growth and Development 2009).

The lessons for African LICs therefore do not lie so much in the planned spending choices; rather, they lie in the capacity to implement those choices. The main problems were that public investments could not be made in the requisite time frame and that programs for the vulnerable were not in place or scalable. Thus, the lessons for implementing effective spending responses in a crisis are assessed, by and large, to be the same key ones for meeting the spending challenges associated with shared growth within a medium-term development context.

Fiscal Policy Lessons from the Crisis

Because uncertainty within the global economy remains considerable, African LICs are again facing external shocks. Thus, it is important to reflect on the fiscal policy lessons from the 2008–09 global crisis. The two most striking lessons are summarized here.

Prudent Fiscal and Debt Policy in Good Times

Although this chapter has described the considerable diversity in the initial conditions and fiscal policy responses by African LICs to the global crisis, many countries had the space for a fiscal response consistent with growth and poverty reduction because of progress on debt and sound fiscal policy in the previous decades. For this large set of countries, the most common fiscal response was to avoid a contraction in expenditures, as reflected in budgets, despite declines in revenues. A subset of these countries even instituted fiscal stimulus programs based on increases in discretionary expenditures. Many other countries were able to keep their expenditure plans intact by accommodating a larger fiscal deficit but choosing not to be more ambitious in terms of increasing discretionary expenditures. This was in part because of legitimate concerns about the ability of additional discretionary expenditures to meet the intended objectives and the potential impact on the credibility of their macroeconomic policies. In particular, the protection of public investment programs oriented toward growth is a notable development, compared with adjustment efforts in African LICs in previous decades in response to shocks.

A smaller set of countries tightened the fiscal stance, however, representing not a response to the change in the global economic situation but a reflection of preexisting macroeconomic tensions and risks of debt distress. Countries with a heavy reliance on revenues from oil and mineral exports were hit particularly hard. Those that had built up reserves during the boom were also in a position to protect expenditures, in sharp contrast to those that had not built up a cushion and needed to contract expenditures (largely public investment) sharply in light of the crisis impact.

Most countries chose not to adjust fully to the shock and revenue declines stemming from changes in the economic situation. Rather, they chose to finance an increased fiscal deficit. The bulk of the additional financing came from domestic borrowing but without threatening macroeconomic stability. It will be important to continue assessing whether this delicate balance can be maintained, how much of the stimulus intended as transitory did not remain in the public finances more permanently, and whether the fiscal stance quickly reversed when the economic situation improved. So far, debt vulnerability generally has not worsened. Nonetheless, the trends in concessional aid will have to be watched carefully for signs of softening, and the inherent vulnerabilities associated with other external finance will have to be assessed carefully.

Meanwhile, assessment of the scope for additional domestic borrowing will have to be updated constantly as domestic markets deepen to ensure no adverse impact on private flows, including crowding out borrowing by the private sector. The impact of the global crisis on Africa may be prolonged. Should this happen, the ability of African LICs to continue with expansionary fiscal policy may be possible only if the debt levels are sustainable. Furthermore, expectations matter! Many governments worked hard over the last decade to establish strong macroeconomic and fiscal policy credentials. With looser fiscal policies and rising debt levels, the risk premium attached to government paper will rise. The extent to which risk premiums rise depends on the credibility of the fiscal policy (and other macroeconomic policies) of the government, affecting the ratings attached to the country's debt. Mirroring the global discussions, measures may be needed now to transition to the long-run optimal trajectory for fiscal sustainability.

The remaining questions are the following:

• How difficult will it be to reverse discretionary fiscal expansion? Evidence from other parts of the world supports the notion that such expansion is difficult to reverse. This is the first major instance in which African LICs overall had the fiscal space to attempt countercyclical policy. It will be important to monitor whether these policies are reversed and credibility is maintained (and whether certain categories of discretionary spending prove easier to reverse), or whether these countries, too, will have to eschew future active fiscal responses (or categories of discretionary spending) out of the realization that an exit cannot be safely assumed.

- How quickly will countercyclical policy responses reduce the output and employment gaps? Countercyclical fiscal policy responses may not have the intended impact in terms of reducing the output and employment gaps in a timely manner. Structural constraints in the noncommodity sectors (including those within the relatively large informal sector) and limited labor market flexibility in African LICs may reduce the impact. Delays in execution, which are particularly acute in the subregion, also may prevent timeliness.[32]

Addressing Public Spending Challenges for the Medium Term

The impact of the availability of fiscal space has been muted because of numerous challenges in implementation of the proposed fiscal responses. Despite plans that protected growth expenditures, execution of those plans was another matter. Only a subset of countries was successful in actually spending as much as budgeted, largely because of structural factors in public investment management. It is important to assess features of managing public investment programs that increase the ability to maintain growth over time and, in times of volatility, avoid an irreversible disruption.

Only countries with well-tested programs to protect the vulnerable were able to scale up those interventions when the crisis hit. For countries wanting to add such programs to their toolkits, it will be important to prepare such programs in noncrisis times when their immediate need is less visible.

In conclusion, most of the challenges in actually implementing higher-quality expansionary fiscal policy in light of the economic crisis are similar to the challenges faced by fiscal policy makers in supporting shared growth within a medium-term context. This finding should be a comfort to those focusing on quality expenditure programs for growth and efficient service delivery.

Annex 6A   Revenue Projections of Select African Lower-Income Countries

For comparative purposes, the principal fiscal shock from the crisis is assumed to be a loss in revenue from changes in the economic environment. Figure 6A.1 shows the revenue loss from both changes in projection, within year, and changes year on year.

Figure 6A.1 Change in Revenue to GDP in Budgets of Select African LICs

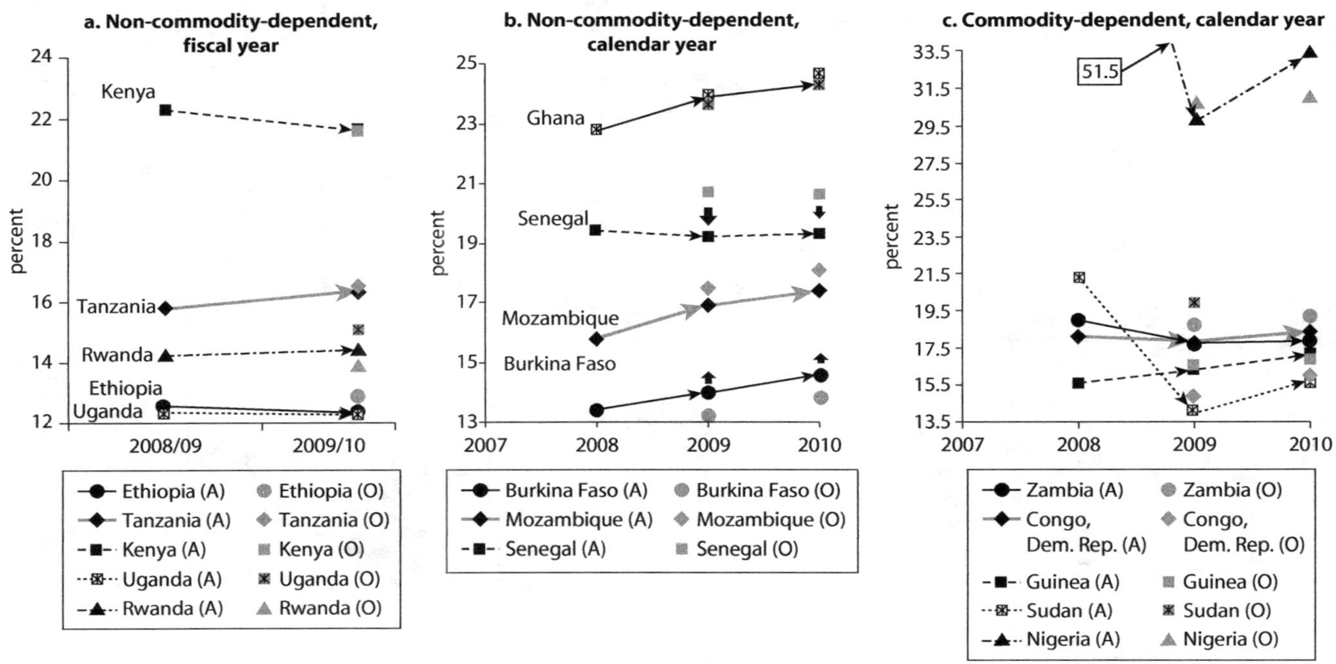

a. Non-commodity-dependent, fiscal year
percent
24
22
20
18
16
14
12
2008/09
2009/10
Kenya
Tanzania
Rwanda
Ethiopia
Uganda
Ethiopia (A)
Ethiopia (O)
Tanzania (A)
Tanzania (O)
Kenya (A)
Kenya (O)
Uganda (A)
Uganda (O)
Rwanda (A)
Rwanda (O)
b. Non-commodity-dependent, calendar year
percent
25
23
21
19
17
15
13
2007
2008
2009
2010
Ghana
Senegal
Mozambique
Burkina Faso
Burkina Faso (A)
Burkina Faso (O)
Mozambique (A)
Mozambique (O)
Senegal (A)
Senegal (O)
c. Commodity-dependent, calendar year
percent
33.5
31.5
29.5
27.5
25.5
23.5
21.5
19.5
17.5
15.5
13.5
2007
2008
2009
2010
51.5
Zambia (A)
Zambia (O)
Congo, Dem. Rep. (A)
Congo, Dem. Rep. (O)
Guinea (A)
Guinea (O)
Sudan (A)
Sudan (O)
Nigeria (A)
Nigeria (O)

Sources: IMF staff reports, various countries.

Note: GDP = gross domestic product; LIC = low-income country; dotted line = change year-on-year; vertical arrow = change in projection; O = original projection for within-year changes; A = actual for year-on-year changes.

Annex 6B   Fiscal Stance of Select African Lower-Income Countries, Pre- and Postcrisis

For comparative purposes, the fiscal stance is described by fiscal expenditure responses to the crisis, ranging from an increase in discretionary spending (notwithstanding the revenue decline that widens the fiscal deficit beyond the revenue loss, defined as stimulus), to maintaining expenditure levels despite the revenue decline (defined as no adjustment), to full adjustment to the revenue loss that avoids any increase in deficit (defined as full adjustment). This is in contrast to a definition based on comparing year-to-year actual fiscal results (this fiscal impulse is discussed further shortly). The details of the analysis for the country sample are given in table 6B.1.

What is being compared under this methodology is two sets of projections for the same fiscal year. Thus expenditures and deficit could have increased between the previous year and this fiscal year (positive fiscal impulse); but if that increase was less than originally planned, it would be categorized as fiscal tightening because the postcrisis response plans were less expansionary than the precrisis plans (such as in Rwanda). Similarly, although the deficit including grants is, by definition, less than the deficit excluding grants, lower projected grants in the postcrisis response plans than in the precrisis plans could result in a larger planned deficit (inclusive of grants) than in the precrisis plans.

Preliminary results for fiscal impulse analysis among African LICs suggest that the two methodologies can be consistent—but in practice they are not necessarily consistent in all cases. For Ghana, the comparative plans methodology suggests fiscal tightening, and the estimated fiscal impulse for 2009 is negative on the whole, based on a large negative impulse from expenditures (–3 percent) not offset by a slight positive impulse from structural revenues (+1 percent). For Kenya, the comparative plans methodology suggests plans for greater stimulus in the economy. Although the estimated fiscal impulse for 2009 from spending is positive (< 1 percent), this is almost completely offset by a negative impulse from structural revenues. Finally, for Uganda the comparative plans methodology suggests partial adjustment. However, the fiscal impulse, compared with the previous year, is positive—both +2 percent from spending and nearly 1 percent from structural revenues (authors' calculations). This approach should be developed further for the African LIC sample.

Table 6B.1 Planned Fiscal Stance of Select African LICs

Fiscal stance	Country	Debt distress risk	Fiscal projection changes, 2009				Country	Debt distress risk	Fiscal projection changes, 2009			
			Revenue	Expenditure	Balance (excluding grant)	Balance (including grant)			Revenue	Expenditure	Balance (excluding grant)	Balance (including grant)
Fiscal tightening	Ethiopia	Moderate	0.5	-4.1	5.6	2.5	Ghana	Moderate	0.3	1.1	-0.8	1.3
	Rwanda	Moderate	0.5	-1.5	1.9	2.0						
Full adjustment	Guinea	High	-0.2	-0.3	0.2	0.0						
Partial adjustment	Mozambique	Low	-0.5	-0.1	-0.3	-0.3	Uganda	Low	-2.8	-3.1	0.2	-0.2
	Sudan	High	-6.3	-4.1	-2.8	-2.1	Mali	Low				
No adjustment	Senegal	Low	-1.5	0.4	-2.0	-1.9	Burkina Faso	High	-0.8	0.0	-1.0	0.4
Stimulus	Congo, Dem. Rep.	High	3.3	8.5	-5.2	-4.0	Kenya	Low	0.1	1.8	-1.6	-1.6
	Nigeria	Low	-1.0	15.2	-16.1	-16.1	Tanzania	Low	-0.2	0.9	-1.1	-1.4
	Zambia	Low	-1.0	0.8	-1.7	-0.9						

Sources: The source of raw numbers for calculating fiscal projection changes is the International Monetary Fund, July 2008 and July 2009, or nearest equivalent date for individual country Article IV documents under the IMF Articles of Agreement; debt distress risk is as of July 2009 when countries were responding to the crisis; from joint IMF–World Bank debt sustainability analysis for individual countries. Some countries' debt distress risks may have changed or improved since then.

Note: GDP = gross domestic product; LIC = low-income country. The 2009 fiscal year is as of mid-2009, relative to projections mid-2008 and percentage of GDP.

Notes

1. Infrastructure user fees have also contributed to overall financing.

2. In a subset of African LICs, the reversal of the food and oil price shocks more than offset the impact of the global recession. For example, Mali's external current account balance improved as a result of buoyant international gold prices and lower oil and food prices. This situation more than offsets the decline in tourism receipts and migrant workers' remittances caused by the global slowdown, and the growth was steady.

3. In October 2009, the World Bank's *Global Economic Prospects* projected a more serious impact scenario for Sub-Saharan Africa, with 2009 growth estimated at only 0.7 percent and 2010 growth projected at 3.8 percent (World Bank 2009e).

4. See Blanchard (2009) for the distinction between changes in economic environment and changes in discretionary policy. See Berg et al. (2009) on the revenue losses.

5. At that time, both North and South Sudan were represented in the GNU.

6. The increase in oil prices since mid-2010 will help shore up the fiscal balance of oil-exporting countries.

7. Guinea benefited from higher gold prices and new mining ventures coming onstream. The Democratic Republic of Congo projected that enhanced revenue mobilization efforts enabled by progress on conflict resolution would more than offset the impact of the global crisis on its mineral revenues. Mali benefited from higher gold prices and the sale of the state telecommunications firm (World Bank 2009g, 2009j).

8. At the 2009 High-Level Workshop on Africa Fiscal Policy for Growth in Light of Global Crisis, participants shared lessons and evidence on which institutional and policy measures were most effective. Those measures included addressing tax expenditures (various exemptions) and broadening the tax base to growing subsectors and beyond the narrow formal sector.

9. As noted earlier, the Democratic Republic of Congo's stance related more to conflict resolution than to crisis response.

10. The exception is Kenya's economy, which stalled in fiscal 2008/09 in the face of postelection violence.

11. These tensions stemmed in part from the food and fuel price shocks that preceded the global crisis and Great Recession (also see World Bank 2009c).

12. Ethiopia had been growing at above 10 percent a year, as had Rwanda in 2008.

13. Exceptions where increases were expected were generally in postconflict countries (such as the Democratic Republic of Congo) for reasons unrelated to the crisis.

14. For example, in January 2011 Nigeria's issue of a US$500 million debut Eurobond was oversubscribed. In March 2011, Zambia received a B+ rating from international credit rating agencies. Senegal indicated it planned to raise US$200 million in Islamic financing in 2011 (World Bank 2011).

15. For almost all countries, data are available for private credit as a share of GDP, but they are more limited for liquidity. For the sample of 15 countries in this chapter, private credit as a share of GDP increased from 12.0 percent in 1999 to 19.4 percent on average by 2009. For a smaller sample for which data are available, liquid assets (or M3) as a share of GDP increased from 26.5 percent to 30.4 percent on average.

16. The income earned by banks on private debt depends on the demand for new loans and on the extent to which the global financial crisis increased the share of nonperforming loans. In Zambia, for example, the increase in nonperforming loans has tightened lending to the private sector.

17. The ratios of liquid liabilities to GDP, private credit to GDP, and bank deposits to GDP increased throughout the region.

18. However, foreign investors, who had been active in Zambia government securities, pulled back more sharply (see IMF 2010b).

19. Ethiopia adjusted during the crisis. The 2010 joint IMF–World Bank debt sustainability analysis shows that it now has a low risk of debt distress—an improvement from the medium risk rating of the last few years—in part because of having introduced gross workers' remittances as a source of enhanced repayment capacity.

20. This is based on the discussions at the High-Level Workshop on Africa Fiscal Policy for Growth in Light of Global Crisis.

21. In the context of the Policy Support Instrument (PSI) with the IMF, the authorities agreed on a 1.5 percentage point decrease in spending relative to budget as of mid-fiscal 2010/11. Any further reliance on net domestic financing through continued use of central bank advances and other forms of direct central bank credit could threaten the authorities' hard-won policy credibility.

22. Although this chapter focuses on LICs, the problem of execution of public investment budgets extended to medium-income countries: observed capital expenditure for African medium-income countries was a full 2 percentage points lower than the planned capital expenditure for the year 2009 (see IMF 2010a). In Cameroon, only about 50 percent of the largely centralized investment budget is executed over three years. For example, 30.8 percent of the 2006 investment budget was executed in 2006, with 16 percent in 2007 and 3 percent in 2008 (see World Bank 2009b).

23. Evidence on the rates of return of completed investment projects is limited. Economic rates of return on closing water and sanitation projects financed by the International Development Association in African LICs were, on average,

19 percent according to *IDA at Work: Water Supply and Sanitation* (World Bank 2010a). As noted in chapter 3, public investment management systems have eight must-have features, both upstream and downstream: strategic guidance, appraisal, independent review, project selection and budgeting, project implementation, project adjustment, facility operation, and postproject review. These features are interdependent. A review of systems as they are actually functioning in diverse settings noted similarities in weaknesses across several dimensions.

24. Based on discussions at the High-Level Workshop on Africa Fiscal Policy for Growth in Light of Global Crisis.

25. In the fiscal 2009/10 budget, a relatively large allocation was made to a conditional economic stimulus at the district level—K Sh 22 billion (about US$280 million or nearly 1 percent of GDP)—aimed at public service delivery more broadly.

26. Although the World Food Program has been providing emergency support for many years (together with recipient governments) and has developed a number of simple community- and household-based measures of vulnerability to shocks, ex post analysis of those programs has shown relatively high rates of errors of both inclusion and exclusion.

27. The government decided against a pass-through of higher fuel prices to domestic consumers and directly compensating fuel retailers for the loss.

28. A study is under way on the possible lessons from the experience with the limited number of programs in African LICs.

29. World Bank (2009a) *Africa's Infrastructure: A Time for Transformation*, showing how inadequate spending on maintenance has contributed to a Sub-Saharan Africa infrastructure deficit and has undermined the effectiveness of capital investment.

30. The agreement covered a 4 percent salary increase and the clearance of overdue payments for past promotions.

31. Corruption is a perennial issue, as laid out in *Silent and Lethal: How Quiet Corruption Undermines Africa's Development Efforts* (World Bank 2010g).

32. The empirical work on Kenya is sobering in this regard, but this remains an empirical question worthy of further analysis.

References

Beck, T., S. M. Maimbo, I. Faye, and T. Triki. 2011. *Financing Africa—Through the Crisis and Beyond*. Washington, DC: World Bank.

Berg, A., N. Funke, A. Hajdenberg, and I. Yackovlev. 2009. "Fiscal Policy in Sub-Saharan Africa in Response to the Impact of the Global Crisis." Staff Position Note SPN/09/10, International Monetary Fund, Washington, DC.

Blanchard, O. 2009. *Blanchard's Index of Discretionary Fiscal Policy: Economic Policy and Debt, Poverty Reduction and Economic Management*. Washington, DC: World Bank.

Canuto, Otaviano, and Marcelo Giugale. 2010. *The Day after Tomorrow*. Washington, DC: World Bank.

Commission on Growth and Development. 2009. *Post-Crisis Growth in Developing Countries: A Special Report of the Commission on Growth and Development on the Implications of the 2008 Financial Crisis*. Conference Edition. Washington, DC: World Bank.

DelNino, C. 2009. *Concept Note: Study on Safety Nets in Africa*. Washington, DC: World Bank.

Fuchs, M., and T. Losse-Mueller. 2010. "The African Financial Sector in Times of Global Crisis." Finance and Private Sector Development, Africa Region, World Bank, Washington, DC.

Gelb, A., and Associates. 1988. *Oil Windfalls: Blessing or Curse?* Washington, DC: World Bank.

Ilzetzki, E. E. G. Mendoza, and C. A. Vegh. 2009. "How Big Are Fiscal Multipliers? New Evidence from New Data." University of Maryland.

IMF (International Monetary Fund). 2009. *Regional Economic Outlook: Sub-Saharan Africa*. Washington, DC: IMF. (October).

———. 2010a. *Regional Economic Outlook: Sub-Saharan Africa*. Washington, DC: IMF. (April).

_____. 2010b. *Regional Economic Outlook: Sub-Saharan Africa*. Washington, DC: IMF. (October).

Kraay, A., and L. Servén. 2008. *Fiscal Policy Responses to the Current Financial Crisis: Issues for Developing Countries*. Washington, DC: World Bank.

Krumm, K., S. Dhar, and J.-Y. Choi. 2009. "Fiscal Response to the Global Crisis in Low Income African Countries." Paper presented at the High-Level Workshop on Africa Fiscal Policy for Growth in Light of Global Crisis, Maputo, Mozambique, December 2–3.

Petrie, M. 2011. "Promoting Public Investment Efficiency: A Synthesis of Country Experiences." In *Promoting Public Investment Efficiency*, ed. Kai Kaiser et al. Washington, DC: World Bank.

World Bank. 2009a. *Africa's Infrastructure: A Time for Transformation*. Washington, DC: World Bank.

_____. 2009b. "Cameroon: Fiscal Policy for Growth and Development." Report 48433-CM, Poverty Reduction and Economic Management Unit 3, Africa Region, World Bank, Washington, DC.

_____. 2009c. "Ghana: 2009 External Review of Public Financial Management." Report 47639-GH, Poverty Reduction and Economic Management Unit 4, Africa Region, World Bank, Washington, DC.

———. 2009d. *Global Development Finance 2009: Charting a Global Recovery.* Washington, DC: World Bank.

———. 2009e. *Global Economic Prospects 2009: Commodities at the Crossroads.* Washington, DC: World Bank.

———. 2009f. *Kenya Fiscal Policies and Institutions for Shared Growth: Lessons from the Global Crisis.* Washington, DC: World Bank.

———. 2009g. *Memorandum of the President, Financial Sector and Public Financial Management DRC.* Washington, DC: World Bank.

———. 2009h. "Program Document for the Economic Governance and Poverty Reduction Credit to the Republic of Ghana." Report 47233-GH, Poverty Reduction and Economic Management Unit 4, Africa Region, World Bank, Washington, DC.

———. 2009i. "Program Document for the Ninth Poverty Reduction Support Grant to Burkina Faso." Report 48468-BF, Poverty Reduction and Economic Management Unit 4, Africa Region, World Bank, Washington, DC.

———. 2009j. "Program Document for the Third Poverty Reduction Support Credit to the Republic of Mali." Report 46814-ML, Poverty Reduction and Economic Management Unit 4, Africa Region, World Bank, Washington, DC.

———. 2009k. "Program Document for a Proposed Financial Sector and Public Finance Management Development Policy Credit to the Federal Republic of Nigeria." Report 49162-NG, Finance and Private Sector Development, Africa Region, World Bank, Washington, DC.

———. 2009l. "Program Document for the Public Finance Support Credit to the Republic of Senegal." Report 48557-SN, Poverty Reduction and Economic Management Unit 4, Africa Region, World Bank, Washington, DC.

———. 2009m. "Program Document for the Second Reengagement and Reform Support Program to the Republic of Liberia." Report 46508-LR, Poverty Reduction and Economic Management Unit 4, Africa Region, World Bank, Washington, DC.

———. 2010a. *IDA at Work: Water Supply and Sanitation.* Washington, DC: World Bank.

———. 2010b. "Kenya Economic Update: Kenya at the Tipping Point?". Update 3, Nairobi Poverty Reduction and Economic Management Unit, Africa Region, World Bank.

———. 2010c. "Program Document for a Proposed Credit to the Republic of Mozambique for a Seventh Poverty Reduction Support Credit Operation." Poverty Reduction and Economic Management Unit, Africa Region, World Bank, Washington, DC.

————. 2010d. "Program Document for a Fifth Poverty Reduction Support Credit to the Republic of Senegal," Report 60373-SN, Poverty Reduction and Economic Management Unit 4, Africa Region, World Bank,Washington, DC.

————. 2010e. "Program Document for a Proposed Credit to Republic of Uganda for the Eighth Poverty Reduction Support Credit," Poverty Reduction and Economic Management Unit 2, Africa Region, World Bank, Washington, DC.

————. 2010f. *Rapid Budget Analysis, Tanzania Public Expenditure Review.* Dar-es-Salaam, Tanzania.

————. 2010g. *Silent and Lethal: How Quiet Corruption Undermines Africa's Development Efforts.* Africa Development Indicators. Washington, DC: World Bank.

_____. 2010h. *Sudan Country Economic Memorandum.* Washington, DC: World Bank.

_____. 2011. *Global Economic Prospects: Maintaining Progress amid Turmoil.* Washington, DC: World Bank.

Afterword

By Blanca Moreno-Dodson

This book has reviewed several methodological advances and country experiences in accommodating growth and social welfare goals in the design and implementation of fiscal policy, taking into account existing vulnerabilities in developing countries and the need to react to external shocks.

Several knowledge gaps and new ideas identified in the preceding chapters deserve additional attention in the context of future research and country analyses:

- Fiscal policy making in developing countries is severely constrained by a multitude of factors, including the difficulty encountered in trying to achieve several objectives simultaneously, the uncertainty about the effects of diverse public spending components through time, the obstacles to enhancing the institutional capacity to manage public investments, and the adverse political economy incentives. These factors—together with limited fiscal space, scarce external financing and official aid, and remaining vulnerabilities to future external shocks—make it absolutely necessary to prioritize fiscal policy reforms according to which reform will have the largest beneficial effects on economic and social welfare. Moving forward, this prioritization should be the focus of the future research agenda on fiscal policy.

- Diverse studies look separately at the effects of public spending and taxation on growth and equity. The simultaneous effects of public spending and taxation on both growth (input accumulation and productivity) and social inclusion (equity and social protection) should be analyzed empirically, particularly in the context of developing countries.

- In future analyses of the impact of public spending, taxation, and fiscal risks on growth and social inclusion, a broader definition of the public sector, including subnational levels of government and state-owned enterprises (SOEs), should be used, based on data availability and country reporting.

- The analysis of public spending on growth—especially at the country level—could benefit from the greater inclusion of subnational public spending data, the use of firm-level data to estimate the effects of public spending at the microeconomic level, and the identification of potentially beneficial public expenditure reforms with the help of internationally comparable benchmarking indicators.

- Effective public investment management requires better coordination and accountability across oversight/central finance agencies, line agencies, different government levels and SOEs, and private sector actors. Additional analysis of the institutional constraints undermining public investment processes and decisions should be undertaken in order to help policy makers achieve tangible impacts on capital assets.

- In low-income and weak institutional capacity countries, such as some Sub-Saharan Africa economies, more effort should be devoted to identifying the structural factors hindering public investment management in order to maintain growth over time and, in times of volatility, avoid irreversible disruptions.

- Implementing fiscal policy requires institutions capable of correcting the perverse political economy incentives facing policy makers by rewarding compliance while making the cost of noncompliance unbearable. Additional emphasis should be placed on analyzing how fiscal policy could lead to growth and improved social welfare by changing incentive properties and improving the governance apparatus.

- Looking forward, in economies with major extractive industries (for example, mineral and energy resources), additional analysis should be undertaken of the effects of fiscal policy on comprehensive wealth, including physical (produced), human, and natural capital assets. Meanwhile, dealing with climate change will be a significant public policy issue in most developing countries. Policy instruments such as carbon dioxide emission fees and auctioning of emission permits can become a major source of fiscal revenue, whereas public investments in greener power generation will likely be more capital intensive and expensive than alternatives. Adapting to a changing climate will present a challenge for fiscal authorities because public investments in "climate-proofing" infrastructure will be subject to deep uncertainties about the timing and extent (and cost) of adaptive actions.

- The development aid provided by multilateral institutions, bilateral donors, and others affects (1) the levels and composition of public spending; (2) efforts to mobilize domestic fiscal revenue; and (3) debt sustainability patterns (loans versus grants, concessional versus nonconcessional). In turn, these fiscal variables affect input accumulation, productivity, equity, and social protection. The impact of different forms of development aid on fiscal policy making, particularly in a context of scarce resources, deserves further attention.

- Finally, based on the findings presented in this book, additional analysis of the expected effects of fiscal policy on growth, social welfare, and wealth should focus predominantly on the medium to long term. Accommodating short-term pressures that may require immediate responses should not alter or deviate from long-term fiscal policy making. On the one hand, short-term policies affect the options available for the medium and long term. On the other, long-term policies affect private sector expectations in the short run, thereby shaping the effects of any policy reforms undertaken after an external shock. Developing countries should devote more efforts to elaborating strategically a medium- to long-term vision of fiscal policy that is consistently and fully integrated into short-term policy measures, even when reacting to exogenous shocks.